THE INTEGRITY OF INTELLIGENCE

The Integrity of Intelligence

A Bill of Rights for the Information Age

Bryan Glastonbury
Professor in the Department of Social Work Studies
University of Southampton

Walter LaMendola
Vice President of the Colorado Trust

Consultant Editor: Jo Campling

St. Martin's Press

First edition 1992
Reprinted 1993

Published in Great Britain by
THE MACMILLAN PRESS LTD
Houndmills, Basingstoke, Hampshire RG21 2XS
and London
Companies and representatives
throughout the world

A catalogue record for this book is available
from the British Library.

ISBN 0–333–52572–8 hardcover
ISBN 0–333–60521–7 paperback

Printed in Great Britain by
Ipswich Book Co Ltd
Ipswich, Suffolk

First published in the United States of America 1992 by
Scholarly and Reference Division,
ST. MARTIN'S PRESS, INC.,
175 Fifth Avenue,
New York, N.Y. 10010

ISBN 0–312–08098–0 (cloth)
ISBN 0–312–10063–9 (pbk.)

Library of Congress Cataloging-in-Publication Data
Glastonbury, Bryan.
The integrity of intelligence : a bill of rights for the
information age / Bryan Glastonbury, Walter LaMendola ; consulting
editor, Jo Campling.
p.   cm.
"First published in Great Britain in 1992 by The Macmillan Press
Ltd"—T.p. verso.
Includes bibliographical references (p.   ) and index.
ISBN 0–312–08098–0 (cloth) — ISBN 0–312–10063–9 (pbk.)
1. Information technology—Moral and ethical aspects.
I. LaMendola, Walter. II. Title.
HC79.I55G53   1992
303.48'33—dc20   92–7976
                                                      CIP

Contents

Acknowledgements

This work could not have been completed without the support provided by The Colorado Trust, for which both authors wish to express their appreciation. Walter LaMendola has received many gifts which contributed to this work, for which he expresses general thanks. The Trust donated the gift of time to complete his writing, yet somehow he most appreciated the continuing encouragement from staff and Board. His cousin, Ronald V. Pellegrini, gave him the gift of confidence in his ideas about computing and invested in them many years ago. His mother and father made many sacrifices all of their lives to give him opportunities that they never had, without any conditions, while his brothers have given freely of whatever was needed. Walter especially thanks his daughters, Julie and Teresa, who must wonder if this work will ever be done. Nancy Van De Mark deserves special thanks. She listened, reacted, consoled and sustained, while tolerating both long absences and long working hours over the past three years.

Bryan Glastonbury wants to express appreciation to colleagues in the European Network for Information Technology and Human Services (ENITH) for continuing support and comments on drafts, to Jackie Rafferty both for general comments and a zealous effort to keep the manuscript free of language which might cause offence, and to Sheena Glastonbury for creative backing and tolerating a noisy word-processor in the pre-dawn hours.

Introduction

Computers and telecommunications, the components of what we label *Information Technology* (IT), are a very recent part of our history. Few of us knew of the existence of computers before the 1950s, and for many an introduction followed the arrival less than two decades ago of mass produced personal computers, such as the Sinclair ZX series in Britain and the IBM PC in the United States. Telecommunications have grown up over the same period, making the world appear a much smaller place.

Tracking back through published materials, we can find by 1970 the beginning of an awareness that these new technologies would change the nature of society. Japan's Computer Usage Development Institute published *The Plan for Information Society* in 1972 (JCUDI, 1972). In the succeeding years we can find a growing acceptance of the potential impact of new technologies, and a realisation that they would impinge on our lives and value systems.

Amongst the first organizations to become concerned about ethical issues in new technology applications were human and welfare services (Hasenfeld and English, 1974). Despite being backward in their commitment to and use of computers and networks, human services staff identified important matters about confidentiality and personal data security. Small groups built up in several countries, like CUSSNet (Computer Users in the Social Services Network) in the United States and CASW (Computer Applications in Social Work) in Britain, and in 1987 a first international gathering assembled in Birmingham, England. It was at Birmingham and in subsequent conversations that the authors of this book came to the conviction that society needed to confront the ethical challenge posed by information technology, and move to place it within an ethically acceptable framework. On a wider stage CPSR (Computer Professionals for Social Responsibility) and ACM SIGCAS (Association for Computing Machinery, Special Interest Group on Computers and Society) were formed in the USA amongst technicians with similar concerns, and ENITH (European Network for Information Technology and Human Services) has been set up in Europe.

The Integrity of Intelligence is in three parts. Part 1 is a scene setter. Its four chapters aim to define the context and subject area, overview selected current information technology developments along with their applications, and outline some of the major issues. Part 2 is about problems and principles. It has six chapters, taking in global matters like technology transfer, the role of big business, the impact of people inside the information technology industry, poverty and the Third World, gender and racial discrimination, and the experiences and attitudes of the general public. Part 3 starts the task of looking for solutions. It contains a wide ranging discussion of the actual and potential role of what, borrowing from Masuda (1980), we have called the *ethics industries*. The book then finishes with a statement of priorities for ethical intervention and a possible Bill of Rights.

This volume is a transatlantic effort, bringing the authors face-to-face with the differences which exist in developments, attitudes, organizational structures and cultures on either side of the ocean. Nevertheless, as we have thrashed out the issues from our own cultural and experiential standpoints, so we have come to believe that despite variations at the margin, the core ethics for the fast-advancing information age are global. Further, we need to take a global overview if we are to see the benefits of information technology spreading across poor as well as rich societies. From this global overview we can then have a clear vision of the principles that have to be embedded in local actions, in the ethical use of technologies in the home, the workplace, the neighbourhood, or wherever they impact on our everyday life.

The authors of this book are IT enthusiasts. Computers, networks and a range of applications are a significant part of our work lives, and increasingly play a role in our homes. If we spend the following pages offering a critique of the way IT is developing, and where it appears to be going in the future, this is because we are committed to making it work, not wishing to see it banished. Our argument is that leaving IT to grow uncontrolled is the path to putting democracy in jeopardy, trampling over people's rights, placing more power in the hands of corporations and governments, dehumanizing society, and subjugating the majority of us to an insensitive machine intelligence. Nevertheless, to move to the opposite extreme, and seek to destroy or ban IT development and applications, is to deny progress, deprive us of immensely valuable facilities, cause chaos in areas of social and economic organization which have grown dependent on the technology, and make many of our heavily urbanized communities both ungovernable and incapable of self-maintenance.

There has to be a middle way, which achieves the benefits of IT, encourages rather than inhibits its advancement, and yet ensures that it works for humanity, all humanity. At present IT is a mixed blessing, good, indeed brilliant in parts, and not just bad, but threatening, insidious and demoralising in other parts. The middle way is ethical IT, responsive to broad social need, sensitive to the human condition, and accessible to everyone without regard to race, beliefs or economic status.

The reader who wants a quick impression of the book will find a summary at the start of each chapter. Those who delve further into the pages will, we hope, be stimulated to tackle some of the issues raised. To aid or inhibit their progress they will find phrases and illustrations from both sides of the Atlantic, and an attempt (please believe us!) to steer clear of specialist jargon. Enjoy.

Part 1
Setting the Scene

1 Intelligence, Integrity and New Technologies

SUMMARY

Human societies have thrived or suffered in relation to the degree of integrity with which our intelligence has been used. Intelligence in itself has often been viewed as threatening, because of its potential for harm, and in consequence a vital role of religions and philosophies has been to emphasise the value of the partnership between intelligence and another human ability, to understand and act according to moral codes. For many centuries human judgement ruled social systems, but the rise of science has undermined human capacities to make right decisions, and put in their place scientific experiment and the accumulation of factual knowledge.

Our argument is that the rise of information technologies in the latter part of this century has not only taken to new levels the empowerment of science and disparagement of human judgement, but also posed a significant new challenge. The combination of computing, media and telecommunication is promoting the development of an artificial intelligence, already near to rivalling human intelligence in some of its activities, and far exceeding any human individual in its global power. Yet it is substantially an unfettered intelligence, lacking the intrinsic morality (whether inherited or learned) which underwrites human judgements.

Information technology offers intelligence without integrity. As such it can take on whatever rules or moral standards its designers and controllers choose. This technology can and in many ways is being used for great world benefit, though many signs suggest that it will also be used to enhance discrimination, the gulf between rich and poor, and new forms of colonialism. If we are to have a technology with integrity, then a moral framework must be worked out, and established quickly, before the charge of scientific progress leaves the world's communities too far behind. We argue the need for a Bill of Rights for the information age, which will provide both a moral framework and the rules of design and application for new technologies.

THE HUMAN CONTEXT

Intelligence, or the ability to perceive, understand and reason, is the quality which humans use to justify their placement on a pedestal of superiority. Along with intelligence comes self-awareness and the notion of personal responsibility, so that we can take credit when things we do go well, blame if they go badly. In order for us to behave responsibly (or with calculated irresponsibility) we must have at hand a set of rights, rules and guidelines, which combine to make up a code of conduct for dealing with all the events of our lives. Formulating such codes has been a central preoccupation of religions, governments and societies since the beginning of the human race. We squabble, sometimes fight over whose code is the right one, who was the creative deity, whether such codes are the province of gods or human reasoning, or whether the adoption of new codes should be a revolutionary or evolutionary undertaking. Despite disagreements, there is a common base to human attitudes, and one component is acceptance that if life is to flourish then intelligence must be used with integrity.

Even so, our age is one in which the relationship between moral values, our way of life, and our purposes, needs to be reassembled. We believe that this need is most forcefully driven by the impact of technological progress. Technology has become a reality which encompasses all of our world and its inhabitants, and is taking us on ever wider explorations. Without challenging or limiting its judgement, we have let technology become our Solomon and soothsayer, witch and poet. There is an enormous and growing gap between the complex technological phenomena that form our everyday lives, and our ability to make these phenomena coherent and intelligible. The common person is bewildered: those who attempt to gain an overview of technology are too often frustrated. We live at a time when intelligence dominates, yet the measured intelligence of humankind is falling in relation to the emergence of machine intelligence (Moravec, 1988). Integrity, a return to appropriate judgements based on core principles of human relationships, has become a necessity.

Integrity can be defined in the traditional biblical sense as wholeness and soundness of moral principle ("Better is the poor that walketh in his integrity . . . . " – Proverbs 19.1). Or we can fix on those terms used to describe a person of integrity, such as open, honest, incorruptible and principled. Whatever the starting point, there is a dynamic relationship between intelligence and integrity, which both enhances the creative potential of the intelligence available to us (whether human or artificial), and combats the scope we all have to use intelligence to promote selfish, undemocratic and damaging behaviour. Well before the arrival of modern information technologies this relationship had been seriously disrupted by the increasing ascendence of scientific methods. A rift occurred between what we now call the sciences and the humanities. Although the rift began as an issue about method, it soon became a dispute over who had a hold on truth; in other words, the most fervent adherents to the scientific method believed that only their way could lead to truth. The application of the scientific method contributed to an era of invention, discovery, and achievement; but it also became a tool used to undermine emotion, induction, intuition and belief as elements in the search for understanding reality, in favour of objectivity, deduction, experiment, measurement and probability. The integrity of human inquiry has been severely dented, to the extent that an eminent scientist can now introduce a book by informing us that "We go about our daily lives understanding almost nothing of the world" (Carl Sagan in Hawking, 1988).

There are two consequences of the dominance of science which concern us here. One is the identification of what powerful sections of society see as truth with the non-human – with machines and measurements. The vestment of computers with "truth", as manufactured but genuine intelligences, puts them on a throne as "The Emperor's New Mind" (Penrose, 1989). Denying a role in the search for social and economic progress to those peculiarly human traits which make up creative imagination, and replacing them with computers and other artifacts, is anathema to some, but many believe and act as though it is essential. We believe that what is really essential is to reintegrate and respect the truth of both science and humanities. In turn method, both the experimental and the interpretive (in fact, of whatever variety), must be servant to meaning. The integrity of human inquiry must be restored.

A second consequence of the disrupted relationship has been the rise of specialization. Partly this reflects the colossal growth in the volume of knowledge, and the impossibility of a single mind containing all of it, or being able to stand back sufficiently to get a coherent overview. However else it may be described, the rise of science represents humanity's obsession with detail, from the microscope to micro-technology. Partly also there is the gradual change in attitudes which allows us still to revere such talented all-rounders as Leonardo da Vinci, while disparaging the generalist in modern life – "Jack of all trades, master of none". We are all specialists now, all feeling a need to claim some narrow area of expertise. Most educational systems have acclimatised to this, and no longer teach future specialists to think about the situation or framework in which their work must take place. The arts, culture, history, even present circumstances of nations and polity, are ignored and subordinated. The consequence is an intelligence confined by tunnel vision, unable to fathom its place in human valuation, everyday life, or ecological context.

The Nobel prize winner, Arno Penzias, argues that anyone planning to work with computers should have a "personal information strategy", designed to keep the computer in its proper place, and assert the controlling role of the human user (Penzias, 1990). He lists ten guides (p. 11), including such nuggets as "Computers are like cars – they're great for speed, but you have to steer them . . . . People run too many errands for their machines . . . . If you don't want to be replaced by a machine, don't act like one."

The Integrity of Intelligence spotlights the importance of the relationship between the two concepts in the title, and sets out to consider the uses and abuses of intelligence, to draw out in a practical way the elements of a code of conduct, and to do all this in the context of new technologies which may or may not possess their own built-in intelligence, but most certainly combine the promise of a heightened use of our own capabilities with the threat of being subjected to ever tighter controls.

The idea of intelligence has always provoked suspicion. There is something not quite right about it. No doubt it is flattering and a compliment to be described as intelligent, but it has to be rationed. As with cleverness you can be accused of having too much of it, especially if it is thought to be used unwisely or improperly. Like knowledge it can bring power and satisfaction, but also unhappiness and corruption. A Chinese poet of the eleventh century, Su Tung-Po, wrote:

> Families, when a child is born,
> Want it to be intelligent.
> I, through intelligence,
> Having wrecked my whole life,
> Only hope the baby will prove
> Ignorant and stupid.

In this context ignorance is synonymous with innocence, while to be intelligent is to be put at risk, to be challenged as to one's moral soundness. Martin Healey (1976), writing of computers in the early days of the silicon chip, called his demonstration machine Dumb 1, ostensibly because it lacked real intelligence, and could only do those tasks of a repetitive nature for which it was given precise instructions. It is tempting to see a deeper concealed motive, aiming to line up computers with the ignorant and innocent, and thereby distance them from issues of integrity. Yet in all major languages there are sayings which point up the responsibility of the human user in any partnership with inanimate objects, like "the bad worker always blames his tools". In such sayings choice, and therefore morality, rests with the user: the tools are ethically neutral.

Such a view of IT might be convenient. Certainly it is simplistic. It would also reflect a distortion of the role of IT in world society. Still more would it deny its future role. One of the longest lasting and most successful confidence tricks in the history of the human race is the perpetuation of the tranquillising view that the equipment we use in our lives, for survival, for life enhancement, for making money, for gaining and holding onto power, has few if any integral moral characteristics. It is a trick because the items themselves, cars and computers, guns and gasoline, regardless of whether or how they are used, represent power, rank and relationships in society. The assertion that it is not what you possess or control that matters, so much as the responsibility with which you use it, is relevant only up to a point. Much of the paraphernalia around us is, in itself, a moral hazard.

Nuclear bombs are a hazard, even if they are never used, because of their potential for causing damage. Cars are harmful, however beneficially they may be run, because of their fumes and their claims on the world's fuel supplies. A life without paper is inconceivable, but paper needs trees, chopping down trees destroys forests, and deforestation ruins the atmosphere around us. The list is long indeed, but in essence we are being given a few core messages. We must be aware of the links in any system, and the way an action at one point spreads its effects in many directions. We need to recognize that many actions, however creative, helpful or well motivated, have a price. The price of great good can be great harm. Our actions may be beneficial to us and our interests, but leave a heavy price to be paid at other times and places.

At this point, as the script makes increasing reference to IT, a simplistic definition is relevant. *Information Technology* is the label given to the combination of computing, media, and telecommunications. The technologies of computing and telecommunication, including their use in mass media, require description rather than definition, and this is offered at appropriate points later in the book. Information is a much more complex concept, especially establishing the differences between data (a raw material of knowledge) and information (the output of data analysis), and between real (human) and symbolic (computer) information. Chapter 3 focuses on our concept of *information*, because it is central to the way we approach information technologies.

INTEGRITY AND IT

Computers and the wider framework of IT are outside or peripheral to some forms of ethical debate. They are not, in any significant way, using up scarce natural resources, though in their transitional stage of implementation they may increase rather than reduce the consumption of paper and production of chemical waste. They are neither global polluters of the environment like agricultural nitrates or gasoline, nor creators of intransigent disposal problems like nuclear waste. They make use of but do not promote the sorts of buildings and electricity pylons which offend the eye. In all of these matters IT is a bit player.

In other matters IT has a featuring role, though not a star part. There are concerns about health risks. Upwards of half a million people in USA alone come into contact with toxic substances in the production of equipment (Glendinning, 1990). Video monitors are an industrial hazard capable of damaging the eyesight of those who spend hours sitting in front of them; wrist and back problems are not uncommon; some users may feel unwell in the prevailing atmosphere of static electricity. Computers provoke issues about education and training. There has been controversy about the part they play in teaching method: they have been used to reduce the need to teach aspects of some subjects, such as arithmetic and statistics, which had previously been justified both for their content and their contribution to "training the mind".

The real impact of IT derives from the contexts in which it is employed, the material it works on, what it symbolises, and how it is conceived as a form of intelligence. Just as with many other new discoveries and their subsequent industrial exploitation, such as the internal combustion engine or splitting the atom, IT applications pose a core dilemma. Some are life-enhancing: others serve to make more effective the tools of control, extortion and, ultimately, warfare. Debate on the peaceful uses of atomic energy has been forever contaminated by knowledge of the nuclear bomb. Will we find, in much the same way, that the positive potential of IT will always have to survive in the shadow of hi-tech wars?

In its application to human communities IT lives on information, and the type of information which most demands integrity in its use is derived from data about people. Human records are the bread and butter of the world's electronic data system. Everything is of interest, and willingly gobbled up into gigantic data stores – our names and aliases, family structure, past and present relationships, qualifications, strengths and weaknesses, the way we make a living, what we spend, what we would like to buy if we had the money, where we go for holidays, the brand of deodorant we use, health problems, ability to get into or keep out of debt, brushes with the forces of law and order, what the police and bank manager think of us, political views, confessions, aspirations, sensitivities and anxieties. Data about people can be and is moved around, consolidated, assessed, sold for high prices, used as the basis for all sorts of life decisions, processed into composite reports, and analyzed for what it says about all of us as individuals. Fundamental issues of human rights arise from concerns about the reasons for this obsessive data gathering, the accuracy and current relevance of the material, the invasion of privacy involved, the care taken to protect confidentialities, the facility with which we can check on what is held about us, the secrecy which often surrounds the whole operation, and the question of who is the rightful owner of our personal secrets.

To many people computers, media, and telecommunications, the partnership which makes up IT, have established a clear relationship to power, wealth, social and cultural divisions, the obsolescence of ageing generations and unskilled groups, and discrimination. In part this is typical of any new invention: it offers an advantage to those who have it over those who do not, whether the haves and have nots are different nations or next door neighbours. Since possessing the novelty is commonly a matter of being able to pay for it, the display of wealth is also apparent. But IT takes these divisions much further. The capability of computers and telecommunications makes their invention more wide ranging in its importance than, say, a new household gadget, because of the influence, privilege and authority which derives from its use. At the level of nation states and multinational corporations IT offers scope for new forms of colonial or even global control, and some opportunity for big organizations to evade the policies of technologically impoverished governments. Within communities IT favours the educated (a knowledge of the English language is almost an essential), and those who have grown up in the new technological age, when their schooling and interests absorbed the principles and practices of computing as a matter of routine. IT has divided the generations like no other development, into those who are part of the information age, and those who preceded and are commonly alienated from it. Cooley wrote of the obsolete knowledge base of all of us who are middle aged or older: "It has been said that if you divide knowledge into quartiles of outdatedness, all those over the age of forty would be in the same quartile as Pythagoras and Archimedes" (1987, p. 27).

If the primary divisions are between rich and poor nations, rich and poor people, and those growing up before and after the advent of the new technology religion, then there are secondary divisions which IT has not created, but has helped to perpetuate and strengthen. Computing, with its origins in electronic engineering, and its applications roots in science, business and government, is a man's world. The extension of the computer into the home and locality is one of the most potent weapons in the male armoury to counter feminism, and has given a new lease of life to the stereotype of the decorative female keyboard operator. There are some shining exceptions, like the serious efforts being made to give people with physical handicaps a route to computer usage, but in general those who have been traditionally disadvantaged are likely to remain or become more so in the information age. Ethnic minorities, especially those depending on their own language, will have greatest difficulty handling computer equipment: the very poor in society will be the least able to get access to the computer programs which provide them opportunity or, at the very least, allow them to calculate their eligibility and claim welfare benefits.

These are predictions, not inevitabilities. The technology exists to allow us to do away with mystique, cope with all manner of language differences and most forms of disability, and to make access as easy as going into the neighbourhood shop. The question is whether there is the will to use technology in these ways, given that most of us, men or women, fit or handicapped, majority or minority, face a real threat from IT if it remains as it seems at present – not a power for the people, but predominantly the equipment of governments and big corporations.

INTELLIGENT MACHINES

In coming years a formidably challenging aspect of computer technology will be the extent to which it becomes an alternative form of intelligence, or, in making claims to artificial intelligence, serves only to reduce even further the impact of human judgement. A tempting diversion at this point is to launch into a discussion of what constitutes artificial intelligence and an intelligent being, but this can confuse the vital issues which derive from the obvious and observable fact that computers can do tasks which would otherwise be done by humans, or tasks which would not be attempted by humans because they were considered too complex, maybe too boring. In this functional sense the computer is a supplement and reinforcement to its user's intelligence. This is not a unique facility, for it places computers in the broad setting of industrialisation, a feature of which has been the continuing flow of machinery and . equipment aimed at making work more productive and permitting ever more sophisticated activities. Part of this continuity is also the dilemma brought about by real improvements in output being at the expense of employment opportunities, and at the risk of over-exploiting both materials and people.

If IT stands out in this context, therefore, it has to be explained by the degree of impact rather than any uniqueness. There have not only been massive productivity increases in some sectors as they have become computerized, but areas of employment have been swept away in the face of new electronic systems. Clerical and administrative processes have been transformed: robots have taken over production line tasks in place of people: traditional communication and manufacturing skills have become obsolete. There are central ethical concerns here around the degree of disruption of people's lives, the destruction of many traditional forms of employment, and the growing level of dependence on computerized systems. Industrial society is thrown into disarray by the effect IT solutions have on levels and types of employment, and thrown into disarray again when the new systems break down.

Whether or not any computer actions can be described as a show of intelligence is questionable from a philosophical, theological or physiological viewpoint. One problem about entering this debate is that the concept of intelligence has been used so often as part of attempts to establish the uniqueness of the human race, arguing that we are distinctive because we and only we have intelligence: once intelligence is defined as a unique characteristic of human beings we both place serious limitations on discussion of the possibility of other intelligences, and get into the moral minefield of trying to conceive of machines in the image of a person. To have a useful approach to computer actions which are, or give every appearance of being intelligent, we must be willing to work with an explanation of the term which avoids defining humans as, *inter alia*, intelligent and intelligence as human.

In reality many computers and computer driven systems, like robots, are able to mimic intelligence, and the outcomes of following through complex sets of instructions are as though they have behaved intelligently. The range of intelligent functions wanted in most forms of employment is much narrower than a person needs for handling independent living or coping with a major problem. Doing a routine job involves the ability to start and stop at given times, to follow rules and procedures, to show manual and mental dexterity at appropriate moments, to be able to react properly when something goes amiss, sometimes to select and plan the sequence of tasks, and to communicate with other workers in the vicinity. Computer programs can and do cope well with all of these requirements.

The forms of intelligence for which computers are, as yet, less acknowledged are most importantly those connected with illogical or emotionally motivated actions, though even here it is necessary to tread carefully. A computer can be both spontaneous and illogical, in that it can be given the scope to act randomly, or make random choices from a range of options. It can be programmed to behave deviantly, and providing it is given information about the symptoms, it can mimic sensitivity. It can, through careful location and connection (such as a micro-processor implanted close to a human heart), interface with and respond quickly and sensitively to bodily signs. The thought controlled computer systems of Firefox remain a figment of the author's imagination, but are conceptually accurate. The success of Weizenbaum's ELIZA program in convincing many users that it was carrying out an intelligent psychiatric interview is a historical fact.

All of this is or will be a programmed intelligence: the machine will take on the abilities given to it by its designer. The societal role of computer designers, programmers and developers therefore grows in importance, in that they are responsible for the way these newly created intelligences behave. We need to focus on the rules, values and standards they have employed. We also have to ensure that the value systems existing within these artifacts which we call computer programs are in accord with real societal codes. Where, for example, do we place the children's game in which the computer user, with varying success, moves a safety net to try to catch babies thrown from a burning building?

There is nothing in theory to stop a computer being programmed to copy the full range of activities of a human brain. In practice computers show relatively inadequate brain power at the present time, but this is a matter of technology development, and intellectual capacities to match or even better a human being will come. Given the short history of computing, the achievements are impressive. Moravec (1988, p. 61) puts computer intelligence in context – "Current laboratory computers are roughly equal in power to the nervous systems of insects . . . The largest supercomputers of the 1980s are a match for the 1-gram brain of a mouse . . . " Where next? Will the 1990s produce the computer equivalent of a dolphin, the 2000s a chimpanzee, the 2010s an averagely capable schoolchild?

It will become still more necessary for societies to know about and control the ethical component of computer design as we move beyond the notion of computers doing as they are told, towards programming a machine with a set of instructions which in effect ask it to take responsibility for its own development, to produce its own operating rules and procedures. It is a logical extension of such a process, and likely to become the simplest approach in practice, to invite the computer to design, and its linked robots to produce, a more effective successor to itself, so establishing a reproductive sequence. The originators, the Adam and Eve of the dynasty, will set some initial parameters, and provide the equivalent of a genetic imprint for generations of machines.

Theoretically we can conceive of self-developing computers opting to move their initial parameters, to change the basic rules, but they will be of little use to any of us if they are not constrained to work within a given framework, much as we have to observe the criminal and behavioral codes of our own communities, or face the consequences of deviance. For effective action the computer must be given as much information as possible about the subject areas over which it is to be asked to span, whether to respond to queries, or seek to advance knowledge. In the same way it has to receive and understand the rules of good conduct, the moral code it should observe in its activities. An especially pertinent part of that moral code will relate to the rules governing our interaction with IT, and the rights we have or should have in the way the power of IT can be harnessed for or against us. In the future we may also have to address the question of rights of the computer, as it becomes increasingly able to make value judgements, add to our knowledge base, and guide us to an awareness of our own illogicalities and inadequacies.

A BILL OF RIGHTS

The argument so far has been that now and in the future we need to be aware of the moral content and implications of information technology. Issues of values, purposes, standards and conduct can be found throughout the IT span, from the design of systems, through the uses to which they are put, to their ownership, and the activities they generate under human control or on their own initiative. Seeking to describe and analyze these issues is the primary aim of this book.

The task of indicating the route to integrity for the intelligence of computers and those people who become involved with them is far from easy. Not only is there wide ranging conflict over ethical standpoints within the world society, but also there are very strong temptations for powerful groups to seek to harness the authority and wealth which their monopoly of control would give them. In a world where there are already strongly drawn up dividing lines between technology haves and have nots, there will be plenty of ambivalence, and some firm opposition, to the idea of trying to instil greater fairness. Many people will see IT as too important and valuable for citizens to have full access to it, or a say in the rules of conduct. As authors and computer users we want to oppose such a stance, and state our arguments.

Furthermore we feel that the task should not be evaded. All of the world's major moral frameworks recognise concepts of social justice and oppose discrimination. Why should IT be left to market and political forces, rather than be placed firmly in the arena of public concern and debate? It has to be recognized, however, that time is short and the need acute. The pace of technological development since the middle of the century has been so rapid, and will continue just as quickly in the foreseeable future, that traditional processes of the gradual integration of new inventions into established life styles have not occurred. For several decades there has not even been enough time to draw up an agenda for reviewing the role and morality of a new invention, before the next generation of technologies comes into sight. In the computer hardware world generations are measured in months, obsolescence in weeks. It is no wonder that so many people can come to feel alienated from the technology around them!

The pace of technological change is not likely to slow down to accommodate these traditional processes of social integration, so if we are to formulate and gain acceptance for a code of conduct in IT we have to do it at the gallop, and focus both on what is already here and what will be here next year or next decade. Simultaneously we must strive to hold onto respect for traditional cultural processes, and analyze how essential components of long established routes to social change and integration can be used to give sense and cohesion to the IT stampede. If computer people are producing for their sixth generation, we should be planning the rules for their seventh and eighth. To do so we need some guidelines, reflecting basic tenets which should be embedded in any detailed operational manual, and which can become the framework for culture specific arrangements. Many societies, such as the British, have shied away from the idea of setting such frameworks in Bills of Rights, preferring to work through precedent and evolution. Many more, including the United States and much of continental Europe, have long traditions of setting out the basic rules of social life in written form. The impracticability of an evolutionary approach in the time span and at the pace that is so characteristic of IT growth, makes it both desirable and inevitable that if ethical issues are to be confronted, it should be with the aid of a written and widely understood code.

The case for a written Bill of Rights cannot and need not be argued solely on the basis of current practicalities. There is another reason closely linked to the place each of us holds in modern society. It is a curious and not altogether comforting observation that at a time when individualism is touted as a characteristic of the most advanced societies, nowhere do we find the individual treated with more hostility. Indeed, the drift toward democracy now prevalent among the Eastern European nations is laid largely upon the economic circumstances which have corrupted the Soviet as well as their own governments, and less upon any inherent commitment to principles of human dignity, individualism, or democracy.

Major social institutions in both eastern and western countries have, for different reasons, progressively interpreted the production and consumption of material goods and support of the accumulation of wealth as the core determinant of public policy. For example, some have looked wistfully at the Japanese wedding of commercial and government endeavour, and the subjugation of the individual, as evidence of the legitimacy of such an approach. Firmness in support of such principles has only faltered when the organization's or nation's economy has itself given cause for insecurity. Rarely does it appear to falter in such a way as to soften the built-in mean spirited attitudes towards forms of behaviour not premised upon financial profit taking and monetary gain. The consequences of these actions for the individual have been unaddressed, other than to hold the individual responsible to recover from them, with limited and variable help from employment, welfare and other support services. In fact these priorities can sometimes foster dependence rather than engender the sort of individual initiative we are expected to show in the face of, for example, computer encroachment on our jobs.

Technology of all types has been used in a number of circumstances to toughen up reactions to the perceived failures of the individual. For example, when individual employees have tried to protect themselves by turning to union activity, technology has been used to help break up collective action by taking over the jobs of striking workers. When workers have been viewed as unprofitable, and therefore a liability rather than an asset, technology has again been used to facilitate redundancies. When failures have been blamed upon labour cost, technology has been used to supplant the individual. When these failures are blamed upon individual deficits, technology has been used to control the individual. Put another way, the "unacceptable face of capitalism", as it appears in corrupt forms of share dealing, or asset stripping, or money laundering, becomes enormously easier through the help of IT. Even where a change is badly needed, as perhaps it was to the outdated production methods of newspapers in Britain in the 1980s, IT too often gets the blame but not the credit.

It is in part because examples of these uses of technology have proliferated over the past few decades, that we have entered an era where technologies of all types are gaining a reputation as intrinsically alienating and destructive of human rights. The anonymous impersonality of IT outputs, coupled with occasional instances of idiocy, inaccuracy or insensitivity, promote the feeling that technology is out of control, and that humankind is its servant (Winner, 1978). It is probably more correct to accept that technology is not itself out of control, but that its rulers (if they seek to exercise control at all) apply technologies in a manner that is outside the influence of the citizen. In short, they act in their own interests, not necessarily in a manner that is respectful of human dignity or democratic principles.

In the more recent past an IT application has been developed that, while substantially contributing to the material economy, has, in form, content, and application, provided powerful tools for generating profitable new activities. This new sector for exploitation is not material: it is our intellectual and social infrastructure. The marketable commodity is data. As Lyotard writes (1979, p. 4) – " The relationship of the suppliers and users of knowledge to the knowledge they supply and use is now tending, and will increasingly tend, to assume the form already taken by the relationship of commodity producers and consumers to the commodities they produce and consume – that is, the form of value. Knowledge is and will be produced in order to be sold . . . " In our first try at understanding and explaining this application we called it data processing technology, then information technology, and more recently, knowledge technology. We suspect that this progression will not stop until it encompasses all intellectual activity as its domain. Such technologies are perceived as building blocks which, when assembled alongside a prosperous material economy, generate new property, new wealth, new empires. There is a real risk that just as in past years common land moved inexorably into the category of private property, the same process will take over a community's intellectual wealth and the cherished necessities of community survival, such as the air we breathe, the water we drink, and the stories we have to tell.

What we are anxious to promote through this book is public debate and analysis about what we consider to be the proper use in a technological society of the principles of democracy, individualism and community life. We will structure these principles as a draft Bill of Rights for the Information Age.

2 Status Report

SUMMARY

This chapter comments on the current state of developments in IT, starting with a brief history of technology progress, noting both significant positives like the provision of useful information, as well as irritating negatives, like hardware incompatibility. The argument is developed that the views of IT from insiders and outsiders are dramatically different. The former is dominated by technical progress, in ever faster or more powerful computer chips, or more sophisticated programs: the latter perceives IT as a mixture of utilities (such as computerized timetables), threats (to jobs), irritations (junk mail) and entertaining trivia (games).

We pursue the view that the governments of the world's richer communities have failed badly in taking a largely *laissez faire* attitude, except where military sensitivities are involved, instead of seeking to handle IT within a coherent strategy for its social integration. Poorer countries have found themselves open to new forms of subservience, arising from their dependence on the new world powers, whether government or multinational corporation, for access to equipment, applications and global networks.

From a technological viewpoint the future seems set to offer continuing progress, with widespread benefit to all of us if a helpful political and moral climate is structured. We argue that it is vital for governments to recognize the risks, and implement policies to cope with them.

MAKING HISTORY

The history of IT has been told elsewhere (e.g. Shurkin, 1984: Randell 1973). In broad sweep, mechanical calculating or computing devices were first designed over a hundred years ago, and were perfected in the early decades of this century. They helped to cope with census returns for governments, life expectancy estimates for insurance companies, salaries and pensions for large employers, and other sturdy tasks. They were faster than humans, and more reliable at the arithmetic, but still slow by today's standards. It was the search for greater speed that led to the switch from mechanical to electrical processing. During the 1939–45 war we wanted to be able to do some work quickly enough to have an impact on the rapid pace of hostilities, like forecasting enemy shipping movements and aircraft interception courses, or decoding secret messages. In practice most successful wartime computing was handled by tried and tested mechanical methods, and hostilities were nearly over before electrical computing became a reality.

Computers were built using hot valves, but they were prone to over-heating and collapsing after a few minutes as valves burned out. The next real advance came with the development of transistors in the 1950s. Most of us will recall the "tranny", the ubiquitous transistor driven radio, but for the likes of IBM the transistor was the spring and summer of mainframe computing. Governments and big companies had big computers, with equally big and important staff, all at very high cost. The computer industry had arrived.

Looking back 20 or 30 years, the technology of the time seems laughably antiquated, breaking down (crashing in the more vivid jargon of the "in-crowd") as often as it did, and cocooned in vast air-conditioned halls. It was a sumptuous deity which all but the priesthood dare not approach, though from time to time we could hire a little of its attention and demonstrate our faith by feeding it with piles of punch cards, in the hope of getting some useful output. Communicating with these monsters was a hard-learned specialism: some computer phrases, like user-friendly, had not been coined, and populist applications, like word processing, did not exist. Nevertheless this short era, barely two decades, this medieval age of computing, set a course which we have followed ever since. It fixed computing alongside so many other human developments, from calculus to law, botany to psychiatry, as a great but unnecessary mystery. Like so many mysteries, it clings to its position through the obscurity of the language and jargon of its users; but unlike others it thickens the fog still more with a long and tenacious tradition of incompatibility. Until different computers, programs and peripherals came along incompatibility was something between people who felt they could no longer maintain a relationship: now it means two bits of equipment which will not, cannot and perhaps were intentionally designed not to work together.

Obscurity and incompatibility look set to characterise IT into the foreseeable future, perhaps because the machines fit the attitudes of those who control them. Technological development is facilitating ever greater devolution and openness in computing, but vested interests want - to retain some of this past mystique and cussedness. As McLoughlin and Clark (1988, p. 169) point out, after their extensive research into technological change at work, " . . . outcomes may be seen as a product of social choice and negotiation, and not as a direct reflection of the capabilities and characteristics of technology". They go on to quote Littler (1982), who argues that technology is flexible enough to allow for choices, "centralisation versus decentralisation; enhancement of skills versus the polarisation of skills away from the shop-floor; rigid controls versus the delegation of decision-making . . . " While the context of their debate is industry, their arguments and conclusions ring equally true elsewhere, especially in government.

Mainframe computers also gave governments of wealthy countries and big companies a start of about 90 metres in a 100-metre race with less privileged groups. For most of their history computers were costly, and their scale was such that only wealthy organizations could justify buying or leasing them. Their range of functions and general capabilities were way below what we expect today, but that early start gave an advantageous foothold in the subsequent development process, a familiarity which could be used to enhance the fears and anxieties of newcomers, and dominate the market for scarce specialist staff.

The revolution in computing which we are now experiencing became possible with the mass production of micro-processors based on silicon chips. They allowed computers to be built which were massively smaller, more capable and cheaper than their predecessors. That a revolution occurred, to superimpose personal computing on the previously mainframe scene, should not be put down entirely to technological innovation. There was increasing experience that mainframe systems were not meeting all of a corporation's needs. The new micro-technology needed exploitation, and its arrival coincided with a generation of young people who were resentful and dismissive of *Organization Man*, and sought new ways to creativity, wealth, and life satisfaction. For many years scholars of organizational systems (Etzioni is an eminent example) warned that the concentration of productive or administrative activity into very large units would give rise to problems of staff motivation. The analysis of bureaucracy, both as a form of organization and a process for conducting business, noted the great benefits for staff, such as job security and clarity of task, while acknowledging that boredom was a distinct possibility, and the loss of imaginative enterprise a risk. This is precisely what occurred, and though most employees did and still do rate the advantages highly enough to outweigh the tedium, a talented few did not.

Personal computing was a triumph of youthful enterprise, and the big companies had to puff and pant to keep in touch before being able to reassert their control. Inventors, designers and developers in their teens and twenties gave us many of the well known names in modern computing

– Apple, WordPerfect, Microsoft and a host of others. Their impact has not been focused solely on hardware, the machines themselves, but on the uses to which the machinery has been put. Major new forms of software, including word processing, spreadsheets and interactive databases, all originated from this source.

The point about changes in computer size, capability and cost cannot be over-emphasized. In 1950 a computer needed hundreds of feet of floor space, air conditioned surrounds, and extensive support staff. It was little more than a sophisticated calculator and processor of coded data, and though cheaper and more productive than purely manual systems, it was a significant item in the annual budget of a government ministry or a large corporation. A computer of the 1990s, doing the same tasks as its predecessor along with many more, and having a greater variety of functions, including such new developments as word processing, needs a standard electricity supply, some table space and a single operator who can leave the machine to work unattended for many jobs. The cost has fallen by a factor of hundreds if not thousands within three decades. Moravec (1988, p. 65) suggests that "Since 1900 there has been a trillionfold increase in the amount of computation a dollar will buy".

Computers could not have gained such a grip on industrial societies without two parallel developments, one scientific, the other more social, political, commercial and cultural. The former is communications technology: the latter our preoccupation, perhaps strong enough to be called obsession, with data gathering. Again there have been significant technology advances through telephone and air wave networks, to satellites and fibre optics. Suffice to say that improvements in the speed and quality of telecommunications has paralleled computer developments closely enough to ensure that global as well as local networking is a major feature of the present day scene.

Despite the hectic pace of technological change, attitudes towards data gathering have tended to be more stable throughout the computer decades. The origin of twentieth century views about data, and its conversion to information, lies in the gradual loss of confidence over many decades in the power of oracles, religions and theoretical discussions to answer the questions a curious human race is prone to ask. For the last hundred years two relatively newer methods of advancing knowledge have held sway – experiment and empiricism. Core procedures in these methods have been accurate measurement and data collection, and throughout these years the virtues of precision and observation have been instilled in generations of school children and new employees. Well before IT became a major part of the economy the populations of industrial as well as many agricultural nations were wholly committed to the principle that data gathering, measuring, and accurate recording were both important and endlessly fascinating.

Governments became preoccupied with measuring their populations, and collecting what we now label as "socio-economic data". Researchers began to spend a decade or more of their lives conducting and analyzing an empirically based social survey. Children and adults occupied the furthest extremes of railway platforms, diligently recording the registration number of any train which steamed past. For those people who began to feel the impact of greater material prosperity, it was as though a focus on the quality of our own lives was not enough: we somehow needed to extend horizons and know about the quantity of everything – How much? How many? What sort? Knowledge, especially quantitative fact, replaced belief as the bedrock of individual and communal security. It was an ideal platform from which to launch IT.

WHERE ARE WE NOW IN THE INFORMATION AGE?

Those who are part of IT development have chosen to structure their past and view their future in terms of generations. They appear attracted by the various meanings of that word – creative, reproductive, and innovative, as well as indicating changing epochs. The generations move rapidly, not in the usual 20 or 30-year span of human procreation, and most commonly relate to developments in microprocessors for personal computers and programming languages. So we have the ages of 8088, 80286, 80386 and 80486 chips, as well as 4th and 5th generation computer programming languages.

It is a confusing picture, and one which need not command our attention. There are other, more detached and helpful ways of overviewing recent decades. From a technology angle we may want to distinguish between the mainframe era (1950s and 60s), the advent of desktop computers (1970s), the mass production of personal computers for work and leisure (1980s onwards), the achievement of agreed standards and compatibility (hopefully the 1990s), and when user friendliness becomes a reality (who knows the date!).

There is an observable trend towards the aim of "computers for every-one", though the uses to which computers might be put in office and home settings seem set to be significantly different. There are also some unanswered questions about whose interests should be dominant, and who is responsible for reflecting the public interest. We already have a situation in which there is exclusiveness, privilege and an attempt to maintain obscurity at the technology leading edge, with more populist ideas catered for at the trailing edge. For the present this gives little cause for concern, partly because technology is ahead of software applications, so that "state of the art" hardware is commonly running programs which older machines can run perfectly well (albeit more slowly and with less presentational panache), and partly because the gap is so small between leading and trailing edges. However, it must be galling to those companies which invest heavily in research and development to see their new products so quickly and effectively cloned, and the temptation to take legal or technological steps to block low cost mass production of up-to-date equipment has to be strong. Perhaps instead of speculating about a coming era of user friendliness, we might query whether there will soon come a time when the "empire strikes back".

Still more useful than a technology-focused attempt to describe the current position of IT, is a person-focused view. How does the growth of computing and communicating look from outside rather than inside the hot-house? Most of us are unlikely to have become aware of IT before the 1960s, perhaps later, but except for the minority who worked in organizations which operated computer systems, the first experience for the majority was to be salaried or billed by way of a bulk printing system. The experience was impersonal, and because of occasional lapses in judgement, like a final demand and threat of legal action for a bill of nil, could become irritating and ludicrous. Customers rarely see any of the advantages in productivity, however substantial they might be!

There were many developments in the 1970s, such as computer timetabling for public transport, computer monitored power distribution, computerized banking, and computer control of stocks, which were undoubtedly important, but impinged little on members of the public in a direct sense. The same can be said about the gradual increase in networks, much of which preceded the launch of communication satellites. The big push from the mid 1970s came with the availability of techniques to personalize standard communications, not so much affecting tax bills and the like, but provoking a vast expansion in mailed advertising, with absurdly exaggerated antics to ensure that the individual approach was recognised. "Dear Mrs Crumble, I should like to tell you Mrs Crumble that you have been specially selected to receive the first news of our new washing powder, Gunge, and what's more, Mrs Crumble, with this personal letter to you, Mrs Crumble, there is a voucher in your own name entitling you to a discount on your first purchase . . . ." TV and computer generated printed advertising campaigns were co-ordinated, and IT began its role as a founder contributor to junk mail and deforestation, and a bastion of gender and ethnic stereotyping.

Not much has changed fundamentally in this form of computerized output in the 1980s, at least from the recipients' perspective. Printed personalized material has got more professional in appearance, especially with the advent of desktop publishing and colour. Some resistance has grown up to the intrusiveness of junk mail, noticeably when the so-called personal letter is followed up with a phone call. Concern with conservation has also gained momentum, though focused on the abuse of natural resources, such as the production of paper for trivial purposes, rather than on IT itself. Generally we have become accustomed to computerized dealings, and take for granted that IT has spread throughout the organization of our lives, from personal finance to health care, from leisure planning to work productivity. We have grown to believe, furthermore, that accepting computerized interactions is worthwhile because we think it has made our goods and services cheaper.

Amongst the most significant occurrences in the 1970s were the development, publication, adoption, and implementation of national computer plans in Japan and France. These were carefully crafted plans built on understanding the impacts of technology upon human beings and their culture, as represented in the works of Mumford (1964, 1967), Ellul (1964), Wiener (1965), Fromm (1968), Orwell (1969), Skinner (1971), and Bell (1973). The plans took into account the dire predictions of technological determinists. They contained active work plans for their societies to implement in order to avoid predicted shortcomings and take advantage of expected benefits. In both cases, the plans addressed the preservation of culture, tradition, individualism, and forms of government through a transition period of society. The plans intended to move their respective cultures successfully through that transition to what they called an *information society*. The plans are landmarks of foresight which we cover in more depth in Chapter 11.

The real face-to-face impact of computers in the late 1970s and early 80s on domestic lives arrived with the home computer and software for playing games. Most of us got our first opportunity to try out a keyboard in front of a TV screen, through the chance to zap aliens, or make a mess out of a simulated aircraft landing. Serious IT applications for ordinary families did start gaining a foothold in the 1980s, especially in those countries who sought to place equipment in schools and use it to communicate curriculum material or stimulate learning processes. It gained momentum as some of the games machines, as well as a range of newer equipment, like cheap clones of IBM personal computers, took on the ability to provide a person with few computer skills the chance to process words and try out other seriously intended programs, bringing into the home some of the benefits of office automation. This is where we are now in our home lives, just at the start of a possible age of opportunity to use IT as something more than an animated comic strip. Home shopping, more sophisticated communications and computerized domestic management are coming over the horizon, but the unavoidable conclusion is that so far there has been no significant development originating from or designed for the serious business of domestic life.

Looking back from a domestic viewpoint we might see the first generation of IT, when small computers were still a fantasy, and big computers tried and often succeeded in worthy tasks, as the age of trial, error and respectability. It was quickly followed by, and we are still in, the era of adverts and games, an age of triviality and trash. The domestic view is also likely to be coloured by resentments, less about the way we interface with IT, and more about the perceived impact on conventional lifestyles. Jobs are at the heart of the debate, based on the accusation that IT has served to increase unemployment levels (except, of course, in the new high technology areas). The truth or otherwise of this accusation has to be gauged in the context of other late 20th century events, like the decline of employment in traditional manufacturing in the industrial world and growth of the leisure and service sectors; the capacity of multinational corporations to move investments and work to locations of potential high profit, often away from zones where there is an existing skilled workforce and union structure; the cost of credit; and the willingness of governments to see employment levels fluctuate as a spin-off of their policies.

In the early days of speculation about the impact of technology (in the 1960s), it was assumed that jobs would be lost: but it was also assumed that the wealthier nations were moving into a glorious future of less work for bigger rewards, and more play. Taken for granted in this scenario was the notion of citizens giving up employment as the biggest single activity of our waking hours. Such an assumption has proved to be quite unwarranted. Far from looking forward to less work, many of us appear frightened of the resultant insecurity, and have made the realistic observation that for most individuals less work actually means less not more wealth. A society in which we have the time for leisure and pleasure, but not the money to afford them, has not been seen as very attractive. Miles *et al.* (1988, p. 240) cite several studies showing that "despite the popular belief that commitment to employment has declined, it actually appears that having a job has become in some respects more central in people's lives . . . It appears that the importance of paid employment as a source of economic and social resources has grown for women in most western societies, while there is little sign of its diminishing for men."

The view from the person in the street is hardly likely to reflect the same range of concerns about IT as those held by executives in major industrial corporations. From this angle there have to be two dominating observations about IT applications: they have made many businesses very profitable, and they have made planned and co-ordinated large-scale operations a practical reality. On both counts any reservations about IT are swamped by the obvious benefits. That the business community should see IT in a favourable light is no surprise, given the range of applications which are so relevant to business needs – the automated office, product flow and stock controls, robot-based production lines, project and investment decision-making, round-the-world communications, and so forth. For the leaders of industry it is a bonus that IT has enabled them to reduce their dependence on the vagaries of a human workforce, and with it the influence of organised trade unions, as occurred in the violent confrontations in the British newspaper industry.

PEOPLE IN POOR COUNTRIES

The populations of the world's poorer countries have, with a few exceptions, been simultaneously both profoundly affected and scarcely touched by IT. The major impact arises from the global viewpoint, where the power of computing, its contribution to manufacturing processes, and still more its liaison with telecommunications, has threatened new forms of colonialism, albeit with a strangely familiar look. The history of colonial exploitation shows a mix of involvement from governments and big corporations. Independence movements from the 1940s have removed much of the direct rule from external governments, though leaving behind for those on the geographic boundaries of major powers some limits as to the directions the governments of ex-colonies could take, especially in their world relationships. A residue of economic dependence and increasing debt has also weighed down poorer countries in their attempts to improve themselves.

The removal of the influence of large private corporations has been still less decisive. The old names – East and West Indies Companies – may have gone, but the spread of multinational corporations, and the activities of banking networks, have more than compensated. These inter-relationships have been enormously aided by developments in IT, and the nature and ethical component of resulting dependencies is pursued in Chapters 5 and 6. At this point it is sufficient to note that many of the dubious practices of traditional colonialism remain and are especially prevalent in the IT industry – the continuing exploitation of raw materials and cheap labour (often now to produce low cost computer components exclusively for use in wealthier countries); use of markets in countries without their own manufacturing base to sell at inflated prices and dump obsolete or low quality goods; willingness to take risks with pollution and health hazards which would be illegal or cause an uproar in a rich community; political and racial discrimination as to who should or should not receive tolerably up-to-date technology and help with using it; a preference to link technology transfer with military rather than civil applications.

The opposite sense, that in which poor communities are barely affected by IT developments, stems from a view from inside the Third World. The governments of these countries may feel that they have to spend scarce currency in an attempt to keep their military and core export industries in touch with world standards, but what value is IT for the general public, when there are no computers available, no knowledge of how to use them, and in many places no electricity supply to run them? There are different categorisations of first, second and third worlds, sometimes based on national income, sometimes on political allegiance, and sometimes on broad geographical allocations. All agree that relative wealth and poverty is fundamental. One study (Gross, 1980, pp. 130–1) offers a table which can be analyzed to show that while it takes 10 million workers in the western industrialised population to generate one per cent of the world's income, it takes 70 million from the second world (in this instance from the, then, communist states) and 200 million from the Third World to produce the same amount. Put another way, on these estimates western industrial communities are 20 times wealthier than their Third World equivalents.

The central issue we have to face here is not just the age old one of haves and have nots, though this is important enough in a world where the gap between rich and poor is getting wider. It is the linked fact that IT is now enhancing the lives of majority populations in the richer countries, but scarcely touching standards in poorer parts of the world. In one sense IT products have joined guns and fighter planes as essential purchases, deemed vital for the government's if not the community's survival: yet this new technology is purchased from the same source of funds as provides for such services as health, education and community infrastructures, and therefore to their detriment. Additionally, from a community perspective, IT has been used mainly to promote the interests of industrialised societies with high disposable incomes: many of the computer applications, whether programs or robots, which are offered to poor countries are irrelevant to their needs. Who needs a machine to assemble cars when labour is plentiful and crying out to be employed? What is the value of the latest version of WordPerfect or an increased array of fonts for your printer, if the real requirement is for basic plentiful distance learning material, and the ability to run it? As we shall discuss later (Chapter 8), a computer designed specifically for a poor country would look and behave very differently from the machines we currently send to the Third World.

What then can we say about the current state of IT from the viewpoint of the populations of the world? Some, those from the wealthier western societies, have already gained much benefit in improvements to social and industrial functioning, but as citizens have been treated condescendingly, and offered a diet of substantial triviality. They have paid a high price in the invasion of all forms of privacy, but if standards of behaviour can be established which replace elitist authority and paternalism with populism and partnership, then there is promise from the future. Simultaneously there are many, regardless of wealth, who feel and are excluded from IT benefits. They have been denied access through political decisions to bar them or their governments, or they have come from groups who have been discriminated against on the basis of race, language or gender.

For the world's poor there may be future possibilities, sometimes in the rather distant future; but it is not easy to identify benefits now. Given that North America and Europe have acted in such a *laissez faire* manner in handling the societal impact of technology growth for their own populations, it is hardly surprising that little attention has been paid to poor countries, except as sources of cheap materials and manufacturing, or exploitable markets. We cannot ignore the plea of the IT industry when it asks – "Why should we have to take responsibility for the impact of our inventions and products on strange cultures in distant lands? Surely these things must be handled by the people on the spot, so that they can work out with us what relationships we can have with them?" Neither can we ignore the experience from poor countries, because it is so like our own – that the flood of new invention, new gear, new programs, is on us, forcing us to make decisions before we can properly use or evaluate the products, before indeed we can gain the knowledge to think about and handle the process of evaluation.

THE FUTURE?

Where are we heading? What will the picture look like at the end of the century? Will the 21st century be the golden age of IT, or will the green backlash succeed in holding back IT, along with other symbols of unfettered market activity, in a reassertion of more traditional, spiritual and environmental values? Will IT become firmly tied to the promotion of human welfare and the protection of the earth's resources, or continue to be judged and developed according to assessments of profit margins and military applications? Are there known plans for IT, or is it all speculation?

Once again it is tempting to cope with those questions primarily from a technological viewpoint, not least because the array of IT journals thrive and fill many of their pages with forecasts and speculation, from who will be first to launch a personal computer with the next generation of chip or operating system, to images of the modern family kitchen a hundred years hence. There is interest and imagination to be found in all of these ventures, but if they are characterised by anything it is the continuing trivialization of IT. The really fundamental questions, about, for example, access and empowerment, are rarely asked, perhaps because they are so tough to answer, perhaps because the insiders are not aware of or concerned about their relevance. The most notable exception to this trend has been the learning done in the appropriate technology arena, particularly with the emergence of the concept of an integrated practice of technology choice as articulated by Willoughby (1990). Such a practice requires the participation of the people whose interests are intended to be served and distinctly recognises an ethical-personal dimension to technology practice.

Sticking for the moment with the technology angle, we ought all to be able to look forward to major progress in three areas, accessibility, compatibility and user friendliness. IT should become more available both because it will get cheaper and because mass production techniques need ever growing markets for survival. Computer companies, perhaps more than any others, including car manufacturers, have thrived on designer obsolescence, and selling state of the art gear to existing customers in the same market place. But there are signs of consumer resistance, ominous from the manufacturers' viewpoint, to the waste and costliness of responding to calls to update – note the persistence with which we have held onto the early IBM personal computer standard, despite industry predictions that they would long past have been consigned to scrap heaps. If the industry is forced to look seriously at new markets, and respond both to cultural traits and stages of general economic development, then success will depend on designs which acknowledge and meet the circumstances and needs of those markets. This pressure for more imaginative design, coupled with price falls, could begin to empower many of those we identified earlier as currently excluded.

There are indications already that the core issues of incompatibility are being tackled, not only as the architecture of equipment becomes more open and adaptable, but also as fewer manufacturers strive to assert their own operating idiosyncrasies. Nevertheless the problem will not go away, though it will change its emphasis. At present the vital question we ask is – will this bit of equipment be compatible with that one? Quite soon we are more likely to assume the equipment is or can be made compatible, or that programs will work on several machines: but we will be concerned with the simplicity, crudity and clumsiness of the link-up, and more fundamentally with the core standard around which compatibility is achieved. There is a pronounced trend in the IT industry at present to become compatible with the standard of the big manufacturers, rather than necessarily to the best standard, and there is little sign that this will change.

From the technology standpoint there are some clear messages to producers and hopes for consumers with regard to user friendliness. Do not necessarily get rid of the keyboard, but give us a better way of communicating with computers and networks. In essence, resolve the technology of talking to the machine or through the phone to the network. Furthermore, let the talker speak many tones, many tongues and a rich variety of accents. Deal with the morass and mess of learning about applications. There is no reason why manuals should be so impenetrable, or on-line tutorials so apparently designed according to traditional methods of teaching 6 year olds. Free us from the mysteries and obscurities of jargon, so that those who want us to buy and use their products can speak to all of us, of whatever race or gender, as though we are real people. Lastly, take responsibility for your products after you have received payment for them, and provide the quality of after-sales service that only a few companies do at the present time.

Most of these comments about access, compatibility and user friendliness are speculative to a degree, but verge on certainty because they reflect tangible plans already in process of implementation. The IT industry has a record of dramatic successes and failures, of fortunes made and lost in weeks, but there are clearly some massive rewards for a known range of technological breakthroughs – for whoever gets to dominate the core standards to which all else must be compatible; for the successful exploiters of new markets and designers of machines and applications ideally suited to those markets; for the introduction of a coherent and serious role for the home computer; for anyone who can make real improvements to communications between people and machines.

However, once we move away from the technology and ask about plans to tackle some of the wider issues surrounding IT – of devolution and empowerment, of equal opportunities, of codes of conduct, of technology transfer, and many others – the cupboard is emptier. We can find an interest (and some misplaced complacency) in data protection, and in the context of computer piracy and hacking moves to make criminal certain forms of IT exploitation by individuals against corporations, but little else. In short there is no strategy for the future of IT, and little sign of any intention to give thought to such a strategy. This comment applies as much to individual governments as it does to international groups. What we are able to observe, given this void in strategic planning, is the continuance of certain features which have embedded within them considerable elements of risk for our future.

Accepting significant national variations, the broad thrust of government policies has been and continues to be non-interventionist about the development of IT. Regardless of the pace of technology change, the prevailing attitude appears to be to let things roll, trusting that market forces will lead to the right outcomes. This may be motivated by many factors, including political philosophies, governmental weakness (especially in the face of a military establishment demanding high technology weaponry), or a level of poverty which diminishes the credibility of political utterances. A significant exception in the past has been government action in hardware producer countries to determine where markets shall or shall not be permitted, based on assessments of each purchaser nation's potential military use of any new technology it can acquire. We have and later will again take up these issues in the context of neo-colonialism and the treatment of Third World or politically unacceptable countries.

A policy of non-intervention has several immediate impacts. Considerable scope is left for producer and major user corporations to accumulate power for themselves, in relation, for example, to unfettered control of pricing policies, after-sales support services, and claims made about IT performance in advertising. It is as though governments have decided that they will never succeed in breaking through the mystique of the IT specialists, and are therefore not going to bother. A possible riposte to this statement is that IT companies are subject to the general regulations and controls each nation has in place to cover such things as cartels, false advertising claims, and so forth. In theory this is true, but the success of such regulatory measures depends on the skills of the staff trying to enforce the rules. In IT such inspectorial and evaluative skills are in desperately short supply for regulatory bodies, and in some countries professional ignorance of IT is more fashionable than professional expertise.

Non-intervention also means that there is no co-ordinated effort made to design and negotiate codes of conduct or industry standards for IT applications. In many areas, especially in system designs for community applications for health, welfare and other human services, there are attempts to draw up and operate according to morally justifiable codes. More significant, however, is the fact that so much IT development has taken place, and is fully documented, yet shows no reference to standards or codes of conduct. IT applications are commonly described exclusively in terms of what they will perform – such as the numbers of variables they can handle, the size of the database, the amount of memory needed, or the speed of response – without any mention of the values that underpin them. For example, WordPerfect, the world's best selling word processor, has extensive documentation. This tells you about what you will see on the screen, but not that if you look at it for too long you will get eye strain: and it tells you how to make a file secret, but does not mention the circumstances in which it might be appropriate to use this aid to confidentiality. Within the program itself there is a substantial and useful thesaurus; but try looking up "man", "woman", "black" and "white" to see the built-in racial and sexist attitudes. As a different kind of example, a leaflet (1988) from the Federation Against Software Theft (FAST), on "the ethical and legal use of software", views the subject as solely about making and using unauthorised (pirated) copies of programs. We can only conclude that wider values have not been considered, or are not advertised because they reflect the narrow interests of the producer rather than the wider interests of society. Amongst the few exceptions is Amercia's Association for Computing Machinery, whose Special Interest Group an Computers and Society has launched (1991) a discussion on a wider thical framework for IT.

It would be possible to go on cataloguing the impact of non-intervention, but the point should have been made by now. Non-intervention equals no strategy; no strategy means that major issues are not being addressed in any coherent or comprehensive way; failure to address such issues both symbolises our inability to plan for a better future, and opens up potentially damaging risks for our successors.

3 The Nature and Meaning of Data

SUMMARY

The most important component of the massive information systems which now exist is data about YOU. This data is gathered in a variety of ways, some open, some more devious. It is then drawn together and cross-referenced to create a dossier of personal information. From the point of view of this new information industry the ideal system is one that contains a comprehensive dossier about every one of us.

We trace, with detailed examples, how data is collected, processed and moved around; how it is then used as the basis for decisions affecting our lives; and the ways open to us to influence this situation. Ethical issues are raised about the IT processes employed in handling personal data, and we argue that there is a risk of errors creeping in, of ways of data management which can lead to a distortion of the truth, and a tendency to keep the public in the dark about what is happening.

Two particular matters are considered in more detail. One is the situation in which personal data is not considered to be the property of each one of us, but, from the moment it is put on a computer system, becomes the property and marketable commodity of the system owner. The other concerns the fundamental and inescapable move away from reality which occurs when our perceptions, feelings and conceptualizations are converted into the artificial representations which make up computerized data, what we have called "convenience labelling".

COLLECTING DATA ABOUT YOU

Have you purchased a new home appliance lately? Let's pretend that what you really need is a new vacuum cleaner. You buy one. As you unpack your new appliance, you carefully put aside the enclosed product information and warranty registration. The machine works well the next morning, so you have extra time to fill out and return your product registration card. It asks for your name, address, and telephone number. It asks where you made the purchase – their name, address, and telephone number. It probably goes on to ask for your age, gender, income group, number of members in household, and whether or not you own your own home. How much a year do you spend on appliances? What prompted you to buy the cleaner? Where will it be used? Why did you purchase this brand? Was it purchased for a specific member of your family? Was the decision to buy this cleaner made by a man, woman, or jointly? Have you ever owned a similar product? What was it? What brand? Do you own another cleaner? What model? Such questions are always posed with courtesy, without any sense of compulsion, and with an explanation that your answers will help the company to a better understanding of its customers' needs.

When you fill out and return your card, perhaps wondering what it has to do with your purchase of the cleaner, you might be surprised to know that it usually goes to a company that has paid the manufacturer for the rights to the data. In due course the data will be computerized and resold to other companies, and you have unwittingly become a participant in a wide network, without your knowledge and outside your control. For example, your data may turn up being sold to a firm which markets carpets. As a result, you may start receiving any number of unwanted mailings and telephone calls. In one case reported in a national news service, a data company sold material obtained from a national weight loss association to a chocolate company, which reported a rise in sales as a consequence of using it.

Most of us probably consider the mailing label as the type of data that is commonly bought and sold in the marketplace. That is just the tip of the iceberg, but we can start there. A typical mailing label will contain a name and address. Some of the data companies (also called list brokers) may also want your telephone number. It may be that they can buy a list of names and telephone numbers already on computer, or they have to go through the directory. It is also possible to obtain lists of names linked to job, place of employment and business phone number. By using a computer program these separate sources of data can be merged to build up a comprehensive route for contacting families, at home and work. The computer can cross-reference and link in any other material that is available, like court records of debts or criminal convictions, or the age and income profile you provided with your vacuum cleaner registration.

This type of collection and work with data represents the fastest growing use of computerized data today, and list selling between businesses and industries has become a major activity. For example, credit bureau income from selling data lists to marketing firms or list brokers, presently at about one third of total revenue, may exceed their income from providing credit references within the next few years. Data is big business for everyone. But what type of data is collected? Is it just the basic factual background material, that we have considered so far, or is more involved?

If we start with the example of a high school student, age 15, in USA, we may be able to trace some of the major sources of data collection. As high school students enter their second year their names will start to find a place on computerized lists, especially if they have been selected for any specific recognition or honours. A student of high academic accomplishments will begin to receive mailings from colleges and universities, encouraging the student to consider them. A little later the student may fill out an application for automobile insurance, and this data will be entered into a database and matched with criminal and credit files before the insurance application will be considered for approval. The student will not know the results of the application check or whether the data is bought and sold in the marketplace.

The student may now want a vacation job, and when applying may be asked questions about medical history, brushes with the police, home life, what parents do, and performance in school. If the company is large, the job application will be stored on computer and another check of the applicant will occur. The check may include credit and criminal checks as well as checks of driving record and personal references. Again none of the outcomes will be known to the student. Our student passes the checks and is employed. On receiving the first pay cheque, he or she goes to the bank and opens an account. Here is another application form to fill in, and if the student wants an overdraft facility, some material about the parents' financial viability may be requested.

While the student is working, playing, studying, and becoming a productive citizen, the marketing of personal data is leading to mailings about subscriptions to periodicals, cassette tape and compact disk buying clubs, and hosts of other consumer items aimed at teenagers. At the point of leaving school the mailings increase. Depending upon social and economic status, the contents of databases, and some further screening by a credit reporting bureau, the mail could bring an invitation to apply for a credit card. Our student still has not left the family home or gone to college, but look at the data already gathered. The computerized files have material on:

Insurance
Driving record
Criminal record
Employment

Medical history and condition
Educational record
Credit
Banking
Home life
Family relationships
Own and family finances
Lifestyle
Preferences and ideologies
Leisure activities
Shopping and consumption patterns
Travel and communications

So far we have shown how personal profiles are established as part of massive data systems. How else can we use the material? To return to vacuum cleaners, as well as using those questionnaires to assemble personal profiles, we can use them compositely to build a model of the way groups of people act to purchase such appliances. We might analyze the data statistically, and find that people with medium family incomes say they spend the most money on appliances, and that in those families the woman makes the buying decision for herself, usually at Acme Hardware Stores. The commercial value of this information is significant.

But what if we take it a step further. As a data company, I have product registration data for vacuum cleaners, but I have also bought hundreds of other such databases. By performing operations upon the data, such as matching, selecting, relating, and modelling, I am now able to offer a comprehensive marketing tool to others. One such tool, developed by Lotus and Equifax, is a piece of personal computer based marketing software called MarketPlace which, using a compact disc that contains data on about 120 million people in 80 million households in the US, allows the user to type in consumer profiles and print out mailing labels for the people who match the profile. The data about each person includes name, address, age, gender, estimated annual income, marital status, and shopping habits.

Such types of data collection, facilitated by computing and communication systems, are commonplace in a modern industrialized society, though the public presentation of MarketPlace led to opposition and its temporary withdrawal in 1990. It is certainly true that many of the valued services that we receive depend upon the systematic and orderly collection of data about us. What this example begins to outline is the pervasiveness of the data collection and the underlying ability to match and model pieces of data for the purpose of creating information which can be used to influence our decision making. Even more to the point, these data are the basis for others to make decisions about us and therefore control and manipulate our everyday life. And yet, as large and wide scale as these data systems are, they must be considered *personal* information systems because they hold data which relates to specific, identifiable individuals.

THE PERSONAL IN DATA SYSTEMS

Laws in different countries generally hold that storing data which relates to specific, identifiable individuals constitutes a personal database, but they often do not go a stage further, to distinguish between differing types of data. While a computer system that collects your buying habits may be intrusive, for example, by sending you mail you do not want, a system which contains data about your mental health or political activities may be used in ways that can cause you serious harm, for example, by releasing your past history of depression to a potential employer. There is some data which people consider to be more personal than others, or that we consider to be intimate and do not want to be shared. Alternatively, there is data which we share, but only in confidence. In some situations, not limited to conversations with a lawyer or doctor, people expect that what is shared will be protected in some way by confidentiality. But how do we know that other people share our view of what is personal?

In a most interesting demonstration of defining personal data, Wacks (1989, pp. 226–238) created an index. This is based upon the extent to which the exposure of data could potentially cause harm to a person. The data is rated by the degrees of sensitivity, low, medium or high. He defines *low sensitivity* as biographical data, and puts in this category basic facts about home, job and educational record. *Medium sensitivity* he describes as judgemental, including reports on us (school, employment) and matters involving a judgement or opinion of another person. Data which is *high sensitivity* is intimate, like our mental health record, where "there is a persuasive case for maintaining that at least some . . . should not be collected at all" (p. 229).

Generally, people are highly sensitive to health, ideological, criminal justice, and sexual data. It is true that sensitivity is difficult to define, and may change not only from culture to culture, but from time to time. However, the combination of the ability to identify a particular individual, the potential to cause that individual harm, and the sensitivity of the data being collected are personal considerations which surely need to be, in almost all cases, under the control of the individual.

It is true that many of the services we need, such as health or social security services, rely on us to furnish accurate and truthful data to them. One might also argue that much of this data could be seen as trivial, as opposed to private or sensitive. Indeed, in some countries (all of Scandinavia, for example), data has been categorized to account for differences in sensitivity. It is also possible to argue that some data is of such import to society, and perhaps being HIV positive presently fits this description, that it must not only be collected but also related to specific individuals. Despite these arguments, the ultimate concern needs to be framed within the context of protecting the individual in everyday life. We can do this by honouring the right of the individual to advise and consent. Not only should consent be the cornerstone of all approaches, buy also people need to have the right to be informed when and where data about them is collected or stored. They need to give their specific consent to any activity which accesses, operates upon and uses this data. They need to be able to access and correct data without risking vulnerability or expense.

The location and correction of data is not as simple as it may sound. It is easiest to understand if we assume that the data is stored in one computer, but of course it is not. The fact that it is traded means that it has passed to many computers, possibly linked in a network, but just as possibly quite separate. Leaving aside the complex practicalities, what is the value of a right to view, correct and sanction the use of our personal data, without a parallel right to be informed of all computers on which it is held?

In order to illustrate these difficulties we can continue the example of our student, who is now a high achieving university student nearing graduation, but needing support, advice, and counselling about moving into a career. Though a hard worker, the student has got involved in other activities, and is worried about a number of matters. Can a campus counsellor help? The counsellor, a psychologist, administers a number of tests which hint at a rather unbalanced character. Consequently, in their discussions, they cover the student's uncertainty about sexuality, disgust with war and government, experimentation with alcohol and drugs, and concerns about the future of the world. These discussions are very helpful to the student. They not only relieve anxiety, but they contribute to a number of healthy decisions to change living patterns. Things feel a lot more balanced, and, as the lifestyle changes, so uncertainties disappear.

The future our student desires is a good beginning position in a large firm of stockbrokers. After interviews for a number of positions, none of the applications succeeds. The student's father has a close friend in one of the firms, so makes a discreet enquiry. The friend reveals the reasons why no job was offered. Apparently, there are some damaging psychological test results which come up in the employment check. In addition, there is a psychological report which describes the student as confused, possibly sexually maladjusted, with occasional depression, marginally psychotic, and a potential non-conformist who may be addicted to drugs and alcohol. After calming down, the student recalls talks with the university counsellor, and also remembers in the first job application agreeing to a recruitment firm seeking a report from that source.

The student is able to find out that the firm is a subsidiary of Greater Data. They admit to having the files in their main computer in Taiwan and agree to a formal request to review them for errors and corrections. In talking to a supervisor at Greater Data, the student finds that they have sold the files to others, and probably those have sent them to others again. In addition, the supervisor explains that while the student has the right to correct erroneous or incorrect data, the correct data will not be removed.

The student has now encountered a number of the major problems we can expect in data collection and retention. The counsellor may have professional values about confidentiality, but does not ensure that they are extended to the computer system. Old data has been retained, with subjective interpretations which, while useful at the time of counselling, were later damaging to the interests of the student. No-one, least of all the student, had been given the opportunity to assess whether old test results and notes were relevant to the present search for employment. Most critically, the student had no knowledge that the data was being kept, no knowledge of the use to which the data would be put, and had not been asked to consent to the use of the data.

DATA NETWORKS

In the incident at Greater Data, the student enters a new world of concerns which involve large multi-purpose data banks and data networks, some of which spread across the world. By computer networks we mean computers and their storage devices in different geographic locations which are periodically or constantly linked by use of computer programs and physical devices, such as cables, telephone lines, or satellites. It is understandably difficult for people to grasp the concentration and activity of computer networks which is presently taking place, but it is an activity which gives rise to real fear. In a recent survey in the United States (Christian Science Monitor, 1990), 79 per cent of Americans voiced concern about threats to their personal privacy. Nearly a third had refused to apply for something because they felt the requested data was too personal. While for most

Americans these fears are probably based upon feelings and intuition rather than facts, the facts support their worst fears. Computer networks are a major contributor to threats to privacy.

If someone has your name, address, and social security number in the United States, it is possible to obtain information from any number of national data banks. A private detective in Austin, Texas, understands and uses computer networks as an integral part of his work. He was hired to track down two suspects who had left a number of unpaid bills behind in a small community in Vermont, more than 2000 miles away. After typing the social security numbers of the two men into his office computer, he used a computer program which connected his computer to one in Cincinnati, Ohio, about 1500 miles away. Once the connection was made, another program began a search of social security numbers for possible matches. Matches occurred and new addresses for the suspects were listed, one in Salt Lake City, Utah (2600 miles from Vermont) and the other in Los Angeles, California (3200 miles from Vermont). In less than five minutes after taking the job, he had found the suspects.

In the United States, it is estimated that the three large credit companies – TRW, Trans Union, and Equifax – each have about 85 per cent of the adult American population listed in their data banks. Different levels of government have joined this industry. An increasing number of state records, including voter registration data, are accessible through computer networking. These data banks are regularly accessed by small information bureaux whose business is responding to data requests, for example, from lawyers, banks, insurance agents, property owners, businesses, hospitals, or car dealers. In Britain this extent of network organization has yet to emerge, but it is likely that similar results are achieved through the "old boys network", where material is exchanged through personal contacts in the club or the masonic lodge. However, in one particular way Britain has outstripped other countries. Originating from decisions made in 1971 to merge existing groups into new large welfare organizations (Social Services Act, 1971), reinforced by boundary revisions to local authorities in 1974 which made many of these organizations still larger, Britain emerged with some of the world's biggest welfare agencies. Some of these have pioneered sophisticated computerised client information systems, with much narrower coverage then general data banks (up to about 20 per cent of the population in some local authority areas), but focusing on highly sensitive data about, for example, personal debts, family malfunctioning, behavioral difficulties and health prognoses.

It is in government that difficulties with data networks most often become public. The widespread use of computing in government acts as a magnifying glass to highlight problems endemic to the evolving capabilities of people to use the machinery in an effective manner. Moreover, these problems are often blamed upon the machinery itself – not upon its engineers, programmers, or users. The belief that a machine has been created that performs erratically, makes mistakes of serious human consequence, and yet controls government decision-making, is a frightening prospect to the public. Even more dismaying is the fear that some of those in the public service – civil servants, soldiers, police and politicians – might be fundamentally unethical.

LEGAL DILEMMAS

Chapter 11 takes up some of the legal aspects of personal data protection, though reference to legal frameworks is relevant at this stage, partly to identify the principles which laws have sought to spotlight, and partly to acknowledge that the sorts of data accumulation and use which we have outlined in previous pages would be more acceptable in some countries than others. National frameworks can be viewed on a broad canvas in the range of national IT plans which were developed in the 1970s and 80s, or with more distinct focus in related legislation.

A 1987 study of national computer plans (Matley and McDannold, 1987) shows that Japan and France were the first in the field, followed by Britain (based on the Alvey Report) and the EEC (Esprit). Significantly the USA is not on the list. Japan and France specifically addressed social issues in their plans, while other countries have tended to focus on matters of economic development and commerce. Nevertheless, almost all western industrial states have taken actions regarding personal information, including the Privacy Act in the USA and the Data Protection Act in Britain. While the EEC's Esprit plan has more of a developmental focus, both the Organization for Economic Co-operation and Development (OECD) and the Council of Europe have identified human rights aspects of data collection and usage. The Council of Europe has established a Convention for protecting personal information.

At root all these actions recognise a dilemma, between the need for growing data stores, including personal data, as a means to economic progress, and the need to protect privacy. A range of measures have been tried out in national legislation, including:

Restrictions on the formation of large databases, or on network links.

Controls on data gathering.

Categorisation of data, according to sensitivity or origin, linked to rules for the use of the different categories.

Controls on data access and use.

Registration and inspection of the purposes of data collection and use.

Procedures for data correction and updating.

Procedures to ensure data subject or wider public access to data stores.

Penalties for the breach of legal requirements.

Definition and designation of what constitutes a criminal activity in this field.

Philosophically the measures embedded in legislation range from the view that commercial interests have primacy, right through to the other end of the spectrum, with the primacy of the potential data subject. At the same time attempts have been made not so much to locate legislation somewhere along a spectrum of possibilities, as to find a compromise or even redefinition of the basic dilemma. Both Japanese and French planners have worked on the notion of an information society being a society without the existence of or need for privacy. There is no need for privacy or secrecy because there is total access to all data. The French plan uses the concept of the "privacy of openness", though whether politically (for example, with nationally sensitive material) or psychologically (as with distressing personal events) such a concept could ever have a real existence is questionable. David Flaherty (1989) offers a detailed analysis of privacy issues in several European and North American countries for any reader who wishes to delve deeper.

A further dilemma for legislators arises from a question which is posed about many attempts to define permitted and forbidden behaviours – "Can such a law be enforced?" Already some problems have been identified with regard to data protection. A 1986 report of the United States General Accounting Office criticized the lack of attempts to enforce the Privacy Act. Comment has also been made about the apparent lack of teeth, or reluctance to use them, by the British Data Protection Registrar. A range of practical difficulties have surfaced, including the complexity of understanding and monitoring the technologies of computing and networking, the problems of data systems crossing national boundaries and therefore moving outside specific legislative cover, difficulties in defining incorruptible categories for data gathering and use, and the shortage of skilled resources to handle enforcement measures.

MORAL DILEMMAS

How about the question – "What is your credit history?" This question is asked of us every time we want to start a bank account, or get into any major financial transaction. One ethically acceptable reaction is to suggest that we must be informed any and every time such a question is being asked, from whom, by whom, at what cost to whom, and told what the answer was. Should we also have a right to force the firm storing the credit data to remove it from their records, if we decide not to operate through bank accounts and instead do all our transactions in cash? How about the right to receive a payment of a proportion of the fee the company charged to those to whom such data was provided: or perhaps we should be able to charge that fee ourselves and have our own method to provide valid data to the enquirer?

Take another example. John is told by the police, when they stop him for rolling through a "stop" sign, that they will ask the criminal justice information system whether he had any outstanding summons or fine payable. The system shows that he has two parking fines unpaid. The record was assembled from the county computer disk using the accounts payable program. The database entries were taken from parking tickets, and entered by a clerical officer, but were never verified by any other person, nor checked for accuracy. The police officer also asked if John was known to be wanted for any offence. The question was sent from the patrol car to a computer system at the state office building which in turn dialled a computer system in Louisville, Kentucky. The computer system in Louisville was running a program which directs a machine to respond to telephone calls and if it recognizes the transmitted sound as a digital message it connects it to a query response program. This analyzes the request and then searches disk 14 for any record of John. John is listed in a record entered on 27/02/75. The entry represents John's arrest for driving under the influence of alcohol sixteen years ago, while still a teenager. That entry is now sent back to the police officer who asked the question. What might the officer decide on the basis of the material provided?

That is, in what ways do answers to questions made to computers determine subsequent actions? How responsible for those answers are the persons who entered the data or wrote the programs? Are the entries and programs now something apart from their creators? Do they have a right to forget about them? Are they responsible for errors? Is anyone responsible for the fact that the police officer will accept the computer output without challenge, and probably come down heavily on John as a result? It should be obvious at this point that if and when the human concern with fairness is brought back into the equation, there must be acceptance of the possibility of a gulf between real truth and what the computer presents as truth. What John has to face is a network of computer programs, all based on unstated theoretical constructs, all taking for granted the infallibility of the others.

Imagine now that you are a worker in an agency that deals with cases of child abuse. You are telephoned late one evening. It is the police. They have received and investigated a call from a person in a neighbourhood some distance away who reported that she heard shouting and crying in the house next door. She feared for the child in the home. The police responded and are now in the home. They have found a woman in a state of distress. She and her husband have recently been separated, and the husband is under court order not to visit the house without supervision. She works at a local shop. Tonight, when she arrived home, the child told her that the father had been there all afternoon until she arrived. She was very angry and took it out on her child. It is not clear to the police what she had done to the child, and the police need to have your advice. You leave immediately for the home.

One of the problems in dealing with child protection is in assessing the risk to the child in staying at home, and the potential damage caused by removal from home. What rules of evidence must be satisfied if computer programs are used to help assess the situation? On the one hand, there are a number of human elements involved in the situation which need to be taken into account, such as the suffering of the child and parent. On the other hand, it is important to have clearly delineated responsibilities for decisions if a computer program is used to assess the risk of leaving the child in the home. Is the worker or the computer programmer responsible when decisions are wrong and the child is murdered?

In the situation that we have described, the worker finds that the woman and child are distraught and have been through a difficult emotional time, that the child needs to go to the grandmother's house for the evening, and that the mother needs some supportive counselling immediately. The arrangements are made and carried out. The police write up their report and indicate that they will talk to the father. The worker goes home and later makes a report which is entered into the agency's child abuse risk register. From this point on, the family will be labelled as one in which suspected child abuse occurred, both in the social services computer system and the police computer system, though there is no suggestion that such an entry serves to assist in the protection of the child during the present situation. However, in a number of cases, such as the one described here, no further reporting occurs. For how long must this computer record be kept? As improbable as it might sound, what would happen if the woman's record were made available to her employer?

In this example the worker provided data for computer entry into a program that had a form of organization which was not ideally suited to the situation. The thrust in developing entry forms in organizations has been to standardize them. The information the worker extracts from a situation is put into categories on a form, broken down for purposes of comparability and administration. In such situations the purpose is no longer to convey the information the worker perceived – the suffering, uniqueness and the humanity of it – but the generality of the situation for reporting requirements. The meaning of the specific situation is lost, its personal and human elements separated and categorized. Another worker who uses the computer program and asks questions of the data will not be able to reassemble anything approaching what really happened that night. Yet the new worker may be required to take actions of real personal consequence to the family.

Humans use computer data as though it is real, and make decisions with real personal consequences. For example, a marketing firm accesses data from your record at the magazine company to determine whether or not they should try to sell you soap. Who benefits? Will you now receive soap advertisements? Telephone calls? Perhaps a rather different scenario for such an event could be like this. If marketing firms want to use your record they get your permission. If your record is used you are paid a fee. If they telephone you they must pay you a fee. The fee must be paid simply to dial your number and interrupt your life, and another fee paid for every minute or part of a minute on the phone. The magazine company must also pay you a fee based upon the amount they charged the marketing company. On first reading such a course of action may sound bizarre: but think again. If we ring up and call on the expertise of a lawyer, then we may receive a bill for the time the lawyer spends talking to us. Our personal histories are our own areas of expertise – at the very least we should have the right to decide whether to make a charge to someone who wants to make use of it.

The use of computer data is leading to new questions about intellectual property rights. In a number of universities course work is presented in electronic media. At present the selection, reasoning, and preparation incumbent upon the teacher in preparing course work (an electronic textbook) is rewarded by copyright protection. But what if IT can be used to track the origin of the course material? Does copyright then revert to the various originators? What if the system allows (as in some cases it does) students to add facts and opinions to the course material? Who is then the owner?

The arguments about the issue are not fictional, but were heard in 1989 during the Oversight Hearing on Computers and Intellectual Property, United States House of Representatives Subcommittee on Courts, Intellectual Property and the Administration of Justice. These discussions have continued in many places both inside and outside of various government bodies. The expert views expressed during the United States hearing often did not confront the full scale of the dilemma this situation poses, but only the part related to who will get rich and under what conditions. There is more! As we have shown in this chapter, there is a growing industry in the buying and selling of data. The tools are easy to use, the computer and telephone like the pickaxe and sifting pan of another era. Data is being mined for information. We are in a gold rush. There are few if any rules for the gold rush, and what rules do exist are inadequate to ensure the preservation of individualism. For what is being mined is no longer the earth; it is humans and their activities. And that is the dilemma. The capitalism of the past two centuries has moved forward with the exploitation of the earth providing its raw material. The generation of wealth was tied to land, to mineral rights, oil rights, water rights. We now understand that the earth is a limited resource. And we have reached sight of the necessary end to many of the forms of exploitation that we have enjoyed, from the near exhaustion of oil to the loss of ozone. Capitalism has lost its fuel.

To change the fundamental link in capitalism between earth as raw material to humans and their everyday life as raw material, we need tools. We have found them in information technologies. It is clear that for this transformation to succeed, we also need to change our ways of thinking about intelligence. In major part, this is what the present arguments about intelligence as property represent. If we examine the history of the development of capitalism, we note that early on a large part of the land was held in common. No one owned it. In fact, private property was a notion that ran against human history and tradition. Yet it triumphed: the commons were lost.

We are in a period much like that one. At this moment human tradition holds that progress depends upon a relatively free and open exchange of data, information, and knowledge – an intellectual open space. In some ways one could argue that this is too idealistic, since it is true that there are laws which regulate contracts, trade secrets, patents, inventions, commercial data, information, and knowledge of all types. But in our schools and universities, we have honoured a tradition of learning, teaching, and scholarship based upon sharing and collaboration. In a number of countries, education is a public good, offered free to all citizens. In addition, sharing and replication of experimentation, conferences, and lively debate are the rule. What threatens to alter that tradition is the perception that human intelligence is the raw material for creating future capital.

CONVENIENCE LABELLING

The examples we have offered in this chapter illustrate a range of ethical issues. We have chosen to put emphasis on property rights because it appears that we are quietly and quickly acquiescing in the assumption that our personal lives, once placed on computer, are the property of the data companies. Yet we have noted other factors of considerable human importance. There is both complexity and obscurity about the processes by which computers manipulate data and produce what purports to be information, advice or recommended decisions. There is scope for distortion and chronic proneness to error. Pressures towards standardization exacerbate distortion and error, as well as conceal the uniqueness of individual circumstances. We are not told and do not know what is happening to the personal material which is lodged in computer systems.

All these things are serious faults, but it remains possible to argue that they could all be rectified, given time, better staff training and technological advances. Yet there is one problem which is fundamental and will not go away because it is integral to the notion of taking matters out of the realm of human judgement into the activities of machines. That process takes us out of reality into representation, out of what our senses perceive and into a language of artificial symbols.

At this point it is easy to move into a philosophical discussion of what is real and what is representation. Is reality something out there, permanent and objective? Or is it what each of us perceives, even though some of us may perceive the earth as flat and the moon to be made of cream cheese? Is the very form of communication we use, language and gesture, any more than a complex set of symbols, incapable of ever conveying exact reality? These are all pertinent questions, but in using the terms *reality* and *representation* at this point we are aiming to distinguish between human and computer perceptions. Human beings have the opportunity of direct perception as a starting point, and then the task of conceptualizing and communicating those perceptions. Computers have no perceptions, and therefore no reality. Accuracy for them is dependent on the quality of the language of communication. They work only on representations, symbols.

The computer operates on data represented by signals, mostly electrical but also laser, biological and chemical. Data can be understood by whatever symbols we choose, perhaps a musical note, a special visual design, or a sequence of letters or numbers. The set of symbols must be limited, because large symbol sets are difficult for humans to comprehend and use, and must be representative. For example, $1000, £1000, sköl, and 2.1417 can be data. There is an elegance and simplicity to a numbering system which contains only ten symbols and their combinations, but where a problem arises is with the quality of representativeness. One of the losses in all symbol systems can be the interpretation of the content of that which is symbolized, its meaning. Symbolic languages are used to represent concepts as well, so names can be applied to ideas and abstractions, and, in turn, they can be explained. Yet throughout history we have sought to combat a system of labelling which offers convenience at the expense of accuracy, comprehensiveness, subtlety and balance. We have opposed using such labels, especially when they serve to categorize people unfairly. We have opposed generic labelling which does not recognize human differences, resented logical categories which create artificial distances between us and our colleagues, and sought to promote individual characteristics even within a collectivist political framework.

Now we are faced with computer languages which are the ultimate in convenience labelling, creating logical structures which relate to reality in much the same way as does, for example, a cubist painting. Who will trust life decisions to the interpretation of that sort of representation, regardless of whether the interpreter is a person or a machine?

Of course not all computer generated information is unreal. Much of it has sufficient accuracy to allow us to ignore the potential weakness of representation. If the computer says the Thai Airlines flight will leave for Bangkok at 1900 hours on Tuesday, the plane probably will take off at or somewhere near that time. We accept that subject to known risks (weather, breakdown, delayed incoming flight) this is good information, and useful to us. We can also accept, without ignoring what was said earlier about the fallibility of programming, data entry and data interrogation, that some material can be represented precisely enough so that what is recalled from the machine is acceptably "real". This includes what we commonly call "hard data", factual material like names, addresses and phone numbers.

Problems begin to emerge in two ways. The first is when a complex reality, made up of a network of precise and imprecise data, is represented on a computer by a rigid symbol set. Some things can be done, like digitizing a Beethoven symphony or a Turner landscape, so that they can be brought back to life almost like the original. Other attempts make some progress, like a two-dimensional picture of a three-dimensional scene: they have truth but not the whole truth. The remainder fail, and the failures include attempts to computerize human emotions and the dynamics of human relationships.

The other area of failure cannot be blamed on computers so much as on those who market and advocate for computer services, in their insistence that by gathering together and putting into structured symbols a range of data about us, they can represent *our* truth, the reality of our lives as we perceive them. They want to tell us what is the best soap for us to use, where and when we should shop, what we should buy, and in many ways how we should conduct our lives. Old maxims like "the customer knows best" are fast being replaced by "the computer tells us what the customer wants". Computers have one enormous attraction for the rulers, political and commercial, in our societies – they seem to provide all the information without anyone having to soil their hands by direct contact with people. For most of us, the ruled of this world, we have to assert the fallacy of the notion of computer reality before it becomes part of the gospel of the information age.

4 The Technological Hare and Social Snail

SUMMARY

Connectivity is now the buzz word" says a computer journal with a large circulation (*Personal Computer World*), reflecting a widely held view within IT ranks. It refers to the notion of getting people and their technology linked and working together, and is a direct contradiction of the suggestion in earlier chapters that far from connections existing between IT and societies, there is a gulf and a significant degree of alienation. In their own environment, with their own horizons, computer people can find connectivity: indeed, they can illustrate the substance of its achievement by pointing to the huge expansion of network links. We argue that for the world outside there is less evidence of sympathetic associations, and more of self-centred and mindless exploitation. Even within the IT world there are major divisions, based on underlying principles of computer system organization and functioning, which impinge on the rest of us. This chapter will probe the relationship between IT growth and the condition of society, analyzing the nature and sources of alienation, if indeed it exists, and developing the argument that technology change has outstripped its social integration.

MYTHICAL CONNECTIONS

The statement that technology change has forged so far ahead that other aspects of social functioning have not and seemingly cannot catch up, needs some clarification and refinement. A useful start is to take a closer look at the assertion through a series of snapshots, starting from matters close to, indeed within IT itself, and gradually drawing away to a more distant but more panoramic viewpoint. An important secondary objective of this approach is to pinpoint divergences within technology change, and note how they relate to a wider society.

A close-up picture shows significant fragmentation within IT development. In the early days there were many diversities in details, but in the context of a central focus on the production and use of mainframe computers, providing power for remote locations (terminals). These were followed by mini-computers, to meet the needs of small to medium sized companies, or add to the capacity of an overloaded mainframe by providing extra memory or taking over some tasks. Then along came personal computing and a gap began to emerge between those whose knowledge, experience and commitment was to mainframes, and those who identified with the exciting potential of micros. There were and are linkages between the two camps, provided by the mid-sized machines (mini-computers like Vax), and by the convenience with which the micro came to serve a dual purpose as a stand-alone computer and a terminal to a mainframe. However, the dynamics of the scene are between a technology (mainframe) which is of diminishing generic usefulness in relation to its cost, and a vibrant ever-changing technology (micro, based on personal computers) which is growing in importance and scope. Without denying that the large powerful computer, whether a modern mainframe or a "Super-computer" like the Cray, has a place in certain specialist areas, involving very large data sets or extremely long complex calculations, almost all of the high profile development involves the desktop computer, including machines for home and office.

Gradually we appear to be reaching the stage when the mainframe computer, serving dumb terminals (that is terminals or work stations which can do nothing independently of their connection to the mainframe), loses many of its tasks to smaller machines. These micro computers can themselves be configured in a number of ways, ranging from being wholly self-contained, through links with a small number of other, similar machines (often aided by a more powerful micro acting as what is called a file server, or common source within the network for programs and memory space), to acting as terminals in a large linked system. Conceptually there are three alternative approaches – centralisation, distribution and self-sufficiency.

A centralized system is the traditional structure. At an early stage of development there was little choice, because the links to the computer proper (keyboards and monitors, and more historically, punch card readers) had no independent computing power. All power resided in the central machine. Self-sufficiency reflects the opposite end of the spectrum. Here the computer system is made up of self-contained micro computers, each capable of handling its own computing tasks, and dependent on connections with networks solely for purposes of communication. The most self-sufficient systems are home computers, simply because they are likely not to be connected to any network, or to be connected only when the user chooses to attach them, via a modem, to the telephone. In an office context it is also often within the scope of the individual user to decide whether or when to make a network connection. A distributed system represents a mid-point, and in purely functional terms offers the widest number of uses. The core of the system is a mainframe or a powerful mini computer, and as each terminal comes into operation it has the scope to handle tasks through the mainframe (like accessing a large store of data, or a commonly used program such as the company's preferred word processor), or work separately with its own programs. In practice most organizations opt for some kind of distribution, but with significant variations in terms of the extent of central control or devolution.

There are strategic implications within the IT industry, because staff groups are not always able to cope with the switch in priorities and skills, and because some of the big players have a long-standing and seemingly hard-to-move commitment to big centralized systems. There are political implications because of the way a typical mainframe system, with a central provider controlling terminals, parallels the authority structure of a cen-tralised organization, keeping control over outlying offices. Many senior managers in organizations liked the systems of the 1960s and 70s because they felt better in command, with the knowledge that the computer system was in their own block, orders could be sent down the lines, and remote terminals did not have the capacity to do anything independently. There are also staffing considerations. Older systems spawned substantial computer services and data processing staff groups, who developed cohesion, and now use it to combat the risks of redundancy or postings to unfamiliar territories.

New micro or personal computer based systems, linked to be able to communicate with each other without going through a central headquarters, and having independent computing capacities, symbolise the devolution of authority. Such systems are cheaper to install, run and update, and have the capacity to promote lateral communications instead of or as well as vertical ones. They are a threat to centralization within the organisation. Hence we have a situation in which cost and the state of technology favour a new route, while vested interests guard the traditional format. The compromise of a distributed system does often work from an organizational, managerial and political viewpoint, though only because some of the biases are not made too explicit. They may well be hidden beneath the surface of the visible form of operation, dependent on what functions are possible. Does the mainframe (that is, the centre of authority) automatically take a copy of all messages sent between terminals? Can a senior manager either eavesdrop on contact between terminals (the equivalent of a telephone tap), or monitor what a user of an outlying terminal is doing? Can the manager do this without the knowledge of the terminal user? Can the terminal user carry out any computing without an automatic record of the activity being made?

This is not the only range of potential divisiveness originating from within IT. Throughout recent years it has been growing clearer that the technology which produces ever better machines, and faster, more accurate communications, is racing ahead of the range of potential applications. The proportion of programs labelled as "prototype" or "on trial" is extremely high in some areas of application, and much of the material which is considered to be fully functioning is known to be error prone. This is true both of programs widely available on the open market, and expensive special designs, such as those in military settings. More significantly, new equipment is launched onto the personal computer market with few accompanying applications to take advantage of the advances in technology (IBM's PS2 was an example), so potentially very powerful computers are running programs which run perfectly well, sometimes more reliably, on older, cheaper and well established work horses.

Two points made in the previous paragraph have wider relevance. The observation that the rate of technology development relates specifically to hardware, and that applications (software) lag well behind, gives rise to a mixed range of emotions. On the one hand there is the enthusiasm many people feel about having a better machine, and a matching keenness to try out what it can do. The focus of so much advertising on the notion of a new improved model shows how potent such attitudes are thought to be. On the other hand, this enthusiasm can switch rapidly to frustration, disappointment and hostility if the new machine does not live up to its promise, or if it is not possible to give it a thorough trial. It is easy to understand the feeling that state of the art computers are something of a confidence trick, given the time lag before applications arrive (or if they do not arrive ever!).

The second point concerns the tendency of computers to make mistakes. While acknowledging that in many instances this really means that the computer user has made a mistake, nevertheless, it is not possible to find a perfectly functioning, foolproof, flawless piece of software. Had we from the start argued that computers (more accurately, computer applications) were like people, and made mistakes, then expectations might have been different. But instead we chose to let the view gain ground that computers are or ought to be infallible, and that once a program got through its teething troubles there would be no further problems. There is a sound principle in consumer protection that a purchase must be what it claims to be and do what it claims to do. If something has a flaw, or is a "second", or can malfunction, then it has to be sold with this made explicit. Society has tended to be charitable and accept at face value assurances that programs will "in the very near future" be made to work perfectly, or that claimed compatibilities will genuinely come about. Will society go on being charitable when the excuse of tomorrow . . . manyana becomes a permanent feature?

It may be that in the future we shall look back and say of this era that it lived in perpetual hope of better software around the corner, failing to realise the fundamental difficulties inherent in program design. Certainly we have tended to assume that the technology represented the real challenge, and that applications would flood in to take advantage of bigger and better micro-processors. In that sense a relatively low priority has been given to programming, and it has received much less investment than hardware development, so there does appear to have been some inadequacy in strategic planning. However, there is a more fundamental reason for concluding that the IT industry has under-rated the problems of applications. Hardware can be handled with some detachment, as pure technology: software is the interface of IT with its users, and the image presented to a wider public.

IT AND THE PAYING CUSTOMER

An effective strategy for software development requires close collaboration between developers, users, and potential users, with some acknowledge-ment of an overviewing role for society as a whole, and the institutions designated to monitor legality and standards. To overview efforts to achieve the first part of this, a link between developers and users, it is useful to make some initial points about machines, before turning to applications.

There is no questioning user involvement in many early computer systems. They were specialist designs to serve particular customer speci-fications – count census returns, break secret codes, track enemy aircraft movements. The customer emphasis was very much on the desired out-come, with seemingly only one major preoccupation about the computing process, or way the outcomes were to be achieved, and that was speed. The American census bureau wanted speed to avoid the embarrassment of not getting through counting last decade's data before the next lot arrived. The military in the Second World War needed speed because breaking codes and tracking movements had limited value if it was not able to influence the immediate situation.

Some traditions emerged in these early years which are still a part of the scene. The concern with speed has, if anything, grown to be an obsession with system developers – micro-processor speed, disk drive response rate, printer characters per second, fibre optic communication speed – without anyone really pausing to ask what exactly all the haste is for. No doubt there are macho customers who want their computers, like their cars, to be faster than the next man's; but is this the basis for a creative response to user needs? In effect the interest in speed has moved its focus from what the end user needed, to what the technology permits. Computer designers are faced with an array of factors which either enable or discourage development. Inhibiting technology takes in the mechanical (as opposed to electronic) features of a computer system, such as the way printer head actions ensure that print-out speeds are desperately slow compared with processor speeds. Another limitation is posed by the standard operating system in the micro world, MSDOS, which sets boundaries to the extent of concurrent activity. In contrast the development of micro-processors has served as a major enabler, both because of the growth in "bit" size (the number of memory locations that can be worked on simultaneously) and clock setting (the pace of these activities). As a result the initial concordance has come to an end, with developers pointing to the scope for a really major breakthrough if technology developments are linked to more fundamental changes in computer systems, like the adoption of UNIX as the operating system, while consumers appreciate speed in the context of their loyalty to the tried and tested, like MSDOS.

An appropriate speed for the tasks to be undertaken is a reasonable aim; however, the speed must relate not only to the task, but also to the context of the system as a whole and its users. Part of that context is the full configuration of equipment linked together in the overall system, such as the computer (or more specifically its central processor), disk drives for storage and retrieval, printer, and the connections through which they work together. In the last resort a system is as fast as its slowest components (not forgetting the keyboard operator), so integrated speed is what matters.

Another part of the context is the human user, who may thrill at the mind-blowing rate at which the processor can function, but at the same time not be clear what buttons to press to get the right operations underway, or sit waiting for a printer to churn out a hundred lines a minute, or, worse, be frantically trying to free a clogged paper feeder. The focus on speed has been too narrowly based, and given too little attention to the system as a whole. As stated, a typical system has electronic (micro-processors) and mechanical (printer, keyboard) components. Designers and developers have taken up the electronic challenges with great success, but been less successful with the mechanical ones.

Turning to applications, and recalling the suggestion already made that within the IT industry there is a real lack of cohesion between hardware and software producers, there has nevertheless been one area where the theory surrounding the construction of the program links programmer and potential user. This is in the design of expert systems. Here a methodology has been identified, bringing together the system developer with an expert in the field which is to be the topic of the expert system. Routines have been identified for clarifying professional expertise and converting it into the rather firmer statements (commonly rules) which the programmer prefers to handle. Continuing interactions between programmer and topic experts (often in a process labelled *prototyping*) supposedly refine the system to the point where it can be put into operation. Yet surprisingly few efforts at expert systems have been wholly successful, and few of the big companies have chosen to get deeply involved. In fact there is growing evidence that the task is extremely difficult, and that the contacts between program designer and topic expert(s) need more subtlety and sophistication that had been imagined (e.g. Miller and Cordingley in Glastonbury, LaMendola and Toole, 1987).

Attempts at wider involvement in software design are hard to find, as are examples of company policies which place emphasis on getting out into the real world to talk in detail with potential users about just what programs they want. The concept of the customer knowing best has little hold in IT. In general the customer gets the programs which excite IT industry staff, or which their marketing people think will sell well. It has to be added that the public has shown little interest and created no pressure to be consulted, perhaps through apathy, perhaps through insecurity and fear at their lack of knowledge of technicalities and jargon. Similarly the world's legal forces and watchdog organizations have kept on the fringes, though the IT industry has sought their support in combatting problems with copyright and the invasion of IT systems.

Software companies might feel aggrieved at the suggestion that their output lacks sensitivity to the views of users, and argue that some applications are so conspicuously successful that it is absurd to suggest that they have not matched just what the user wanted. What about office automation? What about computer games with their amazing graphics? Surely something like word processing is so good and so imaginative, that no amount of consumer involvement would have led to better things? Certainly recognition has to be given to such innovations, but equally likely, if consumers had been consulted, some major applications as well as some hardware would be different. No doubt the compatibility and interfacing of programs would be much better; keyboards would be used more imaginatively, if we still had such things; the home computer might have a serious and valued function. At a later stage (Chapter 8) we want to take up the idea of what a computer system and its applications would be like if they were designed from the viewpoint of a user community, perhaps a Third World community, or one with different gender relationships.

ARE USERS ALIENATED?

Pulling back for a more panoramic snapshot brings into the frame a further range of concerns in the relationship between the IT industry and both its users and the organs of state. The earlier suggestion that state institutions have kept a low profile can be spelled out to include legal matters (such as data security), quality control and warranty issues, the efficacy of advertising, workforce training and welfare, and anxieties about health and safety in the production and use of computers. Some of these points will be pursued in later chapters, but a matter of note at this stage is that IT companies have not always been good employers. Much of this can be put down to the frenzied activity surrounding production and marketing. Too many business have come into being to take advantage of the topicality of a small range of products, only to fade when they are overtaken. Too much has been made dependent on the success of marketing hype, with sales and support staff coping with customer realities in the wake of exaggerated advertising claims about the marvels of particular machines or programs. In the frenzy these may be pardonable excesses, but it has left workers with little job security and some degree of stress in customer relationships.

High performance claims and poor support service have provoked some disaffection amongst users, but this is merely a small sector of a much wider alienation, which encompasses users and members of the public. User alienation, as argued earlier, is generated by linked factors – weaknesses in software performance, possibility of error, and lack of knowledge. While some applications are now so predictably reliable and effective as to engender feelings of security – word processing would come into this category – others lack reliability and accuracy, whether through software or hardware failure, or because of the user's fallibility. Furthermore, when something goes wrong, it is not always clear what it is, and the inferiority of the user, coupled with regular shows of elitist mysticism and arrogance from the IT-literate, predisposes towards a feeling that the user should take all the blame. In part there is a transitional problem which workers in industrialized countries are currently facing, that a high proportion of staff in the environs of IT applications went through their formal education prior to these new technologies appearing on the curriculum. For them there is self-learning (not easy, given the poor quality of manuals) and short introductory courses. Learning on the job, like an apprenticeship, may be attractive and effective if it is thorough and unhurried, but the expectation that someone can operate a program on the basis of a two day course is a sure cause of anxiety, resentment, depression and illness.

At the extremity of worker attitudes is a feeling of total fearfulness and incompetence at the prospect of using IT, sometimes linked to a conviction that some sort of vibes given off by that particular user will ensure that the machine or program, probably both, will collapse. Some people hold sincerely the view that computers can sense their anxiety, and take sadistic pleasure in exploiting it (a documented example relates to a survey of social workers – Glastonbury, 1985). These gradations of alienation, from worry to virtual anxiety-based paralysis pose a challenge and place a responsibility on the IT industry. In the long term both challenge and responsibility must be worth accepting, on marketing terms alone, if not humanitarian. There are many circumstances in which bad first experiences of IT lead to inhibitions on getting further into that field, and so affect investment and purchasing plans.

Drawing back still further, to encompass a wider public, probably the greatest fearfulness has been about the impact of IT on traditional forms and levels of employment. In the early years of rapid IT expansion the strongest efforts to halt the onward flow came from trade unions and those who were convinced that massive unemployment would result. Those fears still exist, though the loss of jobs through IT related causes is lower than earlier estimates. The recent history of IT has coincided with a decade or more of recessions and insecure phases of growth in industrialized countries, so it becomes almost impossible to say how far levels of employment can be linked to the spread of technology, replacing manual activities. Some elements of disruption are clearer, such as the physical movement of employment opportunities to different geographical locations, as traditional heavy industries fade and "silicon valleys" are formed. This has thrown into disarray the skills training and abilities of many workers, and made previously valued expertise look suddenly wholly obsolete. Many workers have not had adequate chances or not been able to respond to retraining. Moving jobs has also disrupted long established and well functioning communities, leading them into decay, and creating both acute and chronic housing shortages in the new employment areas.

Some societies have passed a long way through this phase of disruption – if indeed it can be seen as a transitional era. Others have still to experience it. Just a few have found IT a window to economic growth without the trauma of simultaneously coping with declining traditional industry. The picture is mixed, but what is common to all is that the public is rarely consulted, and have little chance to achieve awareness of what is happening. As throughout the history of industrial development, the consequences of investment decisions made by small groups of business people have outcomes for whole societies which are not expected or not appreciated at the time. Often they are beneficial, leading to real improvements in living standards: sometimes they are harmful. IT has been no different, except that the pace has been too quick and the action too recent to permit any thorough reflection on the likely impact.

One insidious reality, with a bearing on alienation, is that systems which survive and prosper on gathering and using data need access to sources of data. The biggest source is people, and industrialized communities have fallen rapidly into the role of giving IT systems the sustenance they require. As Chapter 3 illustrated, we cannot now fill in a warranty card for a new purchase, or follow up an advertised offer, without being asked to say something about ourselves – our jobs, families, preferred brand labels, shopping habits, where we go on holiday, and so forth. If we want a bank account or a credit card we are obliged to fill in a form about our income, and usually agree to our employer being asked for still more information about us. We are not only asked about ourselves, but about all family members, and we are offered inducements to recommend names of other people who can be approached. Glossy magazines are increasingly handed out free of cash payment, but in exchange for particulars of self and, commonly, job setting. Any of us willing to answer detailed questions on a regular basis about our private lives will get gifts as a reward. Added to all this, many of the unavoidable transactions in our lives – buying a house, having a medical examination, getting married or divorced, going before a court of law – will be fully documented, and more than likely appear in the great data file.

It is, of course, frivolous to describe this gathering process in terms of the insatiable appetite of computers. In reality the information is gathered because people find it useful, can employ it to inform themselves about us, subsequently manipulate and control us; and because some people want data, and are prepared to pay well for it, there is a growing sector of the economy which makes income out of intruding in our lives.

GETTING AN ACT TOGETHER

The title of this chapter links technology with the hare, society's response to the snail. A direct analogy is too simplistic, though there is observable truth in the assertion made frequently in these pages that IT has developed at a great pace, and the corresponding observation that society has tended to sit back and let it happen. A valid general question is whether it is fair or accurate to equate "letting it happen" with a snail-like response. To describe society's reaction in terms of the movement of a snail is to be thoroughly derogatory, making a specific accusation about the lack of speed, and implying lack of direction as well as a supine passivity. In contrast there are all kinds of sayings and peppy metaphors to justify standing back, giving IT its head, letting them run with the ball, make a home run, and push forward the frontiers of knowledge. If the rest of us do not stand back we may be nothing more than a weight on their shoulders, holding back their progress.

IT is viewed as a great thrust forward, and there is undoubtedly a risk that if the rest of us seek to interfere, we shall impede rather than enable the fullest gains. The issue can be summed up in two questions, the latter conditional on the reply to the former. Is IT going in the direction we want it? Picking up the metaphor of the football game again, is IT running with the right ball to the right end of the field? If the answer from all sides is "Yes", then the second question can be forgotten. But if the answer has some negatives in it, then we need to ask whether we should be able to make IT pause sufficiently to change the ball or run in a different direction or both.

The passivity of the snail has left IT open to relatively unfettered exploitation. We have tried to argue, and will develop these points much further in Part 2, that IT has got many things right. The computer, and the ease with which we can now communicate around the world, are marvels of invention, and great benefits to society. At the same time, the IT system the world now possesses has, embedded within it, many of the recognised flaws of twentieth-century life. These concerns have been stated before in this book, and will be repeated later, so important are they to our thesis. IT is elitist, exacerbating divisions between rich and poor: it is often insensitive to issues of equal rights and opportunities, and more broadly to basic humanitarian standards about the way we should treat one another: it is a tool of militarism: it is a means of control which can be employed all too easily to undermine democratic values: and although it has the potential to empower all of us, the early generations of its use show a clear pattern of empowering rulers, managers and employers rather than citizens.

Given such views, it is difficult to justify the image of society hiding in its shell, emerging from time to time to make a few tentative and slow movements. Indeed, it would hardly suffice for society simply to become more reactive, perhaps seeking to monitor and, if justified, set boundaries and regulations around IT exploitations. Reactivity does not change basic directions, except in a very circuitous and wasteful way. What society needs to do is become more proactive, to harness the creativity of IT by guiding (also if necessary funding) it towards desired goals by way of desired processes.

The suggestion made at the start of this chapter was that technology change has outstripped its social integration. The argument has been developed that the pace of technology change, though fast, is in itself uneven, and lacking cohesion, especially as between machines and applications. The record of discussing or planning developments with users or wider communities is patchy, and in many major areas non-existent. The response of users and members of the public has been lethargic, reinforcing the effect of widespread governmental policies of non-intervention except in specific, mainly military circumstances. The result has been that IT has achieved substantial integration into our lives, in the sense that we are now wholly dependent on it for the conduct of social organization, and have accepted passively the replacement of people with machines, in productive work and in our relationships with big organizations.

However, the nature of that integration gives ground for concern. Put crudely it is integration into systems which represent more the economic values of capitalism without a human face, the political values of colonialism, totalitarianism and militarism, and the social values of impersonal bureaucracy. We do not see IT integration with current or 21st century aspirations for warm human relationships, equal opportunities, a decent standard of living for all, good health, education and welfare, conservation of and respect for our planet and all that lives on it, world peace and Mom's apple pie. Such a statement may ring with pomposity, but should serve to point out that such integration as has developed is limited, fragmented, unrelated to a positive philosophy of our future as a world society, and edges into the dark side of our planet.

Part 2
Problems and Principles

Introduction to Part Two

Part 1 set the scene of IT, and sought to clarify our understanding of the subject. It looked at where we had reached with the technology, and where we were likely to be moving in coming years. It analyzed the core business of IT, to store and utilise data, and went on to trace the complex interactions between data and information, as well as some of the issues impinging on people's lives. The final pages moved forward the argument that there is a substantial and, to date, ill-considered agenda of concerns about the rights and wrongs of the seemingly unstoppable advance of IT.

Part 2 aims to pursue those rights and wrongs, tackling a number of questions. What are they? What is their context? How can we best understand and identify them? What attitudes and behaviours do we need to confront if we are to construct a framework for acceptable IT usage? The sequence starts at the macro level, looking at IT development in its global setting, and ends at the level of individual human beings, as actual or potential, intentional or accidental, willing or reluctant users of new technologies. In between there are chapters about the place of IT in business management, and the role of IT developers, designers and distributors. However, a central core develops on the link between new technologies and equal opportunities, with chapters on disadvantaged majorities (that is women and those who live in poverty), the impact of IT on racial and other minorities, and on the role of human service workers, who exist as society's response to the needs of under-privileged communities.

The global context of IT is its contribution to the development of human-kind, the massive creative contribution that has been made. At the same time a number of underlying themes have already emerged which serve to paint the broad strokes in the darker side of the character of IT and IT applications. They include the corruption of the true nature of information, and human concerns about inaccuracy, insecurity, and the loss of privacy. In the coming chapters further themes will come to the forefront, about exploitation, disadvantage and powerlessness. In parts of our society where we experience traditional person-to-person relationships being replaced by machine-to-person interactions, ranging from computerized shopping to the assessment of health and welfare needs, we find a mixture of praise and castigation. IT is praised where it is demonstrably, *from a consumer viewpoint*, more effective, commonly because it has taken over from a human process that was not well done, or not done in a friendly and courteous manner. In Britain, for example, a survey of applicants for state cash benefits who had tried a self-administered computerized assessment of eligibility, showed that a majority preferred the computer approach over meeting with an official, because it was quicker, friendlier and more private (Epstein, 1984).

In contrast some computerized processes have been attacked because of what is seen as a basic flaw in the technology. The fact that an IT application is fair, in the sense that it treats everyone without discrimination, according to the rules it has been programmed to obey, is a theoretical virtue. In human terms it is a mixed blessing. People want fairness, but they want to feel that they are getting a good bargain, and they want fairness to be malleable, maybe to a limited extent, but sufficiently to allow human circumstances to be acknowledged. If the average time it takes to reach the front of a queue is 15 minutes, then it is fair as a general statement that everyone should wait for 15 minutes: but few people would want the idea of fairness to be so rigid that a handicapped or frail elderly person could not be treated differently. That is the perceived problem with IT: it is mechanised fairness, lacking a human face or a human sense of what is proper, even if such sensitivity does appear to bend the rules.

THE PERSONAL AND THE IMPERSONAL

This fundamentally different approach to codes of behaviour between people and machines which underlies our age has two dimensions. The first, often called instrumentalism, we have begun to deal with in the context of the problematic relationship between means and ends. In this dimension we are referring to information technologies as the instruments. They are, in this sense, an embodiment of the ultimate means in today's society, at the very precipice where science fact cascades over into science fiction. As such, they become the subject of deification, myth and ritual. But, in a peculiarly human twist, from a starting position of being the most advanced *means* for getting things done, they have become accepted by many as the *ends*, the new purpose. To the extent that this is happening, IT is displacing the enhancement of human life as the desired end, and substituting a view that the object of progress is total mechanisation, a world run by robots. One effect of this phenomenon is to leave humans with the feeling that there are no meaningful sets of morals and ethics to judge these new targets. This began to show long before telephones and computing machines were produced in the form we now know them, perhaps as early as our first known efforts to mechanize time. But the controversy has focused upon computers, particularly as no other machines have more symbolized and actualized the potentially reduced role of humans. It is tempting to relate this dimension alone to the existential movement, or to the characterization by Sartre of ennui (boredom), or to an experience of meaninglessness, as the dominant human response to the industrial age.

The second dimension of our age is a loss of personality. As we combine with machines, they become us. The movement towards instrumentalism has been a part of an approach towards knowledge that we call scientific. As we argued earlier, this is characterised by a method which has been applied with arrogance and exclusiveness, to the point that other methods of gaining knowledge, like reason and intuition, are dismissed as incapable of leading to right and correct truth. Even within existing frameworks, the partially different methodologies of areas like the social sciences, humanities, homeopathy and others have been and continue to be subjected to heavy criticism – that is, until they adopt a purer scientific method. The scientific method is an instrument of great power and has contributed much to our lives. But it too is an instrument, not an end, a goal, or a purpose.

A part of the scientific method, as we apply it, has the effect of removing that which is human from the process of knowledge gathering, therefore avoiding what the method considers to be one of the major sources of possible error in the results. The scientific method then removes the human from the interpretation of the results, since this could again lead to mistakes. The method lays claim to achieving reliable and valid results, in part, because it has removed fallible humanity and is therefore objective, accurate and value free. To be objective is valued: to be human is viewed, disparagingly, as subjective. To the extent that the human has been devalued in scientific processes, and given the success of science despite that drift, the impersonal has achieved value over the personal. This has been one root of a feeling of alienation expressed by humanists and social scientists alike, a feeling pervasive in some contemporary societies as well.

Yet science has not been the only instrument to contribute to our feeling of alienation by emphasizing the impersonal. Bureaucracy has been the second, acting in the name of standardisation and control (Beniger, 1986). It may be difficult for some to see bureaucracy as an instrument, but indeed, it is a tool to achieve certain ends. "Bureaucracy bashing", making bitter jokes about "red tape", is certainly common, and we do credit large scale bureaucratic organizations with much that is alienating in Western societies, but that is not our main point here. Instead, we wish to emphasize that bureaucracy, as implemented in modern organizations, has been particularly effective in providing stable structures and dependable working systems, but again at the expense of removing the personal touch. For example, it was and continues to be a great advance to have an organization which seeks to award jobs to people on the basis of suitability for a particular role, rather than contacts or patronage. Even though this may sometimes be more true in form than in practice, the negative side of this aspect of bureaucracy is that it stresses performance according to the job description, so denying human flair and imagination. Bureaucracies are directed to deal with people impersonally, as agents of organizational goal seeking. In addition to the obvious harm this might cause to an individual, persons are encouraged, if not required, to see each other only in terms of these organizational goals. For example, if I am seeking life insurance, then the interaction concerns life insurance. The representative of the bureaucracy, the salesperson, may encourage other dimensions of the relationship, but officially only because they might strengthen the chances of commitment to the insurance company. The personal is subrogated to the service of the impersonal, and the rules of bureaucracy have succeeded in having human beings operate un-human models of behaviour.

It is the unfortunate conjunction of these elements which has led to a primary dynamic of our age, a conflict of the personal and impersonal. Information technologies have arrived in time to give the thrust towards impersonality a new powerful stimulus. These technologies threaten most directly to recast all that is of sensory experience and bodily function, as well as that which is personal, into the impersonal, into the object, the machine. Should we challenge this process? Where do we seek to intervene? What are the broad principles we should be pursuing?

5 Global Development

SUMMARY

The main aim of this chapter is to identify exactly what is meant when discussion focuses on the global development of IT, and move on from there to describe the geographical dispersion of IT capacities and draw out themes and issues related to technology transfer. A core observation is that there is no realistic notion of global development, but quite the reverse, given that IT development work has been closely confined to a very small group of countries. There is a somewhat wider spread of IT manufacturing, to take account of favourable resource and labour conditions. If there is a global scene to be described, it is a global market for IT products and applications, and even here it is not a free market, but one bound up with restrictions based, in the main, on political considerations. The role of the military is noted.

The recognition that IT has a very restricted developmental and production base, and a less than open market place, focuses attention on the vagaries of the transfer of technologies between different nations and regions, in particular transfer from rich to poor communities. Problems are noted in gaining acceptance for the idea that there should be a process of technology transfer to poor parts of the world, justified on altruistic or humanitarian grounds. Even where transfer takes place there are techniques of handling it which are creative and helpful for the receiving society, and alternative routes which risk the long-term ability of those communities to make their own way. The argument is made that technology transfer should be based firmly on principles of community growth, rather than on patronage and paternalism.

However, by way of a prologue the chapter takes a closer look at the concept of development. IT progress has been dramatically fast, as in consequence have been the changes to economic and social functioning. In one sense this is attractive and exciting, a real roller coaster, but we ignore at our peril the relationship between technological or scientific change and the much slower rate of change in our minds, cultures and bodies. In the last chapter we contrasted the pace of technology progress with its social integration. Here we are more concerned with the fundamental capacity of human beings and their cultures to keep in step.

THE TECHNICAL, CULTURAL AND BIOLOGICAL THREE SPEED

When we talk about development we have a number of implications in mind. One relates to an increase in knowledge, whether through new discovery, invention, or the refinement of existing knowledge. Another is a more value laden assumption about making progress, either of a positive and constructive nature, like a more effective treatment for an illness, or a negative development, like a potentially hostile action. A third is a statement about a change taking place, often linked to comment about the pace of that change. In this way we talk of development as, for example, the advancement of personal computers in the 1980s, or the changing attitudes on gender issues during the current century, or the gradual evolution of humans from apes over many millions of years.

Apparently there are different speeds of change which occur in technical, cultural, and biological areas (Wilson, 1975, 1978). The average span of technical change is near to forty years: for cultural change it is near to two hundred years: while for biological change it is several thousand years. In this context "span" means the time between a change being initiated, and its recognition as an observable fact. Thus a span covers the time from a new invention, through its development and marketing, to its routine existence as a consumer item. It covers the gap between pressures emerging for a change in individual or community behaviour, and the observation that those pressures have been successful, and a change has taken place. It also refers to the time from the environmental circumstances arising to warrant a biological change, like the impact of global warming on plant and animal life, and the necessary adjustments being achieved, or the plant and animal species which could not change losing their place in the natural order.

Recently there has been concern that the interaction of biological and cultural change is related in a manner not conceived of in our earlier perceptions (Dawkins, 1976). The discussions and debates around this new understanding focus upon the proposals of a new discipline called sociobiology. Sociobiologists deal with the mutual effects of individual, group, community and population evolution – that is all cultural evolution – and their intersection, over the past millennia, with genetic evolution. The context in which this discussion arose began with the work of evolutionary biologists in terms of what they call the problem of altruism. When Darwin proposed his theories of evolution, one of the great laws which he premised was the law of co-operation. This law was discarded as a significant factor in his theory in favour of the law of survival of the fittest. A few people continued to explore the law of co-operation, one of the foremost being Prince Kropotkin. Kropotkin's major work, *Mutual Aid*

(1914), documented acts of altruism, behaviour in which individuals risk their survival for others, in some detail. This is, in fact, a major concern in evolutionary biology which is not confined to human behaviour. In a number of species, such as among ants, social, co-operative and altruistic behaviour occurs regularly. The evolutionary biologists now maintain that altruistic behaviour has a biologic basis. For example, the behaviour of a mother to save her young is to ensure that her traits will have their best chance of continuing in a future population. Since her young have more of a possibility of ensuring that, the mother will die to save her drowning child. Is there a biological basis for all behaviour? Does that biological basis appear as a consequence of or antecedent to cultural evolution? Does cultural evolution operate on a wider range of laws, such as the law of mutual aid premised by Darwin and Kropotkin, than genetic evolution?

Moving closer to IT, what are the possible effects of the fact that different human populations (tribes) are now in more frequent and intensive contact than ever before? Will the rates of change be altered? For example, imagine a situation in which IT has provided a means to communicate the actions of others on a more immediate basis than was previously possible, through massive news networks. Because the consumer is assumed to be attracted by sensationalism, the networks tend to report acts of violence and crime at a much greater rate. Perhaps this influences the behaviour of those people who hear and see what is reported from other places. Perhaps the fact that so many people now exist also increases the rate of crime and violence. There are now more news items available about such acts. Does this in turn influence our genetic coding for crime and violence? At the expense of altruism? At the expense of passing on an altruistic mother's traits in the population pool through the children she saved? How soon before altruistic traits disappear in a given population? These are questions of debate and interest among those who have engaged in sociobiology. For our purposes, the influence of information technologies may be seen to be central to the debate. The use of IT in this example is important and could be subjected to ethical analysis; but even more important are the possible effects that IT has upon changes in culture and genetic evolution.

Harold Sackman (1967, 1971) was one of the first computer theorists to assert a relationship between IT and the new theories of DNA coding. In his work he related the evolution of IT to the evolution of the species by trying to describe the genetic coding of DNA as an instance of a biological IT. In his analysis the stream of evolution which begins with protein continues through the latest microprocessor chip.

Many writers since Sackman have dealt with information technologies as supporting the development of externally possible though not probable forms of intelligence. Postulating a continuum from protoplasm, through animal and human brain cells and nervous systems, to artificial intelligences, is currently the lifeblood of science fiction. Who knows if it will become an accepted fact? However, our concern is with the more mundane human context in which that debate and others like it must take place. The content of that discussion, we feel, must be tied in firmly with human values, individual rights, and a moral code of conduct, and in so doing must not lose sight of the certainty that IT development goes beyond scientific reformation into cultural change, and the possibility that it will impinge on biological processes.

An uncertain relationship of cultural development to evolution has been formally discussed for a number of years. We have further argued that there may be a close link between information technologies and cultural change. Sackman takes us a stage further towards a full triangular interaction. A possible conjecture which falls out of this analysis is that IT has a characteristic not shared by other technologies before it. It could be intimately related to both our genetic code and our cultural process. What are the effects of the choices to use different information technologies upon the individual, the culture, and our biological evolution? Perhaps it is not too far-fetched to suggest that fears of a technology out of control are related to the recognition that technological use changes our societies and cultures. A vibrant example in contemporary life is the television.

Wendy Carson (1989) reports an experience in which students in a classroom in Ontario sit quietly as the US situation comedy *Family Ties* begins. Their teacher wants them to understand what they are watching, and leads the class through a process called deconstruction. This consists, as a first step, in examining the editing, the camera angles, and how images are used. The second step consists of relating the script to the images, and identifying the information they contain. The class identifies a central theme as the conflict between the cultural values of a son and those of a father. The teacher pushes the students to consider the meaning of the conflict to the script writers and producers. Are they in favour of one stance or another? To what ends? What message are they sending out?

In UNESCO's publication, *One World, Many Voices* (1980), a number of experiments worldwide are listed. In all of them the power of television to effect individual and cultural behaviour is recognized. Behavioral change occurs and group actions take place as a result of TV programming. In USA, where 97 per cent of all TV programming is used to broadcast entertainment, violence, and commercials, there is a growing recognition of the need to balance TV presentation. In one case, the suggestion is made that TV could be used as a tool for democratic change, or for penetrating the cultural isolation of the United States. In another case, there is a call to establish community cultural centres with production, broadcast, and cable capabilities in every community. In Britain an organization, founded by Mary Whitehouse, has existed for many years to monitor radio and TV. Its opinions and complaints to the broadcasting authorities are often controversial, sometimes subject to public ridicule, but the fact that they are so widely reported and discussed is a sure sign of the extent of public conviction that what happens on these media does influence people's behaviour, especially that of children. In short there is no question that this technology can and does influence cultural change.

The present use of TV assumes a receptive audience, much along the lines of what one would expect in a theatre. The level of interaction expected in the near future will depend upon the blend of TV with computer technology. The largest single selling game in the history of the United States, now also catching on in Britain and many other countries, is Nintendo. Nintendo is a game that hooks up to your TV. It gives you the ability to run different games much like tape cassettes in a tape machine, and scores of games are available. The player loads the game, which plays on the TV screen, and interacts by using a hand control device. The Nintendo device, not the TV, contains all of the circuitry necessary to run the tapes and control the interaction. The games are based upon the present content of TV and movies, with a high component of violence. Nintendo is very addictive to young people, with average playing times upwards of four hours a day.

In this case the cultural change is probably significant, not least because there is a difference between an adult's passive approach to TV, and a child's ability to interface with violence and militarism through computer games. What is the developmental and cultural impact of conducting a large part of childhood playtime interacting with an electrical device? No one knows. What about the content of the games? What effect do they have? Did the Nintendo Company have any responsibility to find out before they introduced their product? What is their value system?

Nintendo is only a step toward where TV will go. The TV set can easily be internally equipped with a computer chip. In other words, we fully expect that TVs will be sold for home use equipped with computer devices already contained within them that allow users to play games, communicate with telephone-based facilities, and control a myriad of electronic and home devices. At the same time, a manufacturer has recently produced a circuit card for a computer that allows the computer user to watch television programming on a part of the computer screen while working at other tasks. While one would like to believe that such advances will be exciting, complex, and useful for learning and discovery, history and common sense tell us that the benefits will be matched by deficits.

Developments of TV interactivity in the United States have focused upon shopping and advertising, and this is already on its way to other parts of the world where there is substantial consumer spending power. For example, some cable channels are devoted to twenty four hours a day selling, encouraging the viewer to call telephone numbers to receive products. With a computer chip in the TV and a telephone line jacked in, shoppers will not need to write down the call number and go to the telephone. They will not need to have their credit card number ready. They will be able to indicate electronically that they want to order the product. The TV will be programmed to communicate the appropriate information to the seller, including name, mailing address, and phone number. It is also possible that the money for the purchase can be moved from the buyer's to the seller's bank account at that point, completing the transaction. Who needs to have a face-to-face commercial contact any more?

As pointed out in Chapter 3, the data from the transaction will become part of a database. With the advances in TV/computer technology, it will soon be feasible to tailor the items on sale to a particular home to suit the consumer habits of members of the household. Perhaps the database would indicate that the household might now want vacuum cleaner accessories, that they usually purchased from TV in the late evening hours, and that the woman in the home makes the decision. The database then relays the viewing preferences of the woman, and adverts for vacuum accessories could be slotted into breaks in her favourite programme. This example may seem relatively benign, but keep in mind that the same activities can be applied to all areas of our lives, such as political choice. Who will set the rules for this development?

As Ben Bagdikian (1989) has pointed out, five to ten corporations will control most of the world's broadcast stations, magazines, and newspapers well before the end of the century. In other words, the global consolidation which is occurring will result in communication companies whose assets dwarf the GNP of many of the world's countries. If present trends continue, these companies will control the content not only of what we read, watch and play, but also major parts of our interactions. Through this they will exert enormous influence on how and what we consume. They will also control the development and application of new technology. For example, video recorders introduced in Japan which automatically edit out commercials have met with corporate opposition, and the Government has acquiesced to the extent of questioning whether or not such devices meet socially desirable goals. In effect, companies like Sony, Time Warner,

Paramount Communications and the BBC are not just setting the pace: they are also setting our cultural, social, and political values.

PHASES OF TECHNOLOGY DEVELOPMENT

In all accounts of development IT is described as a new advanced way of doing things. What is not always emphasized is that it is a way of doing things as prescribed by a small group of people who control design and applications. The shape of a technology is influenced intimately by the commercial, social, and cultural context in which it takes place. This observation will be a vital feature in later discussion of technology transfer. Can technology be transferred without its cultural context? Is it the same technology, doing the same job, if the context is different? Does a computer in urban USA achieve the same ends as a computer in rural India?

Studies of technology (Kochen, 1981) have reported that development takes place in three phases. When the three phases are applied, it is important to note that they always begin with activities that people are doing on their own, or have identified as things they would like to be able to do. They are usually activities of ordinary everyday life. In the first phase of development the new technology can do some of the things that people can already do for themselves. In the second phase, the technology does some of the things that people can do for themselves better than they can do it. In the third phase, the technology does things that people did not anticipate it could do. In other words, it is planned when technology is implemented that it will have effects that cannot, by definition, be pre-specified. The second phase, when the technology is applied to those things that we could do ourselves, albeit less effectively, is the predominant phase of most information technologies. In this phase IT is being applied to every day tasks in military, science, business, commerce, industry, government, and a fairly abstract and wide range of activities. The "abstract and wide range" includes information technologists who are engaged in using and creating systems that behave as we do as humans. All human behaviour is the agenda of some IT activity.

The range and agendas of IT have raised some questions about the outcomes of the technology, but at this particular developmental stage it is the failures that have provoked widespread questions about the values of the technological directions in which we are travelling. For example, many businesses with powerful computer systems are led by executives who refuse to have a computer terminal in their office. Airport radar computer systems fail and thousands of travellers cannot leave or arrive at a major airport on a sunny day. A frail elderly woman stops receiving social benefit cheques for no reason and suffers without justification. A bank automatic teller machine refuses to give money to a wealthy patron and then eats her access card.

It is important at this point, as IT begins to be more widely used within a social and cultural context and is applied to the achievement of many human goals, that the issues of values and rights spawned by the experiences of failure are tackled. System failures have focused attention for many people on the widespread impact of IT, as an invader of privacy, a controller of society, and hopeful mimic of humans. If and when IT becomes less error prone, and throws up many fewer instances of the unpleasant impact of failures, there is a real risk that less attention will be paid to the whole process of technology implementation.

Ethical problems will be more difficult to address in the third phase of technological development. In that phase IT will begin to do more and more things that we are unable to do ourselves, so have no experience of handling, and will sporadically cause surprise by achieving the unexpected. Unforeseen outcomes are by no means solely associated with IT: indeed, they have received more publicity and debate elsewhere, such as in the unexpected (often unwanted) side effects of new medical treatments. However, they have occurred in IT, and in significant contrast to the medical example, responsibility and liability for the harmful effects of the unexpected have not been visited on IT designers and developers. Market a drug which causes some people damage, or run an airline with a jet that unexpectedly crashes, and legal processes will extract redress. Design and run a computer system which deprives people of their due benefits, and it is just put down to an inconvenient mistake.

Indeed, the capacity of computer systems to make mistakes, even when they have apparently been used perfectly correctly, is one of the unforeseen outcomes which we can now record. There are others. Society was able to predict, for example, that IT implementations would cause problems of unemployment, and create needs for retraining and redeployment of labour: but it did not predict the way in which IT would serve to reinforce gender divisions, or the subjugation of poor communities. In a more positive light, there were few prophets, even as recently as the mid 1970s, who saw the impact of miniaturization (the chip, that is) on the fall in computer prices and growth in home computing.

CONTROLLING DEVELOPMENT

The motivation for invention is complex and not easily open to generalization. New inventions can emerge from anywhere in a spectrum of activities, ranging from a massive corporate plan to the work of isolated individuals. Corporate activity may be based on sophisticated teamwork, or by hiring and offering a creative setting to individuals who are assessed as having the potential to come up with new ideas and ventures. It may be a commercial project involving only private companies, or an effort at state or international level. Where there are known goals, with the prospect of massive rewards for whoever gets there first, rival teams may be in operation. The inventions which are made may be the outcome of careful planning and goal setting: but they may also be accidents, or spin-offs of other activity. If we look retrospectively we can find examples of enormously varied routes to a significant new invention, from the huge amount of step by step work which led to the internal combustion engine or the modern computer, to the supposedly accidental discovery of penicillin. Looking forward, we may know little of the work of individual inventors, but we are well aware of the inventions which are sought, and carry the glittering prizes – cures for cancer, an environmentally acceptable replacement for petroleum, even smarter weapons, and many others.

This is not the place to seek a more detailed analysis of inventions. The purpose in suggesting a diverse and complex scene is to show something of the character of the raw materials of development. Some inventions feed readily into new developments because they have been motivated by developmental potential, and emerge from the same corporate structure that will handle the developmental process. Other inventions are more detached in the sense that they may occur away from and out of contact with developers. More fundamentally the potential of the inventions may neither be recognized, nor viewed as worth exploitation. The point being made is that there may be no reason in purely human terms why invention should not be spread around the globe, but the reality is that inventions will tend to concentrate where developmental investments are being made, and where there is the will and capacity to undertake the exploitation of new ideas.

Politics and business are the main driving forces for global technology advances, reflecting the combined impact of societal and market considerations. Technological advantage is a major component of the competitive edge, and it has often been demonstrated that new technology can determine the survival of the corporate enterprise. The survival of governments will also depend on their ability to keep up or keep ahead, whether in military terms or in the promotion of human health and welfare. The task will vary with the setting. To those countries with a substantial developmental capacity will go the responsibility of receiving the bulk of inventions, and making the core decisions about their exploitation. They will determine both the way in which a new potential is brought into a social reality, and the direction and goals for further advances. These are the leading edge societies who will decide, in their own interests, what a Coca Cola bottle or a personal computer will look like, and how they will function.

Other societies need different skills if they are to be part of the action. They must be able to offer something which is politically or commercially desirable to the developer countries and companies. Political skills focus on maintaining a good working relationship with the developer, whether through processes of close collaboration, or the accident of strategic location, or control of raw materials which can be used in trade-offs. Commercial potential will converge on the size of the potential market for the newly developed product or service, but may extend to a share in component manufacturing or local assembly. Societies without the clout to work on these possibilities must either do without, or show their ability to beg, borrow, steal or counterfeit.

The conclusion to which this analysis steers us is that the concept of global development is a misleading one. Do we get the same result from an observation of the development of IT? By examining the origin of the machines and physical devices utilized as components in IT, it is evident that no global development of those devices has taken place: only a few countries have participated, significantly the USA and Japan, and that situation has continued. The copying, manufacturing, production, and assembly of computers and other linked devices has been established in a variety of settings in different countries, but this has not occurred as a consequence of locally based development work. Rather is has occurred through sub-contracting, and the use of cheap skilled labour to produce low price components. Some countries which have not been able to play a part in the design and development of new information technologies have, nevertheless, found a niche as parts suppliers for the major product labels, or scope to share in the mass production of cheap trailing edge equipment.

We can also ask if global development has occurred in the application of information technologies. One approach used to support the claim of global IT development has been to identify social institutions which have incorporated the application of information technologies into their activities, and to assess their proliferation. Yoneji Masuda (1981), former director of the Japanese fifth generation project, named the developmental stages of computing as they became successively part of different social institutions, identifying, in order, scientific, military, corporate, governmental, and individual stages. If there has been genuine global development, what we would expect to find is that each social institution has relied on the development of its own applications (programs). Science is an interesting example. While it was likely that a scientist might have written an IT application to solve a problem early on in the use of computers, that has become less likely now. A number of pre-written applications exist which are commonly used, so despite an initial phase, before commercial programs were widely available, when many of those wishing to make progress with IT became self taught programmers, we have now fallen back into dependence on the applications output of a small and highly concentrated group of companies. These companies have, in turn, managed to use copyright laws to their advantage, so putting impediments in the way of others who may wish to join.

This picture of a close and narrow control of IT, both equipment and applications, indicates a view of the world which parallels but is not identical to the traditional typology of First, Second and Third World communities. There is a small and elite First World made up of genuine IT developers, with only two certain members, USA and Japan, but a long tail of "possibles", including Britain and several other European nations. There is a much larger Second World made up of countries whose main productive involvement is component manufacture and machine assembly (that is, where Britain appears to be heading), and/or an economic infrastructure, coupled to political acceptability, which offers a viable market for IT products. The relationship of these two categories is complex. There is extensive overlap. Britain, for example, began with every intention of being a First World IT developer, making a major early contribution through the work of such companies as Sinclair and ICL. Now, however, Sinclair has moved off centre stage, and ICL has been sold to a Japanese company. Several countries, Britain and much of western Europe included, have sought to retain a developmental role, while in practice yielding to American and Japanese IT imports: others, like Taiwan and South Korea, have focused more clearly on component manufacture, without so far having significant internal markets. The pattern of national wealth is also not in direct relationship to the IT role. That is, the developer role is not necessarily the one that achieves greatest profits: some of the countries and companies who have performed well in terms of profit levels have concentrated on product exploitation and marketing, rather than the expensive business of product development.

From an IT viewpoint, First and Second World nations are "haves": they have the benefit of IT regardless of whether they have developed it themselves or bought it from outside. Third World nations are the "have nots", those whose political unacceptability has kept them excluded from IT benefits (a diminishing group in view of changes in eastern Europe), whose internal policies have preferred a more isolationist approach, or who simply cannot afford IT when there is a prior need to avoid illness and starvation. The fact that this category is so large is clear indication, in global terms, of the failure of altruism as a motivating force, and in IT terms of the ineffectiveness of technology transfer.

TECHNOLOGY TRANSFER

The scope for technology transfer is, in part, a matter of will. Are governments, rich societies and profitable multi-national companies prepared to make information technologies available free or very cheaply to less privileged communities? The answer has to be that despite a veneer of altruism and generosity, based on small scale projects, they are not. IT is a double edged commodity. It offers benefits, for illness diagnosis for example, which on any basis of acceptable human morality ought to be on offer to everyone: simultaneously it gives potential for great power, especially in military applications, which will only be handed over as a political favour or for a very high price. In the world of power politics the potential human benefits of IT have been swamped by the concerns of international strategy. There are few national policies committed to technology transfer, and international organizations sometimes seem to behave as though the technological revolution is a figment of the imagination. Why, for example, is there no organization for the technological welfare of the world population comparable to the World Health Organization?

Commercial companies have been hindered by politically motivated prohibitions and restrictions on their activities, but on balance have done little better. Insofar as it is possible to discern a general distribution and marketing policy of major IT companies towards foreign communities, it appears to have several unhelpful components. With limited exceptions, like indigenous language versions of word processing software, IT equipment and applications are distributed very much in the design and configuration used for the domestic market, with little recognition of the particular needs of different cultures and societies. Support services to help with installation and system operations get weaker in proportion to the distance the customer is from the distributor country. Perhaps most significantly pricing structures discriminate against Third World countries to an extent that cannot be justified by the additional costs of transport, local taxation and so forth. For many years there has been a tendency for companies with a strong world-wide market position to subsidize domestic customers at the expense of foreign ones. An IBM, Compaq or other "big name" computer produced initially in the USA costs approaching twice as much in Europe, even though it may be assembled there. In India, if it could be obtained, it would cost 5 or 6 times as much. If these actual costs are related to incomes in different countries, the discrepancy becomes absurdly pronounced. A personal computer costing 10 per cent of an average annual American wage works out at 30 per cent or more of a British wage, but reaches the equivalent of about 8 years pay in India.

The statement at the start of this section was that the will to start up technology transfer is just a part of the potential for success. Even where the will exists in abundance, the processes and techniques of transfer involve substantial, sometimes insurmountable difficulties. The core of this issue lies in an understanding of the extent of integration a new technology has with the context from which it emerged. The motives, catalysts, debates, plans and activities which lead up to a new development are part of the human interactions in the surrounds of the developer. In a cultural sense the emergence of a new product is the end of a sequence of stages, including understanding, interpretation, analysis, observation, data gathering, and many other processes, all of which are steeped in taken-for-granted cultural features.

Technology transfer, in its simplest form, is quite different. It is a transfer solely of the technology. What is significantly missing is the human process, the ability of the culture to form and absorb at least part of the meaning of each stage before the next stage begins. Perhaps the stages need not be experienced in the order in which they originally occurred. But no one has examined those stages from a human, cultural point of view, put them into the context of the new culture, and studied the possible effects. Instead, the transfer of the IT has taken place according to the technological needs and wants of the scientific area, corporation, or government.

In addition, receiving countries often get obsolete versions, because the sending country has gone beyond and devalued that form of the technology. The logic of this approach is that the receiving country is behind in technology development, therefore the "behind technology" is appropriate for them. In other cases, the behind or trailing edge technology is all that is made available to that country.

For years the United States and other countries have refused to supply computers to some countries on the basis of competing political philosophies. Other than unofficial market issues of supply and demand, the applications which have developed in that milieu are military and governmental. This has meant that important developmental differences now exist as cultural artifacts of, say, eastern European IT development. For example, we may find that military applications are much more sophisticated than expected, since more of the country's ingenuity has been devoted towards that single area. Or, we may find that the use of computers for governmental surveillance is acceptable and advanced in the absence of any reasonable democratic checks and balances.

The human process, ingenuity, or genius which is necessary to develop an IT and its application within a particular social and cultural context is rarely, if ever, a subject of technology transfer. Usually, it is only the commercial products of the process that are transferred – the machinery, hardware, wire, TV sets, programs.

It is also important to note that the transfer to Second and Third World countries of the manufacturing and production process has significant impact. There should be no notion of largesse entertained here. Instead, manufacturing and production has moved to other countries for economic reasons. Labour is cheaper in other countries. Taxes may be insignificant. Environmental laws are weak and ineffective in most cases. The company in the originating country may not need to pay export or import taxes. The effects on the receiving country can include changes in concentrations of population, disruption of cultural and community life, and accelerated degradation of the environment. The effects upon the originating country are largely invisible, subtle but hardly inconsequential. The widespread technical understanding of the complete production and manufacturing process are weakened. Ideas of how it may be done in a context of respect for the capacity of the people whose culture has developed it are not valued. Employment for the unemployed, for those with limited skills or limited abilities is lost. Not only are there separate losses for each country, but also the interactive effects of, for example, degrading the environment, are compelling.

There is a further question about just exactly what is to be gained by allowing this type of development. Driving social and cultural development through the motivation of a particular corporation's financial gain is quite different to progressing with respect for cultural diversity, human rights, democratic principles, and the environment.

These related problems of transfer which ignore any developmental imperatives, proceed according to the profit expectations of the sending country, convey obsolete and devalued IT, and send a de-cultured schizophrenic technology, are a source of even further difficulties. For example, one manner in which commercial imperatives have been handled is to provide the receiving country with technical advisors or experts. The consequences of this approach have been disconcerting. In a major study of technology transfer efforts (Sande, 1984) which have been accompanied by technical advisors or experts, a significant relationship between the use of outside experts and the destruction of indigenous capacity has been documented. In these cases, the cycle of technology transfer begins with the recognition of a need by either or both of the countries involved. As the decision to transfer the technology proceeds, there is a recognition of the low capacity of the receiving country with regard to the technology. The analysis of capacity leads to the importation of outside experts. If outside experts are not imported, the technology may not be transferred or used, since the commercial imperative is thereby vulnerable, or may be used in unpredictable manners. If the import of outside experts occurs, this leads to a consequent weakening and, if it continues, destruction of the receiving country's capacity for the development of indigenous expertise.

The problems mentioned earlier, in all of their manifestations, as well as the technical adviser solution, have the effect of stripping IT of the richness and variety that can be contributed by the various cultural and social contexts in which it can be applied. They also weaken the ability to achieve social and cultural progress over both the short and long run. For example, a micro-processor company builds a plant for the fabrication of circuit boards and the assembly of co-processor boards in Nigeria. The company flies in managers and engineers. The lower level workers are locally provided. The company employs local women, paying a fair Nigerian rate of pay. They train the women to work in an assembly line plant. They do not have to worry about taxes, laws, benefits, unions, or complaints.

As time passes the women work adequately, but seem depressed, and there are a few instances of public squabbles when men come into the factory with domestic battles, primarily caused by the inability of the women to carry out their traditional roles. Some of the women are attacked and harassed sexually in the environs of the plant. The villages nearby become much more unsettled, with rises in crime, and bad opinions of people who work for the engineers and managers. The women are found to be somewhat transient employees, working for the company for a few months and then, unexpectedly from the company's perspective, leaving to pick up their old tasks. Managers and engineers are in continual rotation, so are also a transient group. Overall some wealth from the wages paid to the women flows into the local economy, but the community is disrupted, valued traditions are challenged, prices rise for everyone, and the plant becomes institutionalized as a resented external edifice.

Now imagine a different scenario. The government of Nigeria invites a foreign company to open a plant to produce and assemble co-processor circuit boards. The conditions of that agreement are to be quite different than in our first example. The company send in a team to work with representatives of the villages and the government, and also to meet with the people in the villages around the area. The company discovers that each village has its life organized around the women being in the village all day. The men leave the village during the day to work in fields. The children are cared for by the women communally. Women handle all of the money, and earn money on their own doing crafts, usually as a group project. Women cook the meals and cater to the men in the evenings and mornings. The team, after studying and talking to everyone, decides to set up a small facility in each of the co-operating villages, using the communal craft rooms wherever possible. The company fails to locate managerial or engineering personnel from within Nigeria, so it contracts with each village to supply engineering apprentices for training. The company builds a central facility for packaging and shipping near the fields where the men work. The central facility contains an education room, where anyone may be trained using curriculum material provided either through the government or the company. Problem solving sessions are also held here, as well as in the local craft rooms, where distance education is also set up. Each village has work group goals and objectives. The work force is stable. The villages are stable. The cultural context is stable. After five years the trainees have progressed to the point where they are leading the work groups and new trainees are asserting their skills. The village begins to offer distance education courses for other villages. Crafts are taught in the courses.

This is all well and good, but what of the problems of economic colonialism? In the second example a precondition to development was that the company agree to an evolutionary process which ends with licensing this product to an emergent Nigerian company, made up of the newly trained local managerial group. The point is, of course, that economic development cannot be seen as occurring without considering the interests of all stakeholders, and this must be done within the context of the global development of democracy and of protection of the environment. For example, the stakeholders in such an arrangement include not only the villagers but the company employees in the provider country. The loss of income and productive capacity for them needs to be considered as well as the possible gains for Nigeria.

The human process and social consequences which need to be considered in a technology transfer activity are extensive. At the same time the contribution to human welfare which can derive from the integrated harnessing of the power of computing and the scope of telecommunications to the needs of local communities is such that the effort and commitment has to be extended. Altruism and equity demand it.

6 IT and Big Business

SUMMARY

The business world has a long tradition of coping with moral issues, sometimes by attacking, ignoring or evading ethical principles, sometimes by compromising or supporting them. IT has little tradition, either of moral corruption or achievement, and comes into partnership with business organizations with an unusually clean record.

The partnership has proved profitable for both sides. Big companies have offered the IT industry a guaranteed market. IT has given business a range of vital new or improved capabilities, to monitor the operations of the company, control staff and administration, and use modelling processes to plan and project ahead. IT began as a tool for senior managers, and although the range has extended, technology's contribution to the tasks and potential efficiency of management are enormous, and managers now exercise a significant influence over developments in IT. We argue that the value and cosiness of the partnership is mutually appreciated, though one outcome has been to leave the rest of us on the sidelines.

POWER IN PARTNERSHIP

Ever since early believers chose to draw the line between God and mammon, business has been viewed as ethically fragile. It is as if those who take the moral high ground want to be able to dissociate themselves, to a greater or lesser degree, from what goes on in the business world. The problem for the moralist is that business is about creating wealth, whether for individuals or whole societies, and wealth is vital for human survival. The love of money may be the root of all evil (1 Timothy), but in the eyes of an earlier biblical scholar, while "wine maketh merry . . . money answereth all things" (Ecclesiastes).

Taking a definition of "business" as organized money making, widely diverse cultures have expressed their own varieties of approval, disapproval and ambivalence. If the Bible is sound history, then money lending was a great sin 2000 years ago, and the basis of much anti-semitism. In strong contrast modern western societies view lending to help people buy their homes and the other necessities of life as a virtue. Many European communities show a traditional ingrained approval of wealth gained in some selected ways (like through ownership of land) and scornfulness of others ("trade" in Britain).

Several other aspects of business have caused trouble. There is a concept of "sharp practice" to denote behaviour which stretches or breaks codes of business conduct. In the relationship of employer and employee there is a long record of accusations of exploitation, and of inconsiderate and insensitive personnel policies. Major political philosophies challenge the morality of the ownership of wealth and property. Big organizations are sometimes viewed as bullies for their behaviour towards individuals. In short, there is no saintly aura surrounding "big business", leaving it vulnerable and exposed to the corrupting influence of IT. Big business is a tough cookie: it has survived the knocks of centuries, and knows how to take its chances.

IT did not work its way up through the ranks in the hierarchy of business: it started at the top. This was not through subtle planning, but simply because only the biggest organizations could afford the vast and expensive early computers. However, once the relationship was established it developed and flourished. Large organizations represented an accessible bulk market for computer manufacturers and system developers, and the big companies in turn could exercise some influence over what was being designed for them. While it would be an exaggeration to suggest that the IT we now have is an outcome of the impact of big business, there are some features which show the working of that relationship, with mixed outcomes for others. Big organizations want system compatibility for internal purposes, but are less concerned with external networks, and occasionally have reasons for preferring inaccessible technologies: such attitudes have weakened moves to overcome those equipment, operating system and software incompatibilities which have hindered so many computer users. At the same time market controllers have maintained an unhelpful commitment to a few obsolete elements of IT, such as MSDOS (a computer operating system), in order to protect the continuing utility of their past equipment purchases.

Such pointers set the context for a discussion of IT and business. What we find is a partnership of mutual convenience. On the one hand is business, with a long history of involvement in controversial issues, and a proven ability to manipulate, wriggle, bully, compromise and just occasionally accede to moral challenges. Wealth and profit making has lived uncomfortably but securely and successfully with a less than clean record of ethical health. Business has both coped routinely with simultaneous confrontations (currently, for example, relating to pollution and conservation), and shown an unerring sense of when to turn away from hostility to a moral argument towards a well-advertised and profitable espousal of it.

On the other hand there is IT, with a brief and chaotic history, few traditions, and scarcely any realisation that moral values have a role to play in social functioning. When business came face-to-face with computers it must have whooped with relief and pleasure. Here was a new way forward, offering the certainty of increased productivity and profit, but with no dark recesses and no strings attached. What a delight to find something without the human problems of a dissident labour force, or the impact on health of dirty manufacturing processes, or the destruction of the environment caused by mineral extraction and waste disposal. IT came along in the 1960s and 70s cleaner than clean, all-American or Anglo-Saxon in concept, and able quite quickly to overcome its initial unreliability. No wonder the business world dusted off the collective air-conditioned bridal suite and put out the welcome signs! The only cloud on the horizon was labelled "unemployment", noting the fear that computers on their own, and still more built into robots, would take jobs away from human beings. Even this was an advantage to many of the barons of business, who saw in IT a means of controlling sporadically troublesome employees and unions.

Once established the partnership prospered, to become even more successful and powerful than anticipated. IT has shown itself more flexible, more able to maintain a fast developmental pace, and more widely usable than the early pioneering investors could have imagined. The IT industry has gone through many turbulent passages, as companies have opened up, prospered briefly, and collapsed, and much of the productive capacity has lodged itself more securely away from Europe and North America in the Far East; but for the rest of the business community IT has delivered the goods. True the predicted unemployment has occurred, most agonizingly in those communities which were so dependent on traditional industry, but business has not suffered the consequences. Companies, whether large or small, have not generally been made to take responsibility for job losses, or even to make the arguments to justify those which are new technology related. There have been no pressures comparable to those which, for example, compel companies to take responsibility for their pollution, or meet the cost of damages to those who suffer ill effects from manufactured products. Society seems to have decided that if IT-led growth causes unemployment, then it is a societal or governmental responsibility, not something for the business sector to tackle.

The apparent impact of IT in allowing companies to escape responsibility for unemployment shows more than anything else the power of this new partnership. IT, like the colour green, symbolises goodness. Things done in the name of goodness must be accepted, and sceptics can be dismissed without recourse to sound argument.

TOOLS FOR MANAGERS

The use of IT in and for business management has many dimensions. The concept of management is diverse, incorporating government, supervision, regulation, administration, and policy implementation. Managerial styles can range between dictatorial and democratic, as well as taking in aspects of individualism, teamwork and corporatism. The organizations which are to be managed can range from small offices to national governments, and multi-national businesses whose budgetary turnover is larger than the national income of many Third World states. The organizations themselves may be compact or geographically widely spread out, specialised or generic in function, high or low profile in their presentation. Relationships between staff, or between HQ and remote locations, can reflect centralization, tight control and hierarchy, or devolution and partnership. The list goes on.

Each of these differing characteristics will have an impact on the kind of IT systems in use (if at all), the purposes they are intended to serve, and the way and extent to which they interact with a wider public. A useful starting point is to seek some broadly based answers to the question – what do managers expect IT to do for them and their companies? An immediate response is that managers expect IT to facilitate the managerial task, by providing each manager with a clearer picture of what is happening in her or his sector of management, with more information, improved capacity for analysis and decision making, and quicker communications. These in turn offer the potential for closer control, for use both reactively and proactively.

It follows that these IT applications may go beyond enhancing managerial effectiveness to have a comparable impact on other aspects of the organization's behaviour. The need for instant snapshots, records of past activities, projections of future possibilities, and scope for tighter control is by no means solely a value to designated managers. A high proportion of jobs have a managerial component, and can benefit from these types of IT service. Overall, however, there must be an expectation that IT investment will be justifiable on the basis of value for money. To achieve this the investment must lead to appropriate increases in productivity and markets, or be matched by reductions in other spending. Whether through saving or improved productivity, the likelihood is of some relationship between proportionate increases in IT spending and cuts in other areas of employment. There are some known vulnerable sectors. IT based clerical, administrative, book-keeping and stock control systems reduce the need for staff to operate manual services. More dramatically, robots can replace humans in many repetitive production line tasks. Thus the development of IT supports for the management process has the effect of changing a company's balance of capital and labour, and switching the emphasis somewhat from person management to equipment management.

Another expectation of an IT system is that it will facilitate extending the range of what is possible within the company, either by doing tasks which could not be done by manual methods, or taking over manual tasks and expanding opportunities by handling them more quickly, comprehensively and imaginatively. In part this is an enlargement of the control capability, allowing more precise planning, tighter margins in stock and production decisions, and, in a more general sense, project management. In part also a computer allied to a fast and effective communications setup offers new facilities, to create models and learn from them. Model building was a rare and time-consuming activity before computer power became available, but now it is common for managers to work on presentations of a type like "If you take actions a, b and c, then the likely outcomes will be x, y and z", or to generate their own modelling interrogations, "If we were to take this course of action, what would be the most likely outcome?". More sophisticated models can deal with highly value laden requests, like "Give me an investment plan which reaches specific cost and production targets with a minimum work force", or "Tell me the impact on productivity of a percentage increase in the number of workers with disabilities who we employ".

The ability to simulate possible future developments, and choose from alternatives, is a very important planning tool. At the same time this new facility brings into the range of accurate prediction and knowledge those matters which were previously incalculable and truly unexpected. Business managers can no longer claim with conviction that they were unaware of the spin-offs of their decisions.

There are forms of modelling with a clear speculative element. Currency and share dealing, as well as full-scale takeover bids, have a major effect on company stability, and with it the security and welfare of staff. Once again this is an activity which has increased dramatically with the advent of IT systems, both in the sense of allowing the speculator much more opportunity to be well-informed and adventurous, and by introducing computer automated buying and selling decisions.

The remaining core justification for IT investment in company management rests with the scope that is available for knowing more about, checking up on, manipulating, and making decisions about the organization's customers. There are special circumstances when the activities of the organization involve the provision of a service which requires information about customers, as is the case with human service agencies, and these are discussed in a later chapter. The point being emphasised here is that IT permits complex human data processing and has encouraged data gathering when it is wholly unnecessary for the company's functioning. What is necessary by way of customer information? A tailor needs a person's measurements to make a suit; a mail order company needs an address to communicate with; some way of responding is needed when, and only when, a customer asks for credit. But is there any case for making this material more widely available, or for gathering still more data for initially unspecified purposes?

A common defence for collecting human material is that it is part of a desirable marketing process of finding out what the customer wants, in order to be able to provide it. The issue of how companies balance their efforts to discover customer wishes with advertising and other routes to influencing customer choice is outside the scope of this book: what is relevant, because it is inevitably handled through computers, is the way a seemingly ethical task – finding out what the customer wants – can spill over so easily and extensively into general collecting, for use in marketing some totally different commodity, or for sale as information.

These reasons for managers seeking to use IT throw up some common themes, which recur in widely varying contexts – the importance of data to give information, and still more data to update or verify previous information; the cash value of raw data and information; the use of IT to increase the speed and scale of activity; the threat to the continuation of person-based processes in organizational operations; greater scope for planning, in a broad sense of the term, to include modelling and predicting: most importantly of all, the use of computerized information to monitor and manipulate all of us.

ORGANIZATION MANAGERS AND CONTROL

References to the groups who interact with the IT industry have so far in this chapter been categorised into employee groups and the public. In seeking to analyze aspects of people control a three-way distinction is more helpful, taking in employees, customers and societies, so that focus can be placed in turn on the activities and treatment of those who work with IT applications, the customers of organizations using IT for managerial purposes, and the behaviour of large, multinational corporations in relation to societies and their governing bodies.

It was suggested earlier that a characteristic of greater use of IT in management is that the perspective alters to place a more weighty emphasis on managing equipment. This does not imply a lowering of emphasis on personnel concerns, and indeed considerable significance is placed on the ways managers behave in their human-to-human communications. Yet at best this picture of the concerned boss can be no more than partial compensation for more fundamental changes brought about by converting space for people into space for appliances. An overview of this would suggest that if a higher proportion of an organization's resources are invested in equipment, then these must be handled in a way appropriate to their value. A coal-face view might well show more preoccupation with the displacement of people, and the way appliances get to be featured. At the extreme a computer or micro-processor based item, especially if it is physically large and the newest technology, like for instance a body scanner, can get star billing – a central location, the most secure and atmospherically kind space, and be set up so that staff must administer to it like a shrine, to be treated with respect if not worshipped. Even routine computer equipment disrupts working teams by ruining work space – cables and eye-straining screens, operators placed to suit the location of power points and the need to keep screen fronts away from strong light, no desk space left for personal mementoes or coffee cups. One of the reasons for the success of FAX is that it is less intrusive, and as a form of communication is much more straightforward.

More threat in the long term could come from the impact of computers on staff relationships, partly because of the intrusiveness of equipment, partly the growth of electronic communication instead of face-to-face, but most importantly because a good computer provides some of those things needed in a satisfying office relationship. It is interactive; it has a nice screen to look at; it can be used for playing games during breaks; it can be more relaxing because it may have faults and idiosyncrasies, but is more predictable, does not have bad moods, and once well known is not a threat; and as a last resort it can be turned off!

It may seem flippant to discuss computers as though they have person-alities, but the point is a serious one. Computers and computer programs (not to mention programmers) do have characteristics, and since few of us have dealings with more than one or two computers we neither know nor are concerned as to whether those characteristics are unique to our machine (that is, very like personality traits), or are shared with thousands of others. They are also interactive, so will respond, albeit in limited ways, and it is therefore possible to have some sort of relationship with them. None of this should come as a surprise. Touchingly human as well as really evil robots have stirred human emotions for many decades, none more than R2D2 and C3PO in *Star Wars*. Less dramatically, but probably of more significance, is the fact that computers share with televisions the small screen, and viewers routinely go through the whole gamut of human emotions in their relationships with TV creations. Having a screen, especially a good coloured one, goes a long way to making a computer a socially acceptable person. Behind the screen the computer programmer, like the TV programme maker, shapes the messages we are given, and plays on our responses.

There is more to the impact of IT on organization management than people-space becoming computers-and-people space. There is the role IT performs, and still more significantly the attitudes which prevail when there are both IT and human options. If computers are undertaking tasks which only they can do, then we usually accept them without question, albeit with a possible backward glance at how this position was reached (such as how many staff lost their jobs). When a task could be done by computer or human, complications can arise. We may be talking about a transitional phase, such as when both manual and computerized office systems function side-by-side, until there is sufficient trust to let the latter take over, or sufficient disillusionment to revert solely to the former. More fraught, however, is where the interface between human and machine is less clear: where, for example, there is overlap because part of a job is done by a person, part by a computer, or where one system is used to back up or check on the other. Two fundamental issues arise at this point – of responsibility and judgement.

A high proportion of IT applications are not fully automated, and still depend on a human sharer, whether to operate the system, or undertake part of the task manually. Who then is to blame when things go wrong? Who can you sue? Can a manager escape liability by pleading that the error was made by a computer? Can the manager in turn place the blame on the computer or software producer, or on the system designer? Is the company and its staff responsible because they share the work with the computer? These are not intended as legal questions, despite obvious legal implications: nor are they simply posing the dilemma about whether blame attaches to the worker or the tools: they are ethical questions which concern workers who have to make decisions and take actions on the basis of computer data and recommendations.

Many workers, especially those with professional qualifications, use their skills, training and experience to make assessments, pass judgements, and recommend a course of action. Some make major life decisions on behalf of their customers (though here we get into a context where the *customer* is more likely to be called a *client* or *patient*). Computers have taken on a special role here, being used to run programs (*expert* or *decision support systems* are the common labels) which seek to enhance the accuracy of the professional's judgement by providing additional material, feed in reminders about organizational, legal or policy factors which the person should take into account, draw attention to procedures to be followed, recommend a way forward, or challenge the professional recommendation. At their most developed they provide an alternative form of decision-making.

Such systems can be used to achieve some managerial purposes. They can represent the interests of the manager, by forcing attention onto considerations which may not be strictly within the professional province, but do have a significant impact. A doctor, for example, using a computer to aid diagnosis and treatment, could be alerted to the cost of certain prescriptions. A welfare worker, handling a case of child abuse, could be reminded of agency procedures and legal requirements. These may well be viewed as helpful intrusions by the IT system. But what is the position when the expert system recommends a course of action which is at variance with that of the professional? Who makes the final judgement? Is it something for the professional to decide, or for appeal to a peer for second opinion, or does the manager take both judgements, check them out for other factors, like comparative cost, and then choose?

All of the issues mentioned earlier about responsibility come up here, sometimes in an acute, maybe life and death form. Which judgement is to be trusted and used? Other concerns are about the role of professionals in society, as computers become more and more capable of decision-making; about the relative responsibilities of professionals and managers when judgements are involved; and about the rights of customers to know and choose whether judgements affecting their lives are made by qualified staff or computer program.

Using IT in customer management has permitted a transformation in the way organizations prepare and present themselves, their products, services, environmental purity and public image. The visible window is advertising, through all widely circulated media, but especially on television, where claims are made that a new art form has emerged. Nothing could be better for business than for the public to believe that advertising is art, and that it should be treated and responded to as such. Art, after all, is creative, given traditionally wide ethical freedom (or poetic license), and far removed from a hard sell. In reality advertising is as hard a sell as it is possible to make, and is based on regular detailed computer analysis of data gathered about people's consumer attitudes, product and service preferences, reactions to existing advertising, views as to what is *good* and *bad* in society, what makes an attractive image, and many other themes. In other words, IT helps organizations discover the ideal image, and then present themselves so as to appear as near as possible to the ideal, sometimes with due regard, though often with scant concern for truthfulness. Thus we have industries which routinely contaminate earth, air and water displaying themselves as in the vanguard of pollution control and environmental protection, while those whose products damage our well-being (tobacco and alcohol companies, for example) like to be associated with sporting endeavour, healthy eating, rustic purity and all that is best in traditional standards.

We have here a crisis of honesty in the treatment of consumers, and although it appears to be about the accuracy and fairness of advertising (and is commonly handled as such), it is really a crisis which has come about through the exploitation of IT capabilities.

Consumers, then, are pressed into giving information about themselves which may subsequently be used to alter their life styles: they are also exposed to a mixture of images about the goods and services they use, and the organizations they deal with, some of which will be truthful, others vague, anodyne and evasive, and still others downright dishonest. Later (Chapter 12) we shall consider what ought to be done to rectify this situation, but before moving on it is relevant to look at the way the really big multinational corporations behave, not just to their customers, but also in relationships with whole societies and their governments.

The multinationals, again depending heavily on IT, have an added dimension of activities surrounding the location of both production and marketing across different cultures, economies and political systems. In part IT helps these organizations achieve significant benefits, by giving managers control over complex production and distribution arrangements on a worldwide basis. Without IT such project management would be difficult to the point of provoking managerial chaos. As consumers we can gain advantage both from the lower prices which derive from economies of large scale production, and from the resources which big corporations can put into developing new products. There is another side, however: IT generated information across the world community gives great power and scope for manoeuvre

The power stems primarily from the ability to move activities across national frontiers, and thus to bargain with governments for preferential terms. Manoeuvrability extends further, to vary pricing policies to market conditions in different countries; to respond to localised changes in levels of demand; to move products which have been criticised or contain banned components in one country to another where attitudes and rules are different; to locate ethically or environmentally dubious activity where there is a sympathetic government; to use the international context as a means to maintaining impenetrable secrecy. Perhaps we take for granted the benefits and notice only the disasters, like Bhopal. Perhaps too we over-estimate the role of IT in all of this, but without the benefit of much more openness we have to conclude that here is another prima facie case of IT abuse.

SECRETS

In the course of their activities, and perhaps even more in their leading edge development work, organizations have secrets. The secrets may be of new inventions and discoveries, or ways of gaining a market lead over competitors; or they may be about people who have something to hide, or some knowledge stored in their minds which others would like to obtain. In the business world what justifies giving something the label *secret* is the awareness that there is someone, or some other organization, which would like to know what is being hidden. What people want they are normally willing to pay for, so secrets have a market value. Occasionally other people's secrets are considered so valuable that any means, including crime, will be used to get hold of them.

Sometimes secrets are conveniently put in a file labelled *Top Secret*, and kept separately from all other data; just as often they form part of a much larger data store, and have to be uncovered through careful sifting. Before the time of computers there were fewer secrets, not because there was any lesser need for confidentiality, but because much less data was stored, it was harder to move it around, and data was rarely analyzed for the gems it contained. Perhaps there was also a more moral attitude towards preserving confidentiality.

IT has transformed the scene, whether in the glamorous world of cops and robbers battling for control of information vital to the salvation or destruction of our society, or in the mundane context of extracting important information from masses of data. The data itself has been miniaturized, so that it can be held, copied or transported with great ease. Large bodies of data, like the client files held by banks and welfare agencies, are almost always held in a framework (that is, in a computer database) which is designed for quick searching, sorting, tracking, pin-pointing and analyzing.

As a result it has become much easier to store and make use of data, so more is collected. Not only are industrial and commercial activities much more likely to be recorded, but, as described in earlier chapters, we have all become the subjects of data.

Of course there is a new and well publicized pattern of crime surrounding the theft and subsequent disposal of secrets, but that is only one end of a spectrum which represents a whole new business, the information business. The spectrum moves from the criminal to the ethically dubious, taking in such practices as head-hunting personnel less for their skills than for their knowledge of the secrets or the computer system of a rival. From there it passes into the somewhat shadowy market in data about all of us, collected whenever we get into any formal economic or societal activity , and traded for the most part without our knowledge or approval. At the other end of the spectrum are the data sources, such as library catalogues, set up openly, and accessible by all of us. Later on (Chapter 12) we shall note the growing attempts to bring this new business within an orbit of acceptable practice, but it is significant how slowly this pressure has been acknowledged, and how contrastingly fast political authorities have moved to outlaw anything which challenges the power base of big business. If we can move so quickly to combat computer viruses, why has it taken so long to act in the vital interests of citizens?

In the forefront of the information business is the framework of IT on which the business depends, so measures to protect data centre round the security of each company's computer systems and communications networks. If the information market is to be profitable, then data as a commodity must be guarded against copying, corrupting and unpaid access. Yet this poses a difficulty for business organizations and for the rest of us. For businesses a part of the problem is the technical and organizational components of a security system. Computers are needed to guard secrets, but at the same time they must be accessible if the data they hold is to be used or traded. As many companies have discovered, there is a fine balance between keeping people out and letting people in. Who is authorised and who is not? Who can just peek, and who can play around with the system? What can be done about the running sore of people who are authorised today, but leave the firm tomorrow to join a rival?

It is technologically possible to devise an impenetrable security system, despite the general assumption that a new lock always throws up inventive minds searching for ways to open it up. The problem is human. It is the keepers of the system, not the system itself, that fail. Yet there is another more insidious difficulty for business managers and owners – ambivalence. What they want is security which works perfectly for their own secrets, but leaks like a sieve for those of their competitors. Getting other people's secrets is often highly desirable: losing your own can be disastrous. A technologically incorruptible security system solves one side of the desire, but destroys the other. Hence the suggestion that there is ambivalence. Do business leaders really want excellent security all the time, or are attitudes to data protection more than a little influenced by whether the current preoccupation is with keeping one's own secrets or getting access to other's?

For the community as a whole the problem with security systems lies in how we handle the contrast between the content of the strong room, and the strength of the locks on the door. In modern society we are conditioned and for the most part willingly comply with processes which gather more and more data. With some exceptions we collude with the principle that the content of the strong room should be all inclusive, not least because data sources (like mail order catalogues and public transport timetables) are very useful for us. At the same time most cultures include strong attitudes favouring privacy, stretching to notions of a right to privacy for views and behaviour which does not affect or harm others. Hence we also collude with the idea that a strong room should be well locked, especially if it contains *our* data. Like business leaders we are ambivalent because we simultaneously guard and search for data. Whatever our earlier beliefs, now that IT and other forms of mass communication have come along to open up the whole scene, and expand the technological potential, we seem to be less attracted by the lucidity and purity of such notions as total privacy or total openness. What we want is the right to be choosy about what we disclose, and nosey about what we uncover. This human reality, and consequent lack of clarity and direction, has helped make it possible for the business world to get on with the task of expanding into data as though it is just another commodity, with few strings attached.

A prolonged obsession with secrecy and nosiness is more commonly associated with governmental bodies than private companies, and not just with totalitarian regimes. Civil servants are the most assiduous gatherers of data, and in many countries the least committed to notions like *freedom of information*. They have a range of justifications for their attitudes which all appeal in one way or another to the general welfare of the nation – the maintenance of law and order, combatting crime and wrong-doing, state security, keeping important matters away from irresponsible elements in society, holding onto the traditional values of good government, political sensitivity, following tradition and rules, and so forth. From the viewpoint of business leaders, governments have an enviable record of successful paternalism which allows them to ask all the questions and take actions without having to give rationale or explanation.

The ambition of many big businesses is to gather to themselves some of the aura of a government, or at least to get themselves associated with governmental sensitivities. Some have been very successful. One strategy is to take advantage of working in a politically sensitive area, like the power industry, which in many European countries can take shelter under a governmental umbrella when showered with questions about the impact of open-cast mining, or the disposal of nuclear waste, or whatever is currently a delicate issue. Another approach is to take full advantage of a mixed economy to form partnerships with public organizations, as has happened in the UK in the shadowy world of private security, where private companies increasingly guard military installations and take on policing functions.

IT has allowed the western world to indulge in a profitable and half-secret orgy of surveillance, gathering data from spoken, written, audio-visual and hearsay sources into computer systems which offer more sophisticated scope for social control than was ever achieved by the dictatorships of eastern Europe. The strength of democratic principles ensures that this data is not used to control our lives . . . yet. But can we trust governments not to be corrupted by the potential power at their disposal? Even more, can we, in a mixed economy, feel sure that private data gathering, surveillance and policing will be kept within acceptable boundaries? The reality is that in the eyes of many people those boundaries have already been swept aside.

7 Developers, Designers and Distributors

SUMMARY

This chapter focuses specifically upon those organizations and individuals who control IT because they know about it, design and produce it. Attention is paid both to the values implicit in the connections of IT companies to the rest of society (that is to the handling of manufacture, distribution, price setting and marketing), and to the more concealed values which are embedded in the types of IT systems and software which are developed. The argument is made that IT, far from being ethically neutral, is substantially value-laden; and while little can be done to alter this at source, because it is integral to the process of IT creativity, the existence and direction of the embedded values should be fully recognized and tackled within the wider society.

ORGANIZATIONS

Many of the fifty largest computer companies are household names throughout the western world. Of the world's top five companies in computer revenues, three are United States corporations (IBM, DEC, UNISYS) and two are Japanese (FUJITSU, NEC). Of the top fifty companies, twenty eight are American, twelve are from Japan, and the remaining ten are European. The computer market is dominated by the Americans and Japanese. If we move to expand our scope to include all information technologies, that is communications, chip and memory production, broadcast media, as well as television and other audio and video devices, the Japanese and Pacific Rim countries dominate production and revenue (Computers: A Global Report, 1989; Computers: Japan Comes on Strong, 1989).

An examination of underlying values portrays Japanese and American companies in an interesting relationship. The Americans value and are successful in research (as to an extent are the British). The Japanese value all aspects of innovation and have perfected production and marketing.

Their interaction has been described as essential: for example, though Bell Laboratories (USA) developed the transistor, Sony (Japan) developed a cheap way to manufacture it and marketed the idea of the small personal radio. The Americans often see research as individualistic. Researchers value publication and scholarly advancement, and are often rewarded with influence on public policy. Research is an independent activity to them. To perform research is the epitome of intelligence. It feeds the cycle of innovation, but it is seen as superior in value to all other activities. It is often disconnected from the activities of development, production, marketing, management, customer relations, and corporation lifestyles. The Japanese value research as an intellectual activity which is a part of and applied to all aspects of thinking; in turn, it is applied to all aspects of the cycle of innovation and life. Research is valued because it benefits everyone and improves their quality of life. The corporation, not the researcher, influences public policy.

Xerox Corporation is an example of an American company that illustrates the American/Japanese relationship and, to some extent, the value differences. Xerox invented the copier and were in on the conception of the personal computer. IT innovations continue to surface which are traceable to work done at Xerox, but the company seemed unable to organize production and markets to take full advantage of their innovations. The Japanese, in consequence, have thrived in the copier market. Japanese engines are found in most major laser printers and components in the best quality personal computers. Over the past fifteen years Xerox has invested heavily in a project known as Xenith, to produce a new kind of technology that combines copying, computing, scanning, facsimile, and printing facilities in a single unit. The initial unit introduced at the end of 1990 costs about $200,000, and the specification takes in paper documents, mail, electronic mail, graphics, fax, and computer data. It will convert anything incoming into digital electronic data upon which any user can work, alter, or transform. In contrast the Japanese companies, Ricoh, Canon, and Sharp, have focused on equivalent machines that can be produced cheaply and ultimately be part of their strategy for the development of personal computing. These machines will be later in the shops, but have a clear vision and will probably sweep the market.

The values which underlie these efforts illustrate a number of important issues. In the American attempt, the Xenith product is suitable for large organizations as a device where centralization and redistribution aids are seen as the primary answer to organizational paper problems. For example, the Xenith vision is one where a government worker could instruct the production of 1000 copies of a legislative rule from a desktop terminal.

While the Japanese vision does not exclude large-scale machines for use in large organizations, the products they are developing are suitable for the work group, and ultimately, the individual. The organizational problem for them is how the work group can be productive in a complex environment. We would support extending this approach to encompass how the individual worker can be more productive and creative.

It is tempting to overdraw both the ironies and contrasts in this situation. In a society which lays claim to individualism and democracy, as well as to personal liberty, IT values are dominated by the skew of technologies as tools of control, primarily of large-scale organizations. In a Japanese society where many of their traditions are the opposite, information technologies are valued as tools of production, focusing upon the work group. While Xerox (and a slightly more expensive Kodak equivalent) may sell a number of large-scale, expensive machines at first, the technology and market will ultimately belong to the Japanese. If we look at this example from the point of view of A. B. Lovins (1980), he might argue that neither Americans nor Japanese have a complete approach – neither is using a renewable resource for their machines. But he may additionally argue that both are exercising human choice in their approach to the technology, and that choice reflects a strategic point of view, a path. The path of the Japanese is primarily a soft technology path: they are striving for a machine that is relatively simple from a users point of view despite its presently extreme technical sophistication. Their goal is a machine that is matched in both scale and quality to individual needs. In simple logic, people are most productive when they have confidence and control in their work place. This is not always fostered by distant, unseen machines; and there is more need for use of the technology at individual productive units than control of it at the copier room. In a larger sense, the design of the technology will influence social and productive relationships; in other words, the form and application of the technology is an important variable in participatory democracy. The democratization of the technology is only meaningful when individual people are in control of machines and technical processes.

The Xenith example we have just discussed is one which fits well with what Lewis Mumford (1966, 1970) called megatechnics and polytechnics in human tradition. *Megatechnics* is technology based upon centralization, large scale operations, and authoritarian principles. Xerox and Kodak have moved along these lines. *Polytechnics* is a technology based upon decentralization, smallness, and democratic principles. Mumford argues that megatechnics cannot be subjected to democratic control, even if the culture is committed to democracy. We note that the development and design of most Western technology applications are apparently subjected to an ethical analysis which is slight, fascistic at worst, or trivial. But who is responsible for such ethical analysis?

INDIVIDUALS

Individuals are responsible. They are responsible to assess and act upon concrete, visible injustices. If they see them. The individuals we refer to specifically in this case are the developers and designers of information technologies. Such people are the subject of a number of published works (Wright, 1988; Fjermedal, 1986; Levy, 1984; Kidder, 1981). One such book, *The Media Lab* (Brand, 1987), describes the social conduct and value base of developers and designers that we will examine later in this chapter. However, we set the scene for that discussion by looking briefly at the intimate social effects produced by the thousands of engineers, systems analysts, programmers and salespersons who work every day with information technologies. Their impact contributes to what we want to term "the failure of the personal".

The personal in our lives is under considerable strain. The conjunction of the problem with information technologies can be looked at in many ways, but nothing is more fundamental than communication. Norbert Wiener (1965) defined the field with the word *cybernetics*, the study of control and communication in animals and machines. As cybernetics has matured, the study of human communication, the interaction of human communication with machines, and the symbolic representation of human communication by machines has progressed.

When computer based communication systems have been marketed they have been advertised as or taken for human communication systems. This error is almost never challenged. We can ask for a communication system, and be pointed to assorted pieces of hardware, software, and wiring arrangements. Laboriously, salespersons will often turn to teaching people that communication systems are composed of a sender, channel, and receiver, with encoding and decoding. When they finish and discover that people still do not understand what their communication system is, they put it down to ignorance, inability to learn, or an opposition to progress. They do not seem to know that they have failed to communicate, or realise that their approach is inadequate to deal with human communication.

One helpful step for the ordinary customer would be to reconstruct the language used in describing the machinery, its use, application, and function, in such a manner as to be specific about what it actually achieved. For example, to say that the computer program activates the machinery is better than to say the computer did it, keeping in mind that some day the computer really might do it. To say that a set of computer programs, accompanied by a supporting group of machines and circuits, using telephone lines, may be able to be used to support a human communication system which intends to share data about job vacancies, is getting too wordy. But it does the work of description a better turn than referring to the equipment as a communication system. Though clumsy, it is more accurate, more descriptive of the human role and problems they will face, and gets closer to describing the available technology. What it achieves can be significant if it clarifies that humans are accountable for the technology and its application, and that the machines only make up a "true" system with a lot of human help. Even more fundamental as a problem of language is the description of machines as information technologies. That very label, which we have used in this book, and others use routinely, is a gross exaggeration.

The use of more precise ways of talking about machines begins to clarify the contribution of humans to electronic data processing. Humans write all of the instructions to run the machines. They organize the communication links. They determine forms of data input and output. Even sets of instructions which enable a computer to be self-generating have human origins. Now, however, consider the complications that can arise when one group of engineers has written a set of instructions to have a disk drive read and write disks in a particular manner, only to find that the resulting set of instructions cannot accommodate other types of disk storage in common use. This is the incompatibility issue. Or, consider the problems of having parts of a set of instructions, which are intended to become a single set, written by many workers in different locations over a long period of time, as occurs in much software development. Ultimately nobody working on the product has a conception of what it is as a totality.

An outsider may find that to be a curious way of writing a single work, but indeed it is done in exactly that manner. An even more curious artifact of commercial approaches to program development is the acceptance of program errors as a responsibility of the purchaser (usually stated in a written disclaimer issued with the program). To the extent that purchasers have accepted such responsibilities, program writing companies are encouraged to offer goods which do not perform as expected. One result has been to encourage marketing and financial advantage to the detriment of product integrity. In consequence it is difficult to separate truth from marketing.

Making long-term profit on software is difficult. A good piece of software needs never to be replaced, though one trick is to convince buyers that they require upgrades or improvements. Another consequence, intended or not, is that software products are regularly introduced which do not work as expected. The consumer is then forced to buy upgrades. Or software will be produced which will no longer run when newer computers come onto the market. We would not want to assert categorically that this is purposeful marketing to generate demand, but it is common.

It is sometimes difficult to spot how quality control has been used in the IT industry. In most industries quality control is not only a production factor, it is part of the development process. In other words, the person who purchases the product expects that the product will have been manufactured as designed, and that if it has, it will work well. Unfortunately, even when hardware and software is produced as specified, it may not work well. Perhaps some fault can be lodged with user expectations; perhaps more with the advertisements that encourage such expectations.

The idea of standards has been discussed many times in IT industries. In a analysis of trends in the IT industry (Frenkel, 1990), one expert saw standards as dominating the computer industry. Others advocate that the concept of standards should be thrown away. Most standards have been adapted to capture the purchasing preferences of the users of the technologies. Put another way, in the IT business, standards are generally equal to what the majority of sellers and buyers want and use, not to some set of guidelines or benchmarks of performance. As an example of this point, consider the history of the floppy disk. All computing systems use some form of media to store data and run software. Early in the development of microcomputers, the floppy disk was adopted for the job. No one could agree on a common size for the disk, and the older eight inch floppy disk drives were used as well as five and a quarter inch drives. Distributors used the different drives as a way of capturing their own audience. A person with large drives needed to purchase from suppliers of large drives and vice versa. At the same time, developers wrote different ways of accessing the data on the disk. Disks written in one format could not be read on other systems: again, a way of controlling the market. Then the IBM PC appeared and swamped the market. Almost all of the designers and developers converged upon IBM as a compatibility standard – primarily because they wanted their hardware, software and data accessible to anyone in the huge IBM market. There were notable exceptions: Apple disks could not be read directly by IBM machines. IBM then introduced a method of writing on the five and a quarter inch diskette which was incompatible with everyone else (the 1.2MB floppy), and defended it as a backup device. Even the accompanying backup software was incompatible and did not work well. In short order, IBM introduced a 3.5 inch floppy on their machines, a floppy which has two levels of data storage. Users found themselves needing to buy a set of different floppy disk drives and disks just to be able to read and transfer available software and data.

What values underlie such behaviour? They are not just that the sale is more important than the social consequences, quality, performance, and use of the product. Here we have innovation and human creativity run amuck: it is tied to market share and short-term profit taking. In this set of values, money, not the product, is the evidence of success. In addition, the sales pitch is made to the buyer, who is often not the user. This is usually disempowering and alienating. For example, how many secretaries are permitted to purchase the computers, displays, and printers that they must use? In an interesting published example of this problem (Otos and Levy, 1984), secretaries in a company did exhaustive research about computers and made recommendations to management, who then purchased completely different machines.

These problems, of substantial interest to our conclusions, are openly and directly experienced. Underneath such problems, there is a more fundamental one, which we discussed earlier as a problem of representation. Perhaps it can be made more clear now. In the case of office automation of writing, editing, and printing, the reality which is used as the basis for the program is that of the programmers. What may seem perfectly acceptable to them may not fit well with the reality of people who regularly do such work.

Word processing offers many examples of this rather abstract principle in practice. The computer keyboard has a limited set of symbols. What happens when the symbol you need is not there? What happens when symbols are imbedded in the text but not displayed on the screen? What happens when you can't see the whole line? Where is it? Why isn't the screen larger or the letters smaller? If a program does not show on the screen what will print on the printer? How important is it to see what will appear on the screen? Ask any typist. It is a part of their immediate experience of success or failure that it be possible to see what they are doing, yet many programs have limited or less than handy approaches to this aspect of everyday work.

There is a consumerist element here. If we were to observe the frustration of typists or discuss matters with them, a number of reactions could be documented. The typists may feel responsible: they may feel that they are being made to look foolish. They may, when the printed product is at variance with what is on the screen, blame the machinery rather than the program, or simply have a feeling that something is wrong without being able to pinpoint it. The point is that the experience of the typist is seen as inconsequential. By ignoring their experience of everyday life, we deny them a form of existence. They experience an impersonality far beyond the minor irritation of a poorly conceived program. A common result, on a larger scale, of the mismatch of realities, is that programs are not used, or workers and management are not satisfied. Workers have reacted to implementations of computer systems in many ways. Some of them are sabotaged, others are filled with useless data (Dery, 1981).

The wider impact of this situation is that workers experience a loss of control of their work. They must adapt their work and their selves to the technology. There is insufficient recognition not only of worker personalities, but also of the totality of staff needs. One result has been a movement toward so called holistic therapies. The underlying motivation for the movement is the correct sense people have that human beings, their environment, and their situation must all be considered in order to understand problems that they are experiencing in everyday life. In part, this may be a contemporary reaction to large scale organizations and the scientific method, but it is wholly understandable as proceeding from the everyday experience we all share. When we are disappointed by something that happens, we not only experience that disappointment within some abstract portion of our mentality called a personality. We feel the disappointment. We may not be able to go to work. We may cry. We may get a headache or suffer from stomach disorder. We may go for a walk and meditate. We may seek solace from others, and, from them, receive nurturing and support.

While we are not intending to deal with all of these problems and variations in this work, we do mean to highlight a few related to IT. Some of those reactions have been documented by Sherry Turkle (1984) in her case studies of the personalities of computer users. In Western society the emerging IT user personalities have been named, with terms such as *nerd*, and have been the subject of media and movie attention. Our concerns are not with these popularizations as much as with the experience of everyday life. For example, when a worker or set of workers is replaced by IT machinery, the tool becomes the worker. The underlying message includes an implicit statement that machines are more valued than the worker, not despite their lack of personality, but in part because they are impersonal.

One of the important aspects of adapting to the machine is in use of space. We have already raised the notion of work space. While many design efforts have taken place since the movement of machines to the work space of the person, there are few if any effective personal computer implementations which are comfortable for clerical staff, even when staff are not housed in open-plan space. Often, machines are placed on the floor in containers. Keyboards are placed in typewriter coves. Monitors are too high, too low, too big, too small, too glaring, facing the wrong direction. The wiring at each desk becomes a nightmare. Yet space is a critical piece of the experience of working life. When the tool one uses at work cannot fit, or fits poorly into a work space, or dominates the structure and content of the work space, one inevitable message is that the machinery matters more than the worker, and the worker must make all the adaptations.

The dimensions of computers were not designed with any particular human or set of humans in mind. Neither were they designed with any thought to the long-term health effects of such machines upon the humans who use them. The health effects may range from radiation, hand disorders, headaches, to stress. For example, researchers may have found a relationship between the high frequency noise emitted by video display terminals and stress symptoms in women. In this respect, one could argue that developers and designers have changed little in their focus since the beginning of the industrial age. Steel smelters, chemical plants, or other work places were not designed to meet the health needs of the humans who work in them. In the case of information technologies even the display devices pose health risks – some known, others suspected, probably more unknown – yet they continue to be used by millions of people, mostly women, each day. Certainly one cannot avoid understanding the message that the health of the worker is subordinate to the use of the machine.

THE TECHNOLOGIST AND DESIGN

The design of the application of information technologies reflects the same values. In case after case, the emphasis is upon the data system not the human. In training for systems designers there is usually no set of required courses which teach human process; nothing about understanding the dynamics of and working with individuals, groups, or organizations; nothing of the applied social science knowledge that we have accumulated; nothing of the values, ethics, and morals of humankind. In effect, a number of people would agree with Marcuse (1964) that the practice of technology is a history that is largely impersonal and inhuman, leading us to a technological society lacking democratic freedom.

Yet many developers and designers focus upon exactly the opposite in their work. They are concerned with the contribution of technology to freedom, human development, and equity. Nicholas Negroponte (Brand, 1987), Director of The Media Lab at MIT, talks of the paramount need to articulate the goal of humanism through machines. Ivan Illich (1973) has been concerned with political and cultural freedom through the use of convivial tools. In his terms, convivial tools are technologies which serve politically interdependent individuals in a society characterized by autonomous intercourse between and among people and their environment. Technology practised in that manner can be viewed as a liberating force.

How can such divergent views exist at the same time? It is certainly related to the differing approaches taken to the practice of technology. *Technology-practice* is a phrase used by Pacey (1983) to describe the application of science and other knowledge to "practical tasks by ordered systems that involve people and organizations, living things and machines" (p. 6). But we also argue that technology practice involves human choice. The idea that there can be a choice is extremely important. It assumes that there exist a number of alternative technological means to achieve objectives, that these may be increased by human effort, and that informed selection takes place with some knowledge of effects.

One example of the manner in which personal values are effected by technical choices is in the area of surveillance. While the tapping of telephone wires and cables has long been a subject of debate, listening devices of much more power are now available. Some devices can be pointed at a domicile from large distances, and every sound heard and recorded. Computer files and computer communications can easily be tapped. TV monitoring is routinely done in markets, stores, work places, banks, and public facilities, presumably to provide security against crime. Fingerprints and voiceprints are used to record individual identities. Infra red and other heat radiation devices are used to discover, locate, and check human movement and activities. Credit cards have evolved to "smart cards". Smart cards are used extensively to monitor poor and vulnerable groups. For example, some food stamp recipients in the USA must now use the card when they shop for groceries. At best, devices are used in socially acceptable manners. Computing devices in individual automobiles monitor automobile movements across a San Diego bridge and produce monthly bills for bridge use. At worst, civil liberties are at risk. Electronic bracelets are used to monitor people's movements, and simple credit card transactions generate a record of where you choose to shop.

If technological choice is possible, the developers and designers are especially accountable. They are particularly accountable for the internal technical or engineering efficacy of a technology, and they are accountable for the external human efficacy of the technology, that is, its efficacy in reaching human goals while operating in the real world. As Cooley (1987) has pointed out, the choice of goals is a political act. The design of technological systems is also an act of social engineering, affecting sets of social relationships and the distribution of power.

PROTECTING THE PERSONAL

The application of computer machinery, telephone equipment, and their associated devices has been historically lodged with large scale organizations. As we have related previously, the military, government, corporations, and, through science, the educational institutions, have been the early and continuing shepherds of these technologies. In each case, the applications which have been developed fulfil needs which are, in the main, impersonal. The technologies have been used in these domains with a great deal of success.

Military applications range from behaviour control, through robotics and mission control, to strategic planning. Indeed, all areas of the military have been affected. In the government, activities which have benefited from application of the technology are surveillance, census taking, budgeting, taxation, fund allocation, criminal justice and police, and social security. In corporations, the applications which have been successful include financial applications, sales, air reservations, insurance and credit systems, banking, point of sale transaction systems, manufacturing, design, process control systems and various robotic applications. Many of these innovations have been accomplished by interaction with educational institutions, where many of the innovative and traditional activities of the natural sciences involve technological applications.

With the possible exception of some of the scientific activities, in nearly all of the areas mentioned above, the motivation for the application is to minimize and improve upon human performance and to reduce human error. The systems thrive when the underlying human process is one of routine and rules. In other words, if passing a product past a bar code means it is sold, then it is easy to design the logic for the use of machines to sell products under those conditions. In these cases the technology application has more likelihood of success when it is designed to exclude human intervention, or, at the least, to standardize human interaction with the designed system. A similar case can be understood to apply for the government in taxation or the allocation of cash welfare benefits. The instructions for the machinery can be set to represent the rules underlying the tax or benefits calculation arithmetic, thereby double checking everyone's tax form or speeding up a complex eligibility test. Mistakes and fraud can be checked in an identical manner.

Development in other areas has been quite different. There are disciplines which have emerged to do rehabilitation engineering, to make devices to supplement existing damaged human facilities, such as legs, hands, and hearing. Some technicians are looking into the manufacture of genes, perhaps of life. Others have begun to look at the manner in which the brain works and to simulate the interactions of the neurons. Some of the explorations have focused upon aspects of our senses, such as the recognition of patterns in physical vision.

The Media Lab at the Massachusetts Institute of Technology in the United States is the preeminent example of contemporary work. The Media Lab is loosely organized into different domains that range from work with images and imagination, speech, and vision, to experimenting with learning and human-machine relationships. The philosophers of the movement, explains Stewart Brand (1987), are science fiction writers. At the time he wrote his book about the Lab, Brand found that Drexler's work, *Engines of Creation* (1986), was having a profound impact. In that work, Drexler posits that information technologies will remake our world or destroy it. Neither of these alternatives seem very attractive to us, but the dialogue at the Lab is important, essential, and needs widening. As Brand points out, designing an ethical robot promises to be a long and interesting problem for the Lab, but maybe the practice will help us understand the problems of being an ethical human being. To have a new hand so you can touch, to have a new heart so you can live, are important and valued advances as long as they are seen as instruments to prolong human experience, sensing, functioning, and, ultimately, the integrity of human intelligence.

Alan Kay is Director of the Vivarium project, associated with The Media Lab, but actually runs an experiment in a Los Angeles public school. Kay is an influential IT designer and pioneer of the personal computing movement. When recently interviewed about his goal of improving the use of computers by working with young students, Kay said (Silverstone, 1990, p. 56):

> "The number one thing you have to get right is values in the home . . . The first order of education is not computers. It's values. Really good learning has existed without technology. If you want to learn sculpture, do you start off with clay or do you start off with a bar of soap? Most art schools will say a bar of soap. Clay has an infinite malleability, yet most people can't make beautiful things with it . . . you have to have an image of good first, and the bar of soap helps sharpen the ability to have that internal image. Learning is more than an adventure game. It's

more than just picking up a particular tool that is going to help you later on. What's important is your outlook on life. It's not just how you get where you're going, but it's the directions you decide to take."

While we agree with such sentiments, in each of the instances we have considered, from military, science, government, and engineering, the technology practice we have presented is dominated by technical rationality. To a large extent, this leads to a situation where human control and choice are progressively limited. This is dangerous because choice, joined with intent, is necessary for values. And values constitute ethics. But the achievements in each of these areas materializes the values which led to their creation: in other words, values have been redefined, not lost. They are redefined in technical terms, serving technical ends, in a technological process. Habermas (1971) has argued that such a process requires the suppression of ethics.

The problem arises when a human situation is made technical – that is, it is defined as a matter of efficiency, or reduced to structure, or rationalized, or seen as instrumental – to the exclusion of the personal and ethical, the social, historical and biological, and the political. We would argue that a different type of technology practice is needed, one that is accountable for the fit between the human context and the technology. We believe it is possible for people to control technology. We do not argue that this is easy or that stories of success are common. They are not. Neither are we arguing that control is reduced to making decisions about which computer to buy. We are essentially maintaining that humans have a set of goals, values and traditions which do not rely upon technology for their existence and derivation. It is these principles which people can apply to understand, control, and direct technology. The problem is translating clearly and systematically our notions of a good life into principles that advance the human ends to which we want IT to serve as a means.

FORMS OF ABUSE

To the extent that we fail to humanize, IT becomes another avenue of abuse against people. Some of the abuse may seem relatively benign, sometimes less so. For example, in many large scale databases, workers cannot change any of the data in the system despite the fact that they know it is incorrect. In a still more damaging example, stocks of housing owned by the government sit unoccupied while families are homeless, and the problem is explained by officials as an inability to get the computer system to catalogue available housing reliably enough. If these are examples of what might be seen as organizations hitting out at the individual, the rise of the computer virus, computer intruders, computer worms, and like activities can be interpreted in part as acts of rebellion by individuals against organizations and authority.

As we have argued, developers and designers must be taught to have a conscious concern for people. The teaching of the practice of technology needs to include training in the assessment of the human context in which IT is intended to operate. As we will detail later, there are disciplines which have developed knowledge in such assessment. These are the human service professions. They share accountability with information technologists and their role will become clearer in our later discussions. But, as a basic principle, we would argue that human goals and technical means cannot be randomly mixed: they need to be fit together through a human process which assesses their psychosocial and biophysical content. In this we are in complete agreement with Willoughby (1990) who argues for the implementation of what he calls an integrated framework for technology practice, one that considers the socio-political, the technical-empirical, and the ethical-personal dimensions. We disagree that in the implementation of this framework the developer, the designer, and the technologist stand as leaders. Instead, we argue the need for a collaborative, participatory process in planning and decision making.

8 Disadvantaged Majorities

SUMMARY

Ibsen provides a slogan for all elitist groups, especially suitable for the computer-wise, "The minority is always right". He also claimed that the majority has the might, but we have found little sign of any majority flexing of muscles in relation to IT. Earlier pages have noted those who constitute the computer-wise – young, male, from industrialized countries, able to handle the English/American language, often with high enough material wealth to have a computing capacity at home, often also self-taught but increasingly a product of modern Western education. It would be harsh to describe them as arrogant, though arrogance is a characteristic of many of their attitudes. Certainly they have and use a specialist jargon, inventing new terms for the new technologies, speaking and writing in initials and acronyms, and making little attempt to explain themselves to the rest of us. They are a new priesthood, without the traditional fancy dress, but with all the rituals and mysticism, and the expectation that we followers will have faith in them. If we are to have faith, and if that faith is to be justified, then we will need growing evidence of a sensitive ministry to two significant population groups.

This chapter will focus on those two large groups of people, majorities in a global sense, who are currently largely outside the brotherhood of IT. One group is made up of poor people, excluded because of their poverty, their consequent lack of education, and, for many of them, their political powerlessness within their societies. This is not a difficult group to place as IT-outcasts, because of the lack of material wealth which puts computers, telephones and the like in the luxury category. They exist within industrialized countries and *are* the societies of the Third World.

The second group is less easily explained because there are no blatantly obvious reasons why IT has become such a male dominated scene, and so effectively kept women out. It would be simplistic to focus on gender relations in IT as no more than a continuation of traditional subjugation, though this is clearly an element. Whether in the broad framework of political, social, legal and religious systems, or in the narrower confines of applied sciences, male dominance is well entrenched. It is hardly a surprise, in a setting where the thrill of inventiveness has overwhelmed all other considerations, to find both the unchallenged assumption that IT systems designed by men should serve to perpetuate male control, and the sort of flippantly patronising attitudes handed down by Dr. Johnson when he described women preaching as "like a dog's walking on his hinder legs. It is not done well: but you are surprised to find it done at all."

As a conclusion to the chapter we look at some "What if . . . " scenarios, particularly seeking to trace the way IT might look it, instead of being developed in a wealthy industrial country, it had taken its values and structures from a different kind of society, based on poor rural communities.

THE WORST OF CRIMES IS POVERTY

("The greatest of evils and the worst of crimes is poverty": G. B. Shaw in the Preface to *Major Barbara*)

A starting point is the premise that what motivates the exploitation (as opposed to the invention) of all new technologies is some combination of a wish to create wealth, gain advantage and power, seek protection or enhance the quality of life. These motives are not always all present, and their relative strength varies with cultural, political, geographic, climatic and other factors. In the sense that they reflect the targets, the desired outcomes of an investment, it should be possible to specify the indicators of performance which allow us to say "this objective has been achieved". In the further sense that exploitation is a process towards desired outcomes, we should also be able to describe the process, and note the experiences of all those who have been involved. It is in the motives and the processes that we can pick out those who have benefitted, those who have suffered, and those who have been left aside. It is in the formulation of the performance indicators that we can look to see the ethical standards that have been applied.

Reviewing those core motives, one, creating wealth, is most commonly associated with commercial exploitation. Some questions are pertinent. Is the wealth new or transferred? That is to say, has the development served to increase the world's store of resources, or was it gained by obtaining riches from somewhere or someone else? Whether the wealth is new or transferred, have there been losers, and who are they? Whatever labels we use, whether we talk of inputs and outputs, creation and destruction, raw materials and finished goods, all new developments depend on resources for production and marketing. What resources have been used? Where have they come from? What has been the effect of their use? In a broader sense, what have been the side effects of the activity, regarding pollution, conservation, health and safety, and other aspects of society and environment? How has the new wealth been distributed? Has it been concentrated in few hands, gone more widely to an increased and well paid group of workers, or been spread across many societies?

The answers to these questions, and the extent to which they are recognised as valid in the developers' assessments of success and failure, will give clear messages about ethical standpoints. Wealth creation has most certainly been an important motive in the exploitation of IT, though looking at the industry as a whole, there is a mix of conventional profit-seeking companies and individual enterprise guided by the excitement of invention. If any single general statement is possible about where IT stands in relation to the sources of new wealth, the use of raw materials, the impact of production processes, and the distribution of the rewards, then it probably has to focus on the lack of attention given to these questions, rather than a particular set of answers. The history of IT development suggests that there has been a genuine creation of new wealth and have not been global problems of environmental damage. In this sense IT has been more creative and had less harmful side effects than many other major developments.

At the same time, as discussed in Chapter 5, the wealth has been highly concentrated in specific locations in a relatively few countries, and there are few strategic plans which concern themselves with the balanced spread of investments or distribution of benefits. Japan is a major exception in terms of its own population, with a broad strategy in place since 1972 linking IT to society, the workforce and long-term investment. The United States has no national IT policy, and although Britain made creative moves with the Alvey project, these went off into technical rather than policy directions.

Gaining advantage and power is both a commercial and a political motive. The advantage can be identified in differing ways: it can be a head start in a race to implement a new opportunity: it can be an improved way of doing something: it can be an attempt to weaken a competitor. All have one feature in common – an object, perhaps a victim to be taken advantage of, or to exercise power over. This motive makes its first clear appearance in IT during the Second World War, and has continued as an element of defence policy ever since. Its arrival in a commercial context is more recent, but it has nevertheless moved straight to the top of the list of priorities for industrial countries and companies. To be in the lead in new technology is to have an advantage over others. Within the industrial world this determines whether a country is an innovator, a front line nation with economic independence, or whether it is destined to be no more than an assembler of parts, a purchaser of the new technology from abroad, and thus a dependent state.

The belief that a lead in IT gives power and advantage, not to mention wealth, is now so strongly entrenched that its maintenance has come to take precedence over the advantage itself. In other words, the performance indicators connected with having an advantage are no longer solely concerned with using the lead as the basis for growth and development. It is also considered vital to keep hold of the lead, by not sharing its benefits, by patents and other legal devices, by an aura of secrecy both about the technology and plans for its use, by designing IT systems with a closed rather than open architecture, and a range of other approaches all designed at exclusion. An example is Britain's copyright legislation (Designs and Patents Act, 1988), which extends literary copyright to computer programs and artistic copyright to screen displays, and in its subsequent interpretation has moved towards the vaguer "look and feel" concept which allows for a breach of copyright even though no direct copying took place. While any fair system will give copyright protection to developers, the "look and feel" provision, which is more strongly established in the USA, closes off whole areas to newcomers. Is it possible to design any new spreadsheet, for instance, which does not have some look and feel of Lotus 123?

The importance attached to keeping the power and advantage of a technology lead has been a central cause of fragmentation and incompatibility in IT, and this notion of intentional incompatibility is itself ethically dubious. At a more political level, there have been, in association with the wish to obtain greater protection, policies of exclusion. Nevertheless, the attitudes of governments and IT companies has been very different. The United States government has used IT as an instrument of foreign policy, both to extend the range of military and other forms of security, and to deny such opportunities to those viewed as potential enemies. In short, national security has dominated any commitment to the importance of free market competition.

IT companies have for the most part been told to keep clear of the countries whose political systems are unsympathetic towards western capitalism, so their own approaches to lead-keeping and protectiveness have to be judged by their record elsewhere in the world. There are relevant aspects here related to design, supply and support, though the core issues focus around pricing policy and market imagination. The pricing policies of IT suppliers openly and unashamedly favour those who can take the largest number of boxes, and discriminates against everyone else. This is the situation as much inside a single market as it is between markets. Superimposed on this is a further level of apparent discrimination against countries or markets who do not come within the favoured group. There are some notable exceptions, like the efforts made by the Japanese to provide for their own domestic market, despite the language complexities, and the cheap availability of some equipment and programs in Far East producer areas, like Hong Kong and Taiwan. But exceptions do not extend into the Third World as a whole, which is treated so uniformly badly that the experience is not far short of the political treatment which used to be meted out to the communist block.

Third World societies are the victims, initially, of unimaginative design and marketing. Despite obvious long term gains from relating closely to such potentially massive markets as that of, say, India, the challenge has not been faced, and the immediate advantages of sticking with the local scene have prevailed. There is no evidence of any creative or concerted attempt to find out what would be beneficial, and therefore marketable, in the Third World. Most of these countries have not been formally excluded from buying equipment and programs designed for western industrial societies, but they have been priced out.

There has been much talk of virtuous technology transfer to Third World populations, but as recalled in earlier chapters, it is a shoddy scene. Coupled with premium prices and a lack of after sales support is a conspicuous shortage of IT generosity to poorer communities. The prevailing attitude towards technology transfer is patronising and paternalistic, based on the presumption that second best or second hand is good enough. Poor countries have become the final resting place for remnants of obsolete technology, often so out of date that there are no longer spares or supported programs to run.

There is some unfairness, however, in seeking to blame the IT industry for the social and economic impact of the modernisation of societies: there is every reason to allocate blame for the trivialization of so many IT applications, and the level of investment in and preoccupation with triviality at the expense of moves more profoundly geared to improving the quality of people's lives. Why is it that computers are so effective in replicating video nasties and war games, but play no part in cleaning the house, giving information about the contents, nutritional values and health risks of foods, or helping solve family dilemmas? Perhaps it is because those who have made a succession of development decisions prefer to play boys games.

Looking at arguments made here and earlier, in Chapter 5, two broad conclusions emerge. Firstly, those factors which drive IT companies and their market policies offer little scope for technology transfer to poor countries. Secondly, the process of technology transfer itself is complex and demanding if it is to be successful. What then are the answers for the world's population of poor people? Obviously part of the answer is to pursue greater generosity and more carefully worked out technology transfer. The fact that these have had failures in the past does not make them invalid for the future. Another part of the answer must be to listen to the messages that come from underprivileged communities. Some negative messages are clear: don't patronise; don't make conditions; don't treat us as technological morons; don't assume that IT which is good for you is necessarily good for us. Clear positive messages are harder to pick out, but two do surface regularly.

One concerns off-the-shelf technology and applications, and the view that packaged final products perhaps have less long term utility than components, parts, at the pre-assembly stage, or the editable manuscripts of the computer instructions which make up programs. The main reason for this approach is that at this stage of assembly there is more scope for flexibility, for making modifications to suit local conditions and needs. An important secondary reason is that assembly and modification play a part in developing indigenous expertise. Expressed another way the components have fewer of the built in values and attitudes of the producer societies than do their finished products.

The second message, perhaps with origins in community work and developmental politics, is about participating in decision making about IT, rather than simply focusing on technology. This is a message about communication, about privileged societies listening and taking notice, and about understanding where the latest aids to hi-tech modern living standards fit in the context of poverty, malnutrition, illiteracy and illness. The technological focus, therefore, is more on the communications aspects of IT, at least in the early stages. What is on the table is a demand to be heard, rather than a request for a computer in a box.

THE POOR FEEBLE SEX

("The Queen is most anxious to enlist everyone who can speak or write to join in checking this mad, wicked folly of *Women's Rights*, with all its attendant horrors, on which her poor feeble sex is bent . . . . God created men and women differently – then let them remain each in their own position", Queen Victoria in a letter to Sir Theodore Martin, 1870)

The power of tradition predisposed IT towards male domination and female subjugation. The continuity which led to the former is that of men filling the ranks of engineers and company managers, so controlling industrial development and production processes. The latter focuses on the role of women as cleaners, typists and decorative personal assistants. Thus it can be argued that the present situation in IT is really not much more than a natural progression of the roles and relationships which existed in older industries passing into a new one, and such an opinion might go on to suggest that decision-makers in IT can hardly be blamed for failing to swim against the tide.

A closer look offers a different picture. The polarization of roles has occurred: men control system development, production management, and most of the senior jobs in marketing and distribution. Women sit at computer keyboards, doing the mundane secretarial tasks, and also find themselves doing stressful and not too well paid jobs on production lines making computer components. There is no doubt which sex does the exciting work and gets the big salaries, and which does the chores for a pittance. However, far from this being a seemingly *normal* position, which males have accepted with resignation or not even considered, there are many signs that men in IT have worked strenuously to maintain their superiority.

Tradition has helped them: so has the way of handling IT in children's education in some parts of the world, where computer studies have at times existed as an alternate on the timetable (for boys to take), running parallel to subjects such as domestic science (for girls). Nevertheless, the growth of IT has also coincided with considerable activity and pressure from women's groups, and some determination has been needed to resist them.

Males have been denied some of the more common grounds for excluding women, such as that the heaviness of the work requires male muscle power, or that it is too dangerous for women, but a rather more subtle suggestion has been spread around. It is that men are somehow more numerate and technical than women: both aptitudes are then indicated as vital in IT, though this is untrue for many aspects of planning and development, and most applications. Women in contrast are said to be (and commonly present themselves as) neither numerate nor technical: they have other capabilities, as mothers and glamorous efficient secretaries, but these do not involve skills which are vital to seniority in IT. Western cultural rituals reinforce these positions. In these societies men cannot admit to an inability to handle calculations or tinker with machinery without creating some aura of shame, failure and, maybe, effeminacy. Women can make such admissions without fear of criticism, and often with cultural approval.

The subtlety of insinuations about female skills is operated in harness with a brash and blatant assertion of the machismo of IT. This is most publicly apparent in the advertising copy used in computer journals, especially those geared to selling business applications. Though many adverts choose not to involve people at all, those that do are wholly predictable. Intelligence, ideas and executive quality are male: decorativeness, nice legs and keyboard skills are female. If men are portrayed in front of a screen, then it must show graphics or figures, but never ordinary typescript. Women just have to look good. If both are in the picture, then the man stands over the woman, or through gesture and expression shows his superiority.

Much more insidious than advertising, however, is the catalogue of software on offer for personal computers, especially programs which find their way into homes. Certainly there are business applications and educational programs, but there are also enormous numbers of games. There are war games, games of personal aggression, of evading attacks, of exterminating enemy, of keeping clear of monsters, of driving racing cars and tanks, and many more, all combining the security of having a computer version rather than the real thing, with scope for unfettered aggressiveness. A display of packaged computer games looks as lurid as any rack of video nasties. These games are made for boys of all ages, 5 to 95, and used by them. For males the computer can look exciting, whether as a work tool or a games machine. For females there is such a paucity of interesting software that the home computer is an expensive bore, and the machine at work no more than a modern typewriter.

It is worth asking why IT has been sheltered from some of the more determined attempts by women's groups to alter the current position. Part of the answer is that there have been other more traditionally male dominated targets to tackle, such as the armed forces and professions, but it might be a mistake to assume that IT is on the list for action in due course. We have already written about the way the IT-wise have established and now protect their exclusiveness, and in so doing have generated insecurities in the rest of us, of both sexes and many cultures. One effect of such insecurities is to deter any group of outsiders wanting to get on the inside.

The build up of insecurity begins at school, not just with the gender biassed timetabling already mentioned, but more fundamentally in the way IT has slotted into subjects which are already established as areas of male dominance, if not male preserves. When the 1981 British Government started the policy of computer provision for all schools, the equipment went to mathematics, an area of documented male strength, rather than to arts subjects. A machine was designated and software developed with good keyboard and statistical potential, but weak on sound and graphics, so reinforcing the deployment. An American study (Sanders, 1987) of the gender division of home computers showed that 37 per cent of boys and 28 per cent of girls had them, but an overwhelming majority of those nominally owned by girls were, in reality, only used by fathers and brothers.

Insecurity and discrimination is reinforced in higher education. In Britain in 1981 22.5 per cent of computer science graduates were women, but as the availability of computers in school mathematics teaching grew, so the proportion diminished. By the end of the 1980s it was down to 10 per cent. Universities and colleges have themselves chosen to deploy their very substantial IT resources towards subjects where there are traditionally large majorities of male students (basically the sciences), and deprived the subjects (arts and social sciences) where there are higher proportions of women.

It is easy to react to such statements by arguing that computers are more useful and appropriate in science subjects. Within higher education there is certainly a strong and arrogant assertion that such is the case. However, this is no more than a man (or should we say scientist) made position. Computers were first deployed in the sciences because the sciences could make better use of number crunching (the main capability of computers at that time), so a demand and market was established for relevant applications, and in the longer term for modifications to the computer systems themselves. As the provision became more explicitly directed towards the initially favoured subjects, so a cosy pattern built up, with ever increasing obstacles to new subject areas wanting to stake a claim. Computer facilities in higher education are gradually becoming more accessible to courses with majorities of women students, especially as more resources are accumulated, and cheap trailing edge technology gives an opportunity to put machines in arts and social science space. At the same time the systems as a whole, and their design, are at risk of becoming very elitist, with high cost facilities for the use of tiny scientific minorities at the expense of more diversified, devolved and balanced arrangements.

Once through formal education the gender basis of IT becomes part of the wider scene in employing organizations. The bequest of the education system in most industrial countries is a male population with significant IT experiences and skills, contrasting with a female population in which only a small minority would consider themselves computer literate, leaving a disillusioned majority of outsiders. Such a situation can only serve to strengthen traditional employment and hierarchical practices in the business community. As far as many women are concerned, the computer in a business setting ceases to be a machine of potential diversity and creativity, and settles down as little more than a disguised typewriter. In this way it is demeaned, and a major opportunity missed.

Computer systems have considerable flexibility in the sense that they can not only be moulded to suit the organizational structure and hierarchy of a company, but can also have a dynamic effect on the dispersal of authority. Summarising an earlier analysis, a strongly centralized company can have its authority reinforced by using a centralized computer system, in which the management group directly controls the file server and its contents, as well as the communications network. A hierarchical company is supported by an IT configuration which enables vertical communications (terminal to HQ) and discourages lateral communications (terminal to terminal except via HQ). Centralization is further strengthened by ensuring that remote terminals are *dumb* in the sense that they have little or no independent working capacity. In contrast an organization with a devolved authority structure is enabled by a similarly devolved IT system, with a higher proportion of self-contained local capacity, flexible communications, and less dependence on a centralised computer.

Another example of potential IT and organizational harmony concerns external contacts. Companies wanting, for whatever reason, to restrict the communications their staff have outside the organization, can aid the process by developing their own unique IT system in a way that is incompatible with others. If the need is to encourage wider communication (as a marketing company might want), or to facilitate home to work links, then there is the opportunity to make use of well established computer and communications operating standards.

These points have been made before, but the reason why such matters are particularly relevant from a gender viewpoint, and why it is so important for women to seek decision making roles in relation to IT systems, is because of the need to tackle the reinforcement of male dominated areas and widen the scope to strengthen the position of women. A broad but generally accurate generalization is that the senior management of companies is likely to be heavily male dominated, even where a majority of employees are female (the position in most welfare agencies, for example). In such a situation strongly centralised IT systems strengthen male managers: devolved systems at least offer a potentially greater role for the rest of the employees. In a similar fashion, a highly internalized and incompatible IT system blocks external communications, significantly home to work, and so denies a work pattern preferred by many women, operating from a home base. Internalized systems also tend to make life harder for those who have simultaneous concerns outside the work base (such as part time staff, or those with family responsibilities), or who need skills which are transferrable because they themselves have to be mobile (again women, who are traditionally expected to follow their male partners around).

There,is as yet an insufficient appreciation of the way IT configurations can and do change power relationships. Discussion here has been about this theme in relation to gender. It can be broadened to cover all aspects of equal opportunities, and many aspects of business management and government. Computer and communications systems are not neutral in these contexts.

WHAT IF . . . ?

A premise of this chapter has been that IT has gradually developed as a tool, weapon and plaything of English speaking males who are not poor and come from (or are favoured by) nations within the orbit of the western world. Without seeking great precision it has been argued that such a generalization is broadly true, and has come about less by careful planning than by the effects of tradition, accident and opportunism. What is being asserted in ethical terms is that IT is and seems set to remain highly discriminatory in its impact on the world community. The discrimination concerns access to IT facilities, the design of systems, the range and design of applications (programs), the uses to which IT is put, and the ownership and control of all the resources involved. In Part 3 of this book we shall seek to present a framework for bringing an end to such discrimination, but before reaching that point it may be instructive to look at "What if . . . ?" questions.

The core question is – What if computers had not been designed and most programs written for males in industrialized societies? What if, instead, they had been designed for poor rural communities, or in response to women's needs? What then would computers have been like? What would they be doing? What would be the range of work and leisure programs?

If there is a stereotype of a computer user for the 1990s, the advertising of IT indicates that he is viewed as a young well dressed executive. He can be contacted anywhere at any time because he has a pager and a portable phone when he is on the move. He may carry a pocket computer, but more likely a brief-case portable, and in his job he will make vitally profitable decisions from his work station, and give his colleagues or bosses brilliantly computer-prepared presentations. He will have a secretary who looks good, and produces desktop published papers within moments of receiving the authoritative command. Occasional glimpses will establish that despite his 24 hours a day devotion to his company, he is morally upright and a good family man. What is implied but not stated is that he speaks or understands

English, and comes from a society in which excellent infrastructures, like health and education services, power supplies and communication networks, are taken for granted.

Let us move our hero aside and describe another image, perhaps of an Indian family, living in rural poverty. They have a piece of land to cultivate, which provides them with much of their own food, and a small cash crop. They have a bicycle and an ox-cart. Their children go to school, but there are real problems with school books. The nearest health clinic is a long bus ride away. They have a power supply for lighting, which is very unreliable, but no phone. If IT was to be designed for a family like this, what would it consist of? How would it work? What would it do?

The first observation is not a response to any of those questions, but a point about price. It would have to be cheap. If a computer system costs 10 per cent of an American salary, why not 10 per cent of the Indian equivalent? Who will face the challenge of designing a durable, flexible, mass produced 50 dollar or 30 pound sterling computer? Alternatively there are many examples of low cost loan schemes, like that run by Britain's Open University, designed to put computers in the hands of those who could not afford to buy them. Who can then support the 50 dollar computer with free or 50 cent software?

The design of the computer would have to suit the infrastructure of the family's community. It would need to be small and light to make it easily and cheaply carried around where transport systems are often inadequate and overloaded, and to minimize the space it took up in, by First World standards, extremely crowded home conditions. It is tempting to suggest that it should plug into the TV set, like the original Sinclair home computers, but this would deprive the family of its TV access (if it had a set) in the interests of a single computer user. Perhaps the notion of a screen is itself out of order: how about image projection onto a blank surface, like a piece of white paper, wall or bed sheet? Then it could be varied in size according to how many people wanted to see it, and equally importantly it would dispense with the need for one of the four bits of equipment normally identified as a basic computer system (keyboard, screen, printer and the box which holds the processing and memory chips, disk drives and so forth).

Powering the computer is a relevant consideration. Electronic equipment operates on electricity, albeit in small quantities, so ability to plug in without overloading the electricity supply is important. However, there needs to be some equivalent of battery backup to cope with frequent power cuts. A possible model is the rechargeable battery used in portable computers, but a more culturally relevant parallel might be the ubiquitous sewing machine, commonly able to run by electrical power, but with the fall back of treadle operation. How about a foot pedal dynamo to run the computer, as an alternative or addition to electricity? Or a computer that could be connected to the dynamo of a bicycle?

It is possible that the notion of a family computer could be challenged. Is the home computer necessarily for the family, or could it be for community use? Does the computer, or a range of computer applications have a place as a community resource, and could it make a contribution to community enrichment? Is there a useful role in rural India for the Community Teleservice Centre?

What about computer applications? The thirst for escapism is as great in India as anywhere else – the Indian film industry is a thriving example. Undoubtedly, however, the thirst for education is stronger. It should be possible to overcome the shortage of school books, and provide educational material much more cheaply than in printed form, by the use of compact disks. They are more durable than traditional floppy disks, hold more, and do not damage easily. Many educational applications would need *read only* material, rather than the combined ability to read and write to a disk. Adult education could be made more feasible in this way, offering courses on a range of topics relevant to rural living. The distance of health services is another factor in the family's life. An on-line health advisory link could be a real benefit, but presumes the existence of an infrastructure able to support a network. Again there may be a rural community rather than family solution.

This attempt to redefine a computer (or fantasize if you wish) could go on, but perhaps the point has been made, that the personal computer as we know it has been designed for western society, to fit that culture, infrastructure and income level. The moment we begin to approach computing from the standpoint of a different culture, so the changes become apparent. The problem for countries like India is that although the technology exists, the wealthy world does not show the interest, imagination or commitment necessary to produce culture-led systems for poorer societies, or human needs-led systems for anyone outside business and government.

9 Insiders and Outsiders

SUMMARY

There are two reasons for using the variables of majority and minority as the basis for dividing up a discussion of equal opportunities. The first is to establish that an IT insider is a member of an elite: most people, because they are female, poor, excluded by political decision, or a mixture of all of these, are IT outsiders. The second is to squash the commonly voiced and patronizing view that in a democratic society deprived or excluded groups must, almost by definition, be minorities. Hence the previous chapter focused on what is clearly a majority of the world's population. This chapter now turns to minorities, and parts of it will be largely descriptive about the efforts made within IT to accommodate some minority groups: but there is a moral, political and strategic context to establish and keep in mind throughout. It is too easy to be seduced by the technological marvels of computer aids for those who are blind or paraplegic, and so forget the real state of affairs for other needy groups.

Following themes from the previous chapter, we look specifically at ways IT is used to help or hinder disadvantaged minorities. The groups studied will include people with physical or developmental disability, ethnic minorities, those who experience mental illness or some other vulnerability, and those who are losing independence as a result of ageing.

MAJORITY AND MINORITY

The reasons for exclusion from mainstream IT benefits are primarily economic, political and cultural. We cannot afford it, our government or an IT provider government forbids it, or our social system makes IT a no go area. Once that framework is acknowledged we can go on to accept that some people are excluded on functional grounds. Either the people themselves have impairments which handicap or block them when they seek to use conventional IT configurations, or the systems used in their community do not provide for a particular characteristic, like the use of a minority language. In many instances these functional situations could restrict access to IT, but in practice do not, because they are not yet in the front line. Most people with a physical or developmental handicap, members of ethnic minorities, or dependent elderly are already excluded as part of the greater deprived majority. These groups contain a higher proportion of poor people than in society as a whole, a higher proportion who have not had the benefits of good health and education provisions, and amongst the fastest growing group, dependent elderly people, a higher proportion of women.

In short those members of minority groups who can get through the majority obstacles to come face-to-face with their specific circumstances are few. What awaits them is daunting. There are strengths and weaknesses in technology developments. People with a physical handicap, for example, have been the subject of much IT activity. In contrast minority or unfashionable language applications have been largely ignored. A blind English speaker will find some effective synthetic speech systems, capable of talking through a variety of screen fonts: but change the required language to Welsh or Hindi or Mandarin and there is nothing. The range of technology applications is so specialized, with so little emphasis on broadening the base of applicability, that the marketplace also offers some nasty shocks. For the most part the market is not big enough to be viable, so there is often little choice of manufacturer, a lot of dependence on charitable "grace and favour" support, and prices are high. It was mentioned in an earlier chapter that a personal computer might well cost the equivalent of 8 years of an average Indian wage. A Kurzweil Personal Reader for a blind Indian (who would have to understand English) would cost around 30 years wages, and India is not the poorest country on this planet.

The politics of selectivity further weaken the position of some minority groups. Faced with awkward decisions about the use of scarce resources, governments are forced to identify priority areas. Unless the prevailing culture gives strong protection to a particular vulnerable group, the chosen priorities are likely to reflect economic factors. Emphasis will be placed on enhancing and supporting those who are important to the economic system – the labour force, and children because they are the future workers. Within the labour force men will get more attention because they fill more of the full time posts and dominate senior positions, while older workers, approaching retirement, run a real risk of being thrown onto the scrap heap. Those who have passed working age, or are thought unlikely ever to be able to achieve able-bodied productivity levels, or (ethnic minorities here) are preferred in an underprivileged state so that they can be channelled into the dirty manual jobs, will get a lower priority. Issues which become or get close to being recognized as human rights in a wealthy society, like rights to education, employment and a full community lifestyle, are too often the subject of exclusion clauses if a face or body or opinion does not fit.

No suggestion is being made here that these discriminations come from explicit open policies. Quite the reverse – most social policies seek to emphasize their non-discriminatory nature, and their concern for those who endure misfortunes. Discrimination shows in unchallenged implicit values, and in the minutiae of policy implementation. Even countries like Britain, with its traditional (albeit currently weakened) commitment to an all-embracing welfare system, is a casebook of examples of discrimination. Shops, banks and other public buildings rarely have counters at a suitable height for people confined to wheelchairs. Steps and staircases are everywhere that elderly or handicapped people are expected to go. Workers lose pay if they cease scurrying around to meet required output levels, and instead talk and move at a less than able-bodied pace. Few social work agencies, banks or law firms have the potential for offering counselling in a range of minority languages.

The list could be extended almost without limit, and IT has plunged into this milieu of largely unintended societal insensitivity with few questions. Modern society is a society for the street-wise able-bodied: IT is a technology for the same people. From that standpoint of prejudice a core question is asked – Who amongst the outsiders qualifies for goodies? Amongst all of those who are not fit persons of the chosen race, who will be given and who allowed to pay for the opportunity of using IT benefits? Continuing with the British illustration, the major welfare agencies (social services departments) operate quite clear priority ratings in their deployment of resources to that society's casualties. Children come first. Old and handicapped people get less attention from less well qualified staff, and face longer waiting lists for a poorer standard of service. Most of the agencies claim allegiance to policies of equal opportunities, but few can cope more than superficially with the needs of a member of an ethnic minority community.

It is difficult to avoid being totally dominated by problems of discrimination when looking at the position of under-privileged minorities. Nevertheless there are other salient issues which affect the potential of IT to respond. In geographical terms some minorities tend to congregate, others to disperse. Most Welsh speakers live in Wales, can be identified as a coherent community, and are in a position to be involved in corporate activity about Welsh language computer applications. In contrast blindness, though it is more prevalent in poor societies with inadequate health and hygiene provisions, spans all race and language groups. The world community of blind people are characterized only by their blindness: they do not have geographical proximity or much scope for wider cohesiveness.

Attempts by IT developers to link with "the blind" will inevitably be fragmented and selective. In the United States consumer groups of blind persons and non-profit organizations have attempted to step in and develop a position which includes links with IT developments. The American Foundation for the Blind has established a National Technology Center. One of the Center's activities is a Job Index/User Network which contains data from more than one thousand blind and visually impaired people using adaptive equipment in a variety of jobs. One manner by which participants share their knowledge and experience is in evaluating both existing and newly developed assistive devices. Put another way, the path forward for IT aided resources for some minority groups is clear and straight: for other groups it is uncharted jungle.

The notions of separateness and integration are relevant at this point. So far we have discussed IT applications for blind people, for example, as though they are specialist provisions for a specific community sub-group. The philosophy of specialist services to meet specialist needs is widely respected, and it would be difficult to visualize how IT developments in these areas could avoid specialization altogether. And indeed such a view has led to progress. In the United States a number of computer scientists like Jean Blazie and John Eulenberg (Williams, 1984) have worked throughout their careers to develop synthetic speech through microcomputers so that blind, speech impaired, and other people with handicaps can speak and be spoken to. Many of the settings for the use of the technology are also specialized, such as the Nebraska School for the Visually Impaired. The school has been a pioneer in the use of information technologies for visually handicapped persons.

However, there is a clashing belief in integration, both in the sense that human needs should be treated in a generic "whole person" context, and that people with handicaps or other special difficulties should spend their lives in the larger community, doing what the community does. In this philosophy having special IT provisions for, say, physically handicapped children, which involved going to a special rather than standard school, would be frowned upon. There is a real challenge for IT developers to come up with systems which meet special needs, interface totally with mainstream systems, and operate in the same context. The basic reason for doing so is that information technologies reinforce and anchor values in a society. What values are at risk here? They can be summarized briefly by looking at values relating to integration, productivity, needs, and stereotypes.

Integration is a difficult construct to define, bound up as it is in the history of racism. Here we mean to talk about integration in a particular sense, that of sharing a set of norms, beliefs, or values so that people can participate in cultural traditions and be members of society. Integration, when realized, encompasses the personal and social values which underpin a person's behaviour and beliefs. When people with handicaps or other minorities are placed in the position of always being treated differently, or living in isolation, they experience a loss of membership. Membership has been called the primary social good awarded by society. Through membership people are empowered. Without it, they are not. They are, to play with words, dis-integrated. In terms of the positive impact of information technologies to provide the opportunity for membership, the obvious course would be to point to the manner in which they have been used to augment speech, or to operate devices which extend physical capabilities.

As we widen our scope to include not only people with handicaps, but racial and ethnic minorities, issues of productivity arise. We live in an age where employment in industrial occupations continues to shrink. The minorities and non-industrialized peoples have especially suffered from this effect. People with handicaps have been excluded as well. For some handicapped persons, issues of work productivity are experienced not so much as a problem of integration as of physical capability and architectural barriers. Laws in some countries have begun to remove architectural barriers. Physical capability has been the focus of information technologies and rehabilitation engineering. Zenith Data Systems and Prab Robotics have recently developed a work station for physically challenged people. The full package price is $49,500 US. The system is one that is described as leading to full productivity. It is unfortunate that the expense of the work station may limit it to use by companies of some size with specific interest in handicapped workers. More unfortunate is the limit to which the work station can be used by persons with handicaps to support their individual entrepreneurship, as few of them could afford it.

Racial and ethnic minorities have a different sort of need. In part, their future economic productivity relies upon knowledge, use, and application of information technologies. Access to information technologies is often limited. In American public school districts, the schools serving minorities are often found to have few information technologies available for students. Aside from status, in educational terms it is essential for everyone to have access to computers. A real cultural gap already exists and is growing, with the majority of the world population finding themselves truly handicapped and disadvantaged through lack of access. Those who have been called the *information poor* of the world, to denote their exclusion from information technologies, are synonymous with the poor of the world, with those who are handicapped, and disadvantaged (Childers and Post, 1975).

It may not be obvious, but the current emphasis upon making computers user-friendly may have the consequence of widening the gap between the IT haves and have nots. Since user-friendliness is aimed at the elite groups of people who now use the technology, it may unintentionally reinforce their values. We have given a number of examples of how this may occur in Chapter 7, but it would be useful to continue one of those examples, that of the keyboard. To make the keyboard less handicapping for people with impairment of language comprehension, having a keyboard with pictures rather than letters has been shown to be a real help. But the major development of icon usage came when Apple discovered that using pictures, now on screen rather than keyboard, is attractive and approachable for the everyday computer user. Since then icons have become part of the mainstream market, without more specialist development for people with impairments.

One of the consequences of IT elitism is the reinforcement of the stereotype that handicapped or disadvantaged people are of limited intelligence. To continue the example of the keyboard, it might be useful to look at reported cases arising from experiences in using Logo, a system pioneered by Seymour Papert, now at The Media Lab. Logo supports a learning environment found to be particularly suited to individuals with learning disabilities and disadvantagement. It puts direct control in the hands of users, and what they do has an effect. In the Logo experience, the user controls a turtle, which can move anywhere across the screen, making figures, symbols, and drawings. It may be the first experience that encourages a disabled person to take on a problem, think out solutions and try them, get immediate feedback, then decide whether to change track or not. Logo can be used with keyboard or mouse, but as we have shown, this may have the effect of excluding some people from using it. At Cotting School in Boston, one way of getting around the problem was to use a box with large buttons rather than a keyboard. This device had marked success, and use by cerebral palsied students sometimes revealed rather remarkable talents in spatial reasoning. The control box with large buttons is now used widely with those who cannot handle a conventional keyboard.

While we are just beginning to understand how much educationally disabled persons may be excluded by our technological choices, the same point runs true for all of us. Stereotypes are powerful belief systems which persuade people that differences in wealth, power, and opportunity are reflections of natural differences in people. In effect, people grow up and are conditioned to accept that inequality and disadvantagement are inescapable, not arbitrary and alterable.

To summarize this framework, disadvantaged minorities exist in every community. At times they are tribes which have not been able to gain a voice in the national or regional community. At other times they are groups who have been disadvantaged because of particular vulnerabilities, life experiences, or disabilities. The disadvantage which follows is not only an economic one. At times, the disadvantage can cover all human needs – from lack of water, food and shelter to lack of health and education, to inabilities to achieve self-fulfilment. Like the disadvantaged majorities described in Chapter 8, disadvantaged minorities include groups for whom societies have mapped out an inferior position and role. One of the circumstances, developmental disability, ascends in direct relationship to the lack of human sustenance, poor health care, and ignorance. Others grow in direct relationship to the chronic impact of poor living standards. A few have been the subject of both token largesse and true social caring, such as physically handicapped people in western nations. In most cases the disadvantage has been accentuated by the progress of information technologies for the privileged, and may continue in that direction. IT, therefore, is not doing anything like as much as it has the capability to offer for many minority groups, and redressing that trend is a task of enormous technological, economic, social, political and moral magnitude.

PEOPLE WITH PHYSICAL HANDICAP

People with physical handicaps, as we have noted, are in a peculiarly privileged position with regard to IT, and, in this regard, are an exception to most other groups of disadvantaged people. Take a real example. A blind paraplegic woman is being driven by a friend along an unfamiliar country road to go on a camping trip (she could drive herself in a car with a radio controlled automatic pilot, but this has yet to be manufactured). The car, for some unknown reason, overheats and stops. It is near evening. By reading the car console map, the friend can find out where they are and how to meet up with their camp party. In fact it is not necessary to move, as the location of the car is now being tracked by a home computer, which has been instructed by car phone to send an emergency message to the auto repair and towing service. However, because the woman is not far from her destination, she attempts to continue on legs. She puts on a pair of automated leg supports and remembers to take her portable terminal link to the car computer. She accesses the braille version of the car console map, which has noted her location. She finds her location with her finger, and traces out the route she wants to follow on the map. The route is recorded by the car, and held in the portable terminal. She tells the car what she intends to do, and gives instructions to lock up when she leaves and notify her when the repair service arrives. The terminal continuously shows her where she is on her route when she wishes to know, by linking with the car console map, and marking her location as compared to the route she wished to follow. At the same time, her location in reference to the car is recorded in case there is an emergency and she will need to request help. As she arrives at her destination, the repair service also arrives at the car. She is notified and gives instructions to her car computer to permit repair.

In this example it is not necessary to imagine that the person is blind and a paraplegic. People who find themselves in similar difficulties today may welcome some of the technological accessories which are described. It may be surprising to know that all of the devices in the example are presently the subject of research and development, with a few available and in use. It is probably less surprising to know that they were not developed specifically for blind paraplegics. Aids for handicapped people often emerge as spin-offs of expensive developmental work elsewhere. For example, the United States military is experimenting with a pilot's helmet that displays a landscape on the visor, with the pilot issuing voice commands and controlling direction with eye movements. This could well be adapted to help someone who is partially sighted, or confined to a wheelchair with extensive paralysis. The technique for car location now exists solely as an expensive security measure, allowing the car to be tracked down if it is stolen.

When applied to the problems of disability, such technologies give the disabled person access to the same motor and sensual abilities as a person who is not disabled. But in compensation, as the example points out, the disabled person may also take on abilities which are presently beyond the range of the normal person, and unquestionably not available to the poor.

There are other IT possibilities which augment the lifestyles of people with handicaps, though not through support of sensual and motor activities. The experience of disabled persons with computer networks illustrates a more subtle form of support. As we have discussed, a physically disabled person suffers disproportionately from being the target of social bias and prejudice, particularly in training and employment. One of the initial ways in which IT has been successfully used to deal with training and employment problems occurred early in the experience of the microcomputer. In a community college on the West Coast of the United States a microcomputer based network was initiated which was connected, by using dial-up modems (devices which use ordinary telephone lines to connect computer signals at one site with those at another site), to both the community college library and training centre. The system also contained a program for those connected to send and receive messages among all participants. Physically disabled people were given microcomputer based systems to use in their homes in order to participate in the network. The system was used initially as the authorities intended, that is for course work and for training and employment opportunities. However, users with handicaps also began talking to each other through the messaging facility. In some cases, this was the first time that they had been able to talk to anyone in a similar situation about their experiences and problems. They began an informal network of communications, exchanging notes, experiences, and hints about the various employment opportunities, as well as exchanging messages which were personal in nature. Because they were not face-to-face, they were able to communicate directly and without distraction from any visible disability, and felt able to develop links which were less tinged by awareness of their disability (Bowen, 1986).

A more recent experience in Canada (Marlett, 1988) has had unexpected results. A project links together more than 700 groups of disabled persons across all of the provinces. One of the surprising outcomes is the variety and vivacity of the types of interests and topics discussed over the computer network. People with disabilities tend to rely upon computer networks as essential and effective means of messaging with others, accessing learning, training, and employment opportunities and participating in groups. Their experience with computer based social networks and computer mediated communication is generally a positive one. As the project proceeded, participants began to group each other in terms of their capabilities and interests, rather than in groups arranged by disease or type of disability. Unlike other computer networks, particularly of the open "bulletin board" type, where the likelihood of interaction with other identifiable individuals is uncertain, this one encouraged participants to form lasting personal relationships. Under that condition, co-operation among participants continues to increase, and to extend to wider areas of their lives. Participants in the network are dealing with each other as persons in a way not possible before the technology was available to them.

Europe has seen other sorts of experiment. HandyNet is a networked database about handicap, with an access node in many countries, and plans to expand it in more accessible ways, such as the distribution of regularly updated CD-ROM versions (compact disks that can be read on a screen). VolNet is a British venture which aims to be more generic. It is an on-line database of information about services and voluntary organizations dealing with disabled and many other community groups. One of the problems, however, for networks with low income users is the cost of the telephone infrastructure on which they depend. In USA local phone calls are free, so therefore are local network calls. In the UK locals calls are charged, and can accumulate to substantial bills.

It is probable that the experience of people with physical disability will continue to be unique, in the sense that they have had a fairly positive experience with technologies. A most compelling outcome of their experience is that they can and need to participate in the design of most devices intended for their use. Handicapped and physically disabled persons must use and rely upon technologies to function in society. Information technologies are not simply toys or expensive baubles for them. They are not discretionary. Handicapped persons cannot cope with the discomfort of a personal augmentive adaptive device which is ill-adjusted, or does not work as advertised. Designers of the technology have already demonstrated that it can allow disabled persons to do things which they were not able to do before the technology was implemented in their behalf. IT can improve the personal quality of their lives.

The technology has also been used to help such people experience a personal power which they have previously been denied. This empowerment can be used to other ends. Remembering that physically disabled persons represent a fairly sizable portion of the population in the industrialized countries, we can speculate that this group have the potential to be a significant political force in the future. It is also important to observe how social resources of a highly sophisticated nature have been directed toward resolving problems of a highly personal, even intimate nature. This has consequences in evoking enhanced self-image, esteem and coping. This has not happened to the same extent for any other disadvantaged group.

DEVELOPMENTAL DISABILITY

The empowerment of the physique is no more challenging than work where a loss of intelligence or learning problem is the experienced disability. Not all of the persons grouped by professionals as developmentally disabled suffer from a loss of measurable intellectual power, but all suffer from a loss of adaptive capacity. This discussion will focus only upon that group of developmentally disabled persons identified separately as having learning difficulties.

The number, size, and types of IT specialists who work with people who have the various physical disabilities are not matched in the disciplines who work with those who have mental disabilities. For the most seriously disabled, models of caretaking exist only to promote a modest amount of comfort in impersonal surroundings. The effects of a life of massive deprivation of this sort have rarely been of interest, although it has been established that nurturing care and environmental enrichment can evoke positive behavioral responses. At the other end of the spectrum are those who suffer only modest learning impairment. Many of these persons are productive members of their community. Most IT for this group has been applied to the development of an assortment of training devices aimed at increasing their adaptive capacities and employability.

Work which deals with modelling the human brain is continuing at a number of places. For example, a cognitive neuroscientist at Johns Hopkins University has simulated a computing machine and type of computer program that learns to read aloud. The model of the computer which is used is one called loosely a neural network, a model based upon our idea of how the brain works. A typical brain contains anywhere from ten billion to a trillion neurons, each connected with from one thousand to one hundred thousand other neurons. The activation of the associations between and among the neurons is responsible, in part, for the great power of the brain. The neural network computer tries to work on all of the available data at one time, unlike a conventional machine which operates on a few pieces of data at a time. The computer programs are also different, attempting to find patterns, generate rules, and solve problems. Rules for solving the problem emerge in action: they are not put into the computer program. For the most part, work in this area has proceeded slowly with some sign of success.

It is possible that applying the same amount of resources to this activity as to physical disability would bring quicker and more substantial results. Instead much effort has gone into the development of genetic tests which indicate any problems with the genetic makeup of the unborn child. Genetics probes deeply into the identity of individual human beings. For example, courts have come to accept genetic evidence as positive proof of identity. Progress in genetics is closely tied to the development of information technologies. Without them, modern genetics could not proceed. Geneticists across the world are now engaged in a massive project to sequence all of the DNA in the human genome. By screening a person for all hereditary flaws, presumably one could have a clinical genetic health test. What we soon must face are the ethical issues around the use of gene therapy to alter the genetic makeup of the unborn child. In the case of people with learning difficulties, will they be made whole? In what way will intelligence be subject to engineering? (Suzuki and Knudtson, 1989).

MENTAL ILLNESS

Supplementation of intelligence is a completely different issue to the one faced in mental health disciplines. In this area we are dealing not so much with the brain as with the mind. The manifestations of mental illness are behaviours which are out of the ordinary, sometimes dangerous to the mentally ill person or to others. Because the definition of mental illness relies in part upon social norms and acceptability, at many times in history mental illness has been used as a label to justify the removal of political dissidents from society. The use of information technologies to diagnose mental illness would probably need to accommodate such social definitions and would raise a number of civil liberty issues.

The causes of mental illness are not all known. Historically, mental illness has been treated as magical, spiritual, biological, or behavioral in origin. Investigations of cause and origin have continued, and information technologies have been applied to the task. For example, they have been used in experimentation which demonstrated that some forms of mental illness are biologically manifested. These advances in biological measurement have contributed to proposals that sensors and drugs be implanted in people, to respond to a biological marker, activating the release of the drug. In other proposals, the sensor would trigger implanted electrical devices, which might produce a shock or calming vibrations. It has also been proposed that sensors be implanted which register data in distant places, tracking the location and condition of the patient.

Perhaps the widest area of IT application by mental health disciplines has been in psychological testing. Computerized test interpretations are commonplace. One effect of automation on testing is that commercial enterprise has become heavily involved, as part of confidential staff screening processes. This has the consequence of changing the free and open research and development which characterized the fields of psychological testing up to now. Success with automated testing has been most pronounced in self-report measures. There is some concern that automated testing can do more harm than good, particularly in areas of unsupervised test interpretation. It is also true that few tests were designed specifically for the computer. One group of psychologists has done so, and others have begun work to incorporate interactive video into the testing situation. Although we know of no one who has begun to do observation during testing using IT, this is in fact possible. In other words, it is possible to use the computer to record the person's reactions, movements, and speech during the testing situation, with or without their knowledge.

Information technologies have been used with increasing frequency in direct patient treatment, primarily in the form of computer aided education and training. Paulette Selmi (Hedlund, 1985) conducted an experiment in which a set of computer programs, collectively called MORTON, were used to treat persons suffering from depression. The computer programs were as effective as human therapists, while those not treated by either method showed the least improvement. Current treatment intervention applications are mainly confined to behavioral, cognitive, and educational ends of the spectrum of available treatments. It is in these areas that programs can be highly structured with clear rules. Direct patient treatment which involves open ended, psychodynamic treatment modelling has not maintained similar progress, relying as it does on unstructured, interpretive decision making in each individual instance. Such applications must wait for the development of more sophisticated tools, depending as they do upon the free flow of everyday conversation, the appraisal of the therapist of all sensory cues, and the therapist's continuous judgements of the effects, singular and cumulative, of their intervention. However, this type of work is occurring, even though it is outside of the mental health disciplines. Fjermedal (1986) has written a stirring portrait of the researchers and their beliefs. It is not surprising that they believe that humans will learn to build a brain. What is surprising and ethically provoking is the assertion, indirect though it be, that humans can build a mind (Edelman, 1987).

AGEING

As we look at the situation of elderly people in the Western world, we can observe that people are living longer. As they age, they are more vulnerable to injury, infirmity, disease, disability, and impoverishment. When people experience these vulnerabilities, they take on characteristics of the groups we have just discussed, physical disability, mentally illness, and learning difficulty, as well as of general illness. For example, injury at this age takes much longer to heal, and may result in chronic immobility. Alzheimer's disease may lead to periods of behaviour resembling mental illness or handicap.

IT has been used in a number of positive ways with elderly people. Perhaps the most compelling example is that of SeniorNet (Furlong, 1989). SeniorNet is a nonprofit project based at the University of San Francisco. Mary Furlong is the founder and Director of the project. She describes the purpose of the project as one to create and support an international community of computer-using senior persons. SeniorNet has developed an "electronic city" which SeniorNet members enter using a telephone, modem, and computer. There are twenty SeniorNet sites in the United States with about two thousand members. People trade messages about politics, meals, hobbies, anything. There are inter-generational projects with elementary schools in which children can access histories and photos. The network is also a way of connecting to other databases and libraries.

Other applications of IT have not led to unequivocally positive results. Nowhere is this more clear than in the application of information technologies to the health problems of elderly people. On the positive side, a number of systems exist which allow an elderly person living at home to signal for help in an emergency. Sophisticated programs have improved diagnostic testing and medical treatment. On the negative side, the use of expensive IT in health fields has been one of the primary contributors to the effect of making resources scarce and driving up the cost of contemporary health care. In the United States and Britain this has featured in the debate about the limits of public support for health care.

One of our problems in Western society is a tendency to accept values which assign elderly people low social estimation. They are at risk of being seen as a burden on society. In the prevailing view of the political right, to be old is to be useless. One should take a few vacations after retirement then fade into the sunset. It is not difficult to imagine that IT could reinforce a different set of values. If the elderly person is seen to have much to contribute to society in life experience, history, accumulated wisdom, common sense, tradition, and continuity, then IT can be used to support those values. As we have discussed, we anticipate that IT has a future role in assisting us to manipulate mortality by augmenting, replacing, or controlling our senses and our bodies, through genetic repair or direction, and by tinkering with our intelligence. That these have absolute application to the situation of the ageing person is undeniable, as they have application to all of us.

MINORITIES

We have sought to illustrate the experiences of a few minority groups, yet still feel constrained to repeat that these are minorities within privileged societies. A person with a handicap can only expect IT support if he or she lives in a wealthy community, where resources are available and value systems sympathetic. Most of those we have chosen to call "minorities" live in societies where IT deprivation is the rule. Except through some quirk of fate or international charity, their prospects of enjoying the benefits of what IT can offer are remote. We may feel good about someone whose impairments are reduced with mechanical and electronic aids, or the availability of a computer chat line for people confined to homes and wheelchairs, but be in no doubt that they are a tiny minority of those who have to endure handicap or debilitating illness.

We have scarcely touched the surface of the depth of global need, despite the fact that at a technological level there are really sophisticated worthwhile capabilities. From a political standpoint the weaker members of poor countries currently have little hope of coming close to IT solutions to their needs. Earlier in this book we asked why there was no international policy or organization active in these areas. If there is to be hope in the future, surely it lies with global collaboration which can seek to address the needs of the world community of people with handicaps.

10 Consumers and IT: a Love/Hate Relationship

SUMMARY

Consumers of IT are a mixed group, taking in buyers, users, those who are the subjects of personal data files, and those who, at least as far as they know, have no contact with these technologies. The relationship between IT and the public is complex, and characterised both by mutual dependency and, on the part of the public, suspicion. The value of IT in the organization of our lives is countered by resentment of its dehumanising tendencies. We expect it to provide a dependable infrastructure for our daily lives, so that we can take for granted, without question, that the correct salary cheque will arrive on time each month, the airline booking will be reliable, and the morning weather report accurate. There are many aspects of modern industrial life which depend on IT for their smooth operation, but where we rarely stop to ask if IT even has a presence. At the same time we do get concerned when things go wrong, when the computer has a fault, makes a mistake, or appears to be doing something we do not like.

This chapter starts by looking at our relationship with IT and the ways it is used by those who govern us. It then goes on to raise the issue of public rights, delving again into the problems which arise if personal data is never allowed as the property of the individual concerned. We debate whether there is a case for a show of public passive resistance to data gathering, to put an end to this form of commercial exploitation. Possible elements in a scheme of public protection are discussed, followed by an analysis of the many ways IT could be advanced in support of individual and local community living.

HOW DO WE FEEL ABOUT IT?

If there is a single general assumption made for us it is that IT is a good thing and a necessary thing, but can expose us to some risks, so we need a little protection. The assumption is made *for us* as a world population because nobody has chosen to ask us: indeed, modern societies are far too

140

dependent on IT applications to take the risk of inviting a citizens' view. We might demand changes which, from the viewpoint of governments and companies, would represent major restrictions both on current activities and future developments. Before looking further into this proposition, it would focus the scene more clearly to define "us", the consumers of the world. All of us belong to one or more of five categories:

1. People who are wholly outside the orbit of IT applications. These *outsiders* will come primarily from the poorest countries. Their governments may buy computer guided missiles for the military, or computerized control systems for the national airport and airline, but those who come into this category will have no contact with IT in their home lives, work, contacts with business and government agencies, or ways of communicating.

2. Those who have direct access to IT systems as *users*. They may have hands-on or less direct access, but in their domestic or work lives they make use of IT capabilities. They include the purchasers of IT equipment and programs, and those who are in the business of collecting data about the rest of us. A vitally important sub-group are the developers, designers, producers and distributors of IT.

3. Those who are on the receiving end of IT, and are fully aware of it. These are *informed recipients* of IT applications in the sense that they are well aware that their salaries are paid monthly through a computer controlled system, or that they use a massive and sophisticated computer network to book their summer holidays, or that they get so much junk mail because they are on computerized mailing lists.

4. People who are on the receiving end, but are unaware of any part being played by IT. We can label them as *unknowing recipients*, but the group will include both those who are unaware because they are unacquainted with IT, lacking a knowledge base, and those who are unaware because they are not being told or are being deceived. How many of us know whether we are under electronic surveillance or whether we get regular offers from money lenders as a result of a computerised assessment? Would we get an honest answer if we asked?

5. Those who are the subject matter of IT data stores. Material about people, which can be processed and analyzed to produce significant information, is the life system of much IT. In western industrial societies it is safe to say that we are all *human computer fodder*,

in the sense that we are on computerised mass mailing lists in government and the commercial sector, and other data is held about us, such as a rating of our credit-worthiness and our record of paying bills and taxes. In such societies we cannot send a cheque to a worthy cause, or buy something with a credit card, without that fact being recorded. As the snippets of data pile up, so a profile can be constructed of our behaviors, and from that a range of inferences can be made about our attitudes and lifestyles.

It is clear from this typology that we may have a complex relationship with IT, some of which we know about and can control, some we know or suspect but cannot influence, and some we know nothing about and can only imagine. Alternatively we may have no relationship at all, feeling relieved if we so wish, but more likely feeling deprived, given the correlation between the strength of IT developments and a society's wealth. Of course we may think we have no relationship, but can we be certain there is no secret file?

The nature of our relationship with IT establishes the framework for the chapter. Two themes, representing the opposing extremes of the relationship spectrum, have been tackled elsewhere. Chapter 7 took up the situation of IT developers, designers, manufacturers and distributors, and several chapters in Part 2 have focused on IT deprivation. Later in these pages we need to look at the impact and outcomes of the relationship which forms the central block of the spectrum, given the diverse role many of us have as users, recipients and subjects (or should we say victims?) of IT. In this process it will be relevant to approach the different contexts for the relationship, those of rulers and ruled, commercial suppliers and customers, and of a shared community push towards better ways of life. In the context of government we will ask about the extent to which political value systems, democratic or totalitarian, influence the uses of IT applications. Issues of control, enablement and entitlement feature centrally. In a market context we shall consider how far IT can be treated simply as a consumer product, with goods and services that we can buy, and applications which innocently provide just what the customer wants. A core issue, already raised earlier, will be that of property, not so much about computer equipment and programs, as about that human computer fodder. Who owns the raw material, the facts which make up these enormous data banks? Who owns the information which is extracted from them?

It is in the government and commercial contexts that we can observe the reality of IT usage. These are the real worlds that those of us in materially wealthy societies experience. These are also the contexts in which we are deemed to need some protection. Answers will be attempted to a range of questions. Why do we need protecting? What are the threats we face? What are the appropriate safeguards? What progress has been made with their implementation? Is real public protection possible without seriously disadvantaging efficient government and economic growth?

The third context mentioned earlier, IT in the framework of shared community enhancement, has more ideals and less experience to back it. Perhaps enhancement reflects an over-optimistic approach: maybe a more realistic set of objectives would be based on damage limitation. Can we limit or neutralise the potential challenge IT makes to progress on equal opportunities and community relationships? Can we then look more creatively at ways IT can strengthen both the material and human framework of community living? Is there a coherent blueprint for IT as a benefit in our lives, as well as in our government and economy?

In the introduction to Part 2 we argued that IT has a lead role in a continuing process of dehumanizing, depersonalizing society. That process started with commitments to earlier forms of mechanization, combined with the growth of bureaucracy as the ultimate in mechanistic administrative systems. What began was a prolonged cultural change (which in due course could promote biological change as well) in which essentially human techniques are being replaced by machine based techniques. A human approach to any topic can be described as using a flexible combination of reason, intuition and emotion, aided by sight, hearing, touch and smell, all influenced by mood and the sense of personal and relational well-being. A mechanistic or instrumentalist approach, in contrast, is what we call scientific. It has that label because it leads to decisions based on what we choose to call fact or "hard data" – that is the results of measurement or experiment. It excludes anything which can be perceived as irrational or inaccurate. The tools of the approach are either actual machines, or procedures, like bureaucracy, which are structured with machine-like precision. The qualities, for many people the virtues of this approach are all connected with stability. Processes like the working of an engine can be described in precise detail, in the knowledge that the engine always works in the same way. The engine, like bureaucracy as a system of administration, is predictable, reliable and replicable. It enables standardized outputs which do not fluctuate and do not discriminate. Keep the system well maintained and it will go on delivering the goods until a better machine is designed.

In contrast a human approach is seen by its detractors to lack stability. Humans, without the help of machines or fixed procedures, cannot cope with standardization. They are not predictable or reliable outside narrow limits. They are addicted to the tools of irrationality. At the same time the bureaucrat is forced to acknowledge that much is lost in the removal of the "human" element – flair, imagination, an understanding of when things could be done better, the level of sophistication, a sense of when an outcome is not quite fair, right or sensible although all the correct rules and procedures have been followed.

Into this changing culture, in which a cloud of insecurity has built up over human capabilities, and a halo of dependability and good sense over science, has come this new technology to strengthen and speed up the change. IT is such a decisive influence that we have to stand back and ask whether the change is in our best interests, and to analyze what the growing gulf between human frailty and machine dominance is doing to us. There is a sense of proportion to be retained. Computers are a human creation, and remain under human control. Yet they are becoming more competent and versatile in societal functioning, and we shall be able to use computers to design better computers, as well as better machines of all sorts.

We have some choices (theoretically at least) in how we want to relate to IT. We can embrace it as something which may increase control over our lives, but will also take on much of the work that has to be undertaken for social survival, and leave us free for leisure and personal development. We probably cannot demand an amicable divorce because IT will keep on pestering us rather than leaving us alone, but we can smash it up and reject the scientific advance it represents. Alternatively we can seek a constructive relationship, accepting the potential of IT, but on condition that it is slotted into the framework of human needs.

Maslow (1954, 1962) has developed a hierarchy of these needs, which move from subsistence concerns, to concerns relating to work and productivity, to self-fulfilment. Through these activities a person experiences life, a personal life, and achieves meaning. A major part of life experience is guided by the access afforded to the individual to make choices about the future. For example, poor persons may predictably be found to be educated in situations or schools where advanced information technologies are not available. To this extent their personal access to information technologies is a social issue, influencing the character and potential of their later contribution to their community.

The association and relationship of the personal life with the community takes place across all areas of community; that is, in socialization, as in school, in social integration, as in government, in production and distribution, as in wholesaling and manufacturing, and in social control, as experienced through community practices of reward and punishment. The concrete experience of community is one of the two major elements in empowerment and in promoting healthy participation in everyday life. If information technologies are increasingly used in each area of community life mentioned here, those who have not had access to these technologies will not be empowered.

They will lack empowerment not only because their concrete experience of community life has been ruptured, but also because they are no longer awarded the primary social good, membership. Membership is the second element of empowering individuals and providing a basis for a democratic society. When concrete experiences of community and membership are a part of community life, participants can work and contribute as well as disagree, confront, and collaborate with equity. Surely this is the creative and support role we should seek for IT, and through it a relationship which can maximize shared progress, and minimize technology alienation.

THE RULERS AND THE RULED

Governments of any nation have some easily identifiable responsibilities, for internal and external security, and for the quality of life of the populations they rule. Important variables do come into play which shed light on how the leaders of the nation view their tasks. Foreign policies can range from aggressive confrontation and a willingness for military action, to well established neutrality linked to principles of pacifism. Internal affairs can be based on explicit codes of conduct and citizen consent, or on coercion. Intervention in the nation's economy can be minimal, clearing the decks for an all-out free market scrap, or across a spectrum to direct state control of industry. Attitudes to citizens can indicate a respect for laws and for freedoms of thought, speech and action, or span to what we would label a "police state". The leaders themselves can genuinely act out their belief in a responsibility to the entire population, or see their power as an opportunity to establish dynasties and increase private bank accounts.

Readers will be aware of examples of all of these possibilities, and be equally aware that IT is a universal tool, for repression as well as freedom, for exploitation and enablement, for militarism and social welfare, for law enforcement or lawlessness. In this sense IT has the potential for good or bad use. In reality two broad thrusts in governmental IT applications are observable, whatever the type of government, and to an extent whatever the level of its wealth. The first is an extension of the sorts of computer facilities employed in office automation. This includes developing the ability of a government to keep the computerized equivalent of a card index on its citizens, or on those who are deemed to warrant attention, like managers, property owners and political opponents. Address lists and the like will enable communications. More detailed databases will allow for files on convicted offenders, or any other specialized area of personal or social data that government wants. Spreadsheets for budgets and project management programs have a place. Governments are administrative organizations writ large, and have comparable needs for IT aids.

The choice and extent of IT involvement will vary according to the type of government objectives in operation. If through preference, or through poverty and the lack of an administrative infrastructure, the rulers are easy going about their administrative prowess, then massive IT systems are not so important. Many countries cope adequately with limited computerization and extensive use of traditional manual methods, and although nations like India have a more obviously visible problem of information overload, because of the masses of paper clogging up offices, computer data overload is a more insidious difficulty in the longer term. Where the government wants a tight and heavy management of its citizenry, then it has little choice but to move heavily into computerization. IT can certainly be a boon to totalitarian regimes, or where challenges are presented by the large size or cultural diversity of the national population.

The second initial priority is likely to be more technologically sophisticated and much more secretive, in that it links IT with the maintenance of a routinely updated military potential. Governments have less choice here. If they want a military capacity that is credible, then the question of comparability with what other nations possess becomes an immediate issue. Trailing edge applications are perfectly adequate for routine administrative matters, but state of the art technology is a requirement for military work.

If the initial phase of computerization is about national security and improved administration, the next will have a more detailed impact on the quality of life of the population. The issues identified here are about enablement and entitlement: that is about the rights citizens have within the political and governmental context to participate in governing activities and enjoy the benefits of government in their interests. The IT strategies involved are essentially about communications, internal technology transfer and the use of data stores. A country's communication network has real and symbolic political importance. Over the centuries governments and those attempting to replace governments have seen control of communications as vital – the central post office, the telephone exchange, the radio and TV stations, and now, of course, the networks carrying any form of electronic communication. Whoever is in charge of these facilities can pass news and instructions to the population, make public claims, block external links, and generally maintain a framework for administration. The core difference between IT and its predecessors is that, like TV and radio, IT can be a form of mass communication, but uniquely it is mass two-way – send and receive. Until recently the only form for enabling community participation in government decision making has been to take note of incoming mail, demonstrations, petitions and opinion polls, or to organise plebiscites on specific issues. We now have the technological potential to consult very widely and frequently, and get a rapid analysis of community views. IT is challenging governments that call themselves democratic to acknowledge the newly available scope for democratic consultation: to date there are some notable exceptions, like the State Government of California's use of the referendum, but no widespread signs that the challenge is being taken up. A realistic inhibition for the early 1990s will be the cost of the network infrastructure, though much can be done in conjunction with conventional TV. As time passes this excuse will grow thinner.

A common justification of innovative military or wider scientific investment (like space probes) is the extent of spin-off which will benefit all our lives. Control systems for military aircraft can be used for civilian travel; new ultra smooth shock absorbers for tanks can go into cars; new ways of packaging foods for astronauts can show up on the supermarket shelves for all of us. The broad theory is one of polar development: a major infrastructural investment in, for example, oil refining or steel production, or a specialised developmental thrust in a new technology, will serve to stimulate and expand activities on a much wider front. The expansion will result from the need for new activities to support the core thrust (coal for the steel mill, plastics for the computer plant), from technology transfers, from marketing opportunities, and from new income coming into the local economy.

The idea is not new. It was used in the economic regeneration of Europe after the second world war, with some successes on balance (like car production in Naples, Italy), and some which the local community might well view as failures (like another Italian effort, the petro-chemical investment in Gela, Sicily). The question is whether it has sufficient relevance to IT. The history of computer development has a military interlude which was of considerable importance – building the original valve driven electrical computers in the mid 1940s – but the bulk has a civil context, from academic research (Babbage onwards), through the need for a quicker way of coping with census material (Hollerith in the USA), to the whiz kids of recent decades. The phenomenal progress in information technologies that we have lived through has almost certainly taken place because the enthusiasm, inventiveness and imagination put into it has a broad, sometimes ill-defined range of objectives and directions, rather than a specific closely focused target. Could we argue with any conviction that the investment in, for example, NASA has produced more valuable spin-offs for society as a whole than the fragmented efforts which have resulted in hypertext, WordPerfect, home computers . . . ?

Governments have not, for the most part, made claims of innovative developments in administrative systems. A common experience is that state agencies have lagged behind commercial companies in the uses of office automation and more specialized IT applications, such as computer aided design and project management.

The issue of technology transfer in this context concerns the extent to which governments have encouraged and funded the development of IT in community based public sectors, like schools, hospitals and welfare agencies, or in the institutions of local administration. We have argued that a sign of a truly democratic government is its willingness to establish and use a two-way communication system. Another sign might be internal technology transfer activities, though we question whether in the field of IT governments have much to transfer, so that their primary role becomes one of helping to pull in technologies from non-governmental sectors. A third sign is a positive attitude towards sharing data and information. Governments collect colossal quantities of data, mostly about people but also about the environment, community facilities, the economic infrastructure, jobs, housing, and on and on. Some of this is private because those who are subjects of the data would want it to be so; some is genuinely sensitive for reasons of state security, both civil and military; a vast amount does not challenge the needs of confidentiality. How far are governments open to sharing access? How communicative are they with the information they draw from data analysis, about poverty levels, for example, or the extent of ill-health resulting from pollution? One of the startling exposures following the collapse of communist regimes in eastern Europe was the extent of industrial pollution and its impact on health and infant mortality, almost all of which had been a closely guarded secret. The data available to the governments of these countries may well have been less than accurate on such matters, because they had been excluded from use of western technologies, but with IT there are no excuses.

A more specific aspect of sharing is about the government's regulations and intentions regarding the services it operates. An example is social security. In most countries there is a state run scheme which offers benefits in cash or kind for people who can give evidence that they meet the criteria of need, whether through unemployment, chronic illness, refugee status or some other reason. In some instances of social security payments, such as state retirement pensions for elderly people, the government takes the initiative, identifying those who qualify and making arrangements for payment. More commonly, however, the initiative rests with the citizen who has to make an application and demonstrate eligibility before a benefit is granted. It is documented that many people are unaware of possible benefits, while others find the hurdle of applying for them too complex, so it is common for well below 100 per cent of possible beneficiaries to take up the offer. IT systems have real potential here, both to help governments who are motivated to take on responsibility themselves for finding out who qualifies and making the payment, and for aiding members of the public in assessing their possible eligibility. The UK is one of several countries where there are effective computer programs for calculating benefits eligibility, and there is no doubting the role of programs like Maximiser or the Lisson Grove Benefits Program in raising take-up levels.

What emerges over and over again when looking at the activities of governments is that IT is an opportunity and a challenge. As an opportunity it is double edged, because it is so potent as a tool for totalitarianism as well as for open government. IT is a challenge because it gives governments the technology to move further along the track of putting their democratic principles into practice, if they wish.

CUSTOMER RIGHTS?

Ivan Illich wrote that "In a consumer society there are inevitably two kinds of slaves, the prisoners of addiction and the prisoners of envy" (Tools for Conviviality, 1973). We could develop his thought to say that in such a society it is the dream of producers to excite addiction amongst their customers, and envy with desire amongst those who have not yet succumbed. The role of the consumer is a dependent one: release from dependence is possible only by ceasing to be a consumer. In IT the dependence is particularly strongly entrenched, since it is not just based on the supply of hardware and software, but on regular information and updates, help with understanding, support and service. Computer and software manufacturers have not made such a big marketing splash in the shopping malls as they have in mail order trading, a trickier and more dependence generating way of shopping for the customer. The galaxy of mail order catalogues and catalogues-cum-journals rivals motoring for shelf space on the magazine stall. In the USA the monthly *Computer Shopper* now exceeds 750 large 10 by 13 inch pages. Accepting such dependence imposes great responsibilities on IT designers and producers, but we also need to ask what responsibilities consumers have in this relationship, and what rights they can claim in their consumer status.

With IT, however, we should go further than viewing consumerism solely as an attitude of customers towards suppliers. IT has customers who buy and use IT products: it also has citizens who, with or without their permission, with or without their awareness, become fodder for information systems, the source of personal data for turning into personal information. Most of us are further pestered by that phenomenon of the late twentieth century, computer generated junk mail. The arrival of word processing and its supporting utilities (mailmerge in this instance) opened up the prospect of all of us receiving personalised versions of mass produced letters, and desktop publishing has put the production of cheap newspapers and glossy advertising brochures within reach of the smallest one-person companies. IT may not in itself use up the world's scarce resources, but this one application is decimating the world's forests.

As customers our responsibility is to apply pressure. There are signs of an assault on junk mail, at least with the gradual extension of a right to be taken off mailing lists. In relation to the computer industry, however, we as a consumer group have allowed our lack of knowledge of IT to be enlarged and embellished by the industry into a belief that we are too ignorant/busy/feminine to know what we want. As a result the industry tends only to consult with big customers – the major purchasing corporations. The rest of us are fit to be stopped in the street and asked about the kinds of personal hygiene products we want, or the TV programmes we prefer, but not about computers and software.

The central issue for customers, however, is personal information. The term *customer* has been used here quite intentionally, though in previous paragraphs *customer* and *consumer* have been used interchangeably. *Consumer* is not a pertinent label because it so clearly implies being on the consuming end of an activity, whereas in IT database applications the people we choose to call consumers are in effect the producers and suppliers of the relevant data. *Customer* is a more suitable label because of the prospect of viewing customers as simply those in a commercial relationship, as consumer or supplier or both. Members of the public are the customers of IT companies in the sense that they are the providers of personal information.

Personal information is gathered in a variety of ways, most frequently as an adjunct of some other activity, as already detailed. In all of these we give information about ourselves, and quite often we wonder what relevance the questions we are asked has to the matter in hand. Why is my employer's name and address relevant if I want to be a bank depositor, or my age if I want to give to a fund for starving Ethiopians? As members of the public we regularly spend time providing data, swallowing any feelings we may have about the privacy of what we are writing on the form. We do this without payment, although that data is subsequently used to target us for sales pitches.

Personal data is property. This much is acknowledged by the act of treating it as marketable. Whose property is it? Banks, shops, charitable agencies and others appear to assume that it is their property, donated to them by a willing public, who also donate their time to write the data and receive the consequent sales efforts. Is that the correct ownership of the data? Should we be expected to give our time freely to commercial companies? Surely personal data is the possession of the person concerned, just as much as is her or his income, clothes, garden tools or whatever. In partnerships, like marriages, there are matters connected with the division of possessions, if that becomes an issue, and most of the public are required to donate part of their possessions by way of taxes to the central or local government to meet the cost of running the nation and providing community services. Neither of these, however, challenges the principle of personal property: indeed, they reinforce it. In that case, should we be expected to donate personal data? We may trade it in exchange for something we want, like a bank loan. or we may, if we feel generous, hand it over as a gift. If those transactions are accepted as valid, then they operate within the core premise that our personal data is a matter for each of us to handle. How many companies who are inclined to bluster about the need for personal information in the context of arranging a service or buying a commodity would pull out of the transaction if told that they could not have the tradable information except at a price? How many good causes would refuse donations? How many banks would decline to receive deposits or arrange loans? As long as only a few of the public take this line, then the strong world of commerce will treat them as eccentrics and assume that anyone who declines to give personal material is a nut or has something to hide, and should therefore be turned away. If, in contrast, substantial groups decided that they would not co-operate with data gatherers except at a negotiated price, then commercial attitudes would soon change.

We argued earlier that a comparable view is worth considering about intrusive sales pitches, based on mailed, phoned or personal contacts.

Is there any reason why a commercial company which wants to take up a person's time with sales talk should not pay for that time and attention? To an extent this is acknowledged. It is common to offer inducements, through discounts or gifts, especially as the selling merges into market research (that is, a combination of selling and data gathering). The IT which makes possible the whole edifice of personal data stores, and the wealth that they generate, can hand back some of the profits.

Redressing the balance between the public and organised commerce in these ways would have a significant impact on an IT sponsored activity which seems to have got out of control. It would make the use of junk mail much more selective, perhaps to the point where it ceased altogether to be "junk", and reduce the use of trees to make paper. It would ease pressure on overloaded communications systems, perhaps making post and phone services more efficient and sensitive to members of the public. Perhaps most importantly it would create a new respect for the public, who could be treated as people instead of fodder.

PROTECTION

The view that the public needs protection in some areas of personal data usage has been asserted for several years. The BBC comedy series *Yes Minister* voiced the theme (Lynn and Jay, 1984, p. 83), when Jim Hacker, the fictional Minister of a fictional Department of Administrative Affairs was faced with an article he had written before joining the Government – "if we are to protect the citizen . . . three measures are urgent. One, no Civil Servant must have access to another department's files without specific signed authorization . . . Two, unauthorised snooping must be made a criminal offence. And three, every citizen should have the right to inspect his own personal file and get errors corrected." As a Minister, of course, his views changed!

Protection has been viewed as necessary in democratic societies, for commercial as well as government held personal data, to prevent abuse and unwarranted breaches of confidence. In theory it is possible to approach the framework of protection from two angles, from the point of collection, and the point of usage. The most direct protection of the citizen would arise from establishing standards of conduct in relation to the collection and storage of data. A code would have a number of components, like for example:

1. There would be a process for establishing the minimum personal data required for those interactions the citizen has with public and private organizations.

2. Any organization would have to meet certain criteria in order to be free to enter the data in a computer file. Those criteria might include limits to access, or to the network links of the computer being used, or to inter-machine transfers; but the core criterion would be the written approval of the data subject to computerization.

3. The individual who has given permission would have the right to view the file, have it corrected or updated, or have it removed. To facilitate this, an organization must send a printed copy of the file to the individual annually.

4. All citizens, including those who have declined to allow personal material to be computerized, would have the right to interrogate a file index to check whether or not they appear.

5. No personal material gathered in the context of a transaction may be manually or electronically linked to data on the same person, or person's family, gathered on a separate occasion.

6. Personal data may be hired or borrowed from an individual, but remains the property of the individual. Such data may not be purchased or received as a gift, and an agreement to hire or borrow may not be traded or passed to another organization.

This type of approach to providing an infrastructure for interactions between citizen and organization, assuming it is set alongside appropriate channels for enforcement, gives the citizen substantial control over whether and what personal data is held, scope to negotiate hire of the data, and a clearer picture of the limits to its use. At the same time, it is a route which virtually castrates IT generated personal data, to the extent that its value to organizations is severely limited. Networking and data processing are restricted, and massive database build up effectively blocked.

The clauses listed above are an intentional overstatement, designed to illustrate the ease with which a code of protection can determine the relationship of citizen to organization, in this instance by giving the citizen a dominant position. It serves to show how the second approach, the one which has been adopted by most countries to have tackled the topic, tips the relationship balance towards the organization. This approach is based on the assumptions that nothing should be done to restrict the implementation of the technological potential of computing, and that control measures should be retrospective, taking effect after something has been seen to go wrong, rather than preventative, at the point of data gathering.

Jim Hacker's view is basically in line with what has happened, though with a few significant variations. The initial premise has been widely accepted, that data gathering can go ahead with minimal hinderance (perhaps a government register of who is collecting personal material, alongside a brief anodyne statement of what will be done with it), and that the data once collected is the property of the gatherer, and as such a marketable commodity. The rights of the citizen are usually limited to viewing the file and having inaccuracies corrected, though access may be denied if the data is categorized under law and order or national security. For the most part the notion of privacy has been ignored, and replaced with the view that since there is no practical way of making computerized data confidential, all that can be done is to let the individual see what personal secrets are on the file. Some professions (medicine, law) have sought to challenge this trend, but others have not. In a social work agency, for example, highly emotional personal matters about the client's collapsing marriage or children's behaviour, which would have been divulged only to the counsellor, will now be open to the myriad of agency staff who are authorised users of the agency's client information system.

Governments have shown themselves reluctant to place any serious restrictions on data transfer or market transactions, providing they are conducted under a cloak of secrecy or reasonable discretion. The main reason for this has to be that central and local governments are themselves in need of data, and occasionally not averse to selling some of their own, so favour the development of suitable networks. However, what Jim Hacker called "snooping" is another matter altogether. Of course Hacker viewed snooping as an activity carried out by one civil servant into the data files of another department, unaware of the meaning which was to be given to his name. The snooping which is being picked up and made into a criminal offence in many communities is that carried out by an outsider, the hacker, into an organization's files. Hacking has developed something of an aura of excitement, of comic-book thrills and military secrets (like the film *War Games*). In real life there is a spectrum of activity, with a criminal component linked to computer fraud, and much which represents little more than a technical challenge to break into a supposedly secure computer system. Yet there is an aspect to hacking which does symbolize public resentment at being expected to supply personal information for computing, seemingly getting so little benefit from it, sometimes being harmed by it, and knowing that there is a whole section of the economy making a lot of money out of it. In the eyes of many members of the public the real snoopers are not individual hackers, but the mass of companies in the information business. At the high profile tip of the iceberg are the eavesdroppers with their listening devices and telescopic cameras, who aim to feed newspapers and the rest of the information industry with juicy intrusions into the lives of well known people. Beneath the surface is the more mundane but equally determined process of snooping into all of our lives.

It is hard to come to any conclusion other than that, where protection measures have been put in place, they are as much to do with guarding the power base of the information industry as with helping those in the community who want to keep their private lives private. The task for society, in searching for a more balanced approach to the relationship between the individual and the organization, is to find a route which genuinely protects the citizen, but not at the cost of blocking technological progress. We have to keep in mind that while IT has given practical scope to fulfil the profitable urge to delve into people's lives, IT also improves the quality of life. Taking a sledge hammer to the computer is not the answer.

IT FOR THE PEOPLE

There is a sequence to the way major technology advances are implemented. They start as expensive novelties, especially in the unreliable early stages of the technology, to be used only by people and organizations who can afford both to pay for the new invention and simultaneously maintain the traditional method. This is as relevant an observation, say, of the development of electric lighting as it is of IT. As the invention becomes more reliable and widely available, so it gets cheaper, and gradually spreads to the point where it is seen as a necessity for the whole community. Who would doubt that an electricity supply is now an integral part of a nation's social and economic infrastructure, and is high on the agenda of those countries where there is not yet a nationwide provision?

What of IT? The early stage of expensive novelty has passed. A substantial degree of reliability has been achieved, and prices have fallen massively, partly as a result of bulk production, but much more as a consequence of the flow of improvements and inventions, especially the microprocessor. In addition the restrictions posed by the large indivisible scale of early computers has been overcome, so that systems can be scaled with great sophistication to serve everything from the individual to the multi-national corporation. Will IT move to the next stage? As with electricity, will it achieve the status of a social and economic necessity to the extent that widespread provision is a target of all societies? This is a harder question to answer because it pushes forward further questions, about whether IT *warrants* the status of being part of a total societal infrastructure, in the way electricity is, and whether there is *motivation* in society, government and industry to accept a wider community role for it.

IT will warrant a full community role when developments and applications reach the point that society cannot survive in or progress from its current state without it. There is no problem in perceiving the threat to any society posed by the loss of water, or to any industrial community by the loss of electricity. Similarly we can readily imagine the great inconvenience to current society, and reduction in living standards rather than survival threat, posed by, say, the sudden disappearance of plastic. Can we imagine computers or telecommunications achieving such a position? To a considerable extent IT already has. We have noted earlier how dependent modern societies are for their organization and administration on computerized systems and communications. Rail and air traffic, holidays, television, tax collecting and the payment of salaries, just to mention a few, would collapse if all microprocessors were withdrawn. But can the same be said about community living? As consumers we would suffer the impact of the breakdown of these major systems, but our home and neighbourhood lives have moved much less into technology applications. We still choose to do manually many things which could be computer aided, like cooking, growing fresh vegetables or talking with a neighbour down the street.

IT has become part of the infrastructure of a modern industrial society, but in an unbalanced fashion. Despite the capacity of IT for functioning at any scale, it has become the tool of large-scale operations, which in practice means the tool of government and private organizations. In economic terms IT dominates the supply side. Is this accidental or intentional? In part it is a reflection of the way IT developed. Micro-technology and the personal computer came onto the market only after the large mainframe computer was well established. Nevertheless, the personal computer has not become associated with domestic activities in the way the mainframe is linked to big business. There have been developments in home or neighbourhood computing, but they are dwarfed by the increasing commitment to tailor what are called "personal computers" to business uses. In practice the personal computer has been a tremendous boon to small organizations, and a valuable extension to the mainframe for the larger agencies. Despite some emphasis on the educational potential, personal computers as tools for the home have been largely trivialised into games machines.

This is where arguments about motivation become relevant. In western societies there is a strong middle class commitment towards making the best uses of technology in educating children and maintaining a middle class lifestyle: but there is less evidence of communities as a whole showing an urge either to get greater control over IT or to expand the range of useful local applications. To an extent the motivation to use IT in community life is matched by a wish to retain some traditional values and ways of doing things. This can be seen in many examples, ranging from peoples' irritation at having to deal with their local telephone company through computer generated standard letters rather then personal contact, to the outright rejection of computerized building designs which maximise efficiency while ignoring the intangibles of style and visual attractiveness. The public assault on the architecture of the 1960s, 70s and 80s is the first significant backlash against a technology dominated existence.

The ambivalence or lack of interest in IT amongst the public is an important convenience for the nation's managers, whether in government or private business. They are aware of the scope IT offers for more effective and detailed administration, of the extent to which it is a power base, and of how the IT industry has directed its developmental thrusts towards their own rather than community interests. They have a vested interest in maintaining or strengthening the imbalance in society's application of IT. The view for the individual is disconcerting. Computer equipment is available cheaply, but except for games and some educational material, applications are for "business". More blatantly the IT journals are not full of descriptions of developments or ideas about how computers can be used in the home or community, but about how they can play an ever more imaginative role in business.

If communities are to counter this bias, or be helped to counter it, then some new approaches are needed to break into the cosy circuit which has now tied IT in so closely with organizations. First of all there is the creation of a market which will attract developers, especially in the field of computer applications. This is not easy because, from our present perspective, it is so difficult to conceive of the domestic or neighbourhood equivalents of the core applications which transformed the business world, the automated office. The notion of an "automated home" tends to be seen as somewhat fanciful and futuristic, based too much on the vision of a robot combining the resourcefulness of Jeeves and the endurance of a domestic slave. The realistic advances which have been made have often avoided a head-on confrontation with the domestication of IT, and looked instead at the neighbourhood or small community, and at the interface between the community and small business people, like the local farmer, hairdresser, or one-person home based agency.

An example is Community Teleservice Centres (CTSCs), originating in Scandinavia through the work of Lars Qvortrup and others (1988), but now extending to other parts of Europe and the Third World. Their focus is on rural regions, on villages and small urban communities, where economic (and consequently social) development is inhibited by isolation from major technological facilities. The aim of CTSCs is to provide locally based IT resources, hardware and relevant software, in accessible places, for the use of the whole community. A village CTSC might have some computing equipment in a local school or community centre, linked to regional and national networks (library, government information services, etc.), and with programs for basic computer training and help with the sorts of economic activities which occur in the locality. There is a person responsible for the facility, recruited from the community, and a user support group. Farmers can come in to use programs which help them with stock control, or monitor experiences with the local use of certain crops or growing methods. Anyone can come in to word process. A small urban CTSC operates on a wider scale, perhaps by the addition of technology courses for locally unemployed people, or the production of material by and about the community, which leads to a greater sense of well-being and cohesion. Evaluative work on CTSCs has found that they extend IT skills, improve people's understanding of IT potential, and increase the local market for relevant IT products.

Running parallel to efforts to develop community markets, and to give that development a helpful push, there is a need at government level (central and local) for an active strategy for community IT. Looking around the world we can find all sorts of relevant parallels. Many countries have policies and services for the maintenance of family life. Poorer societies have strategies for ensuring the spread of schools, clinics, water and power supplies. What can be observed is a dynamic interaction between the pulls of centralization and devolution. The enhancement of family and community life may incorporate a centralized provision (like an old age pension), but the fine tuning is through devolved processes which allow the local quality of life to be handled according to local needs and circumstances. This will happen through the community centre, the local health clinic, activities linked to the local school and sports club, church, mother's union, and all the other components of a complex local network. What governments have to decide is whether they will accept the potential role for IT in this devolved framework, and so make available resources, which in turn stimulates the market; or whether they see IT as essentially an instrument of control and large-scale administration, to be kept in centralized hands. A balanced strategy for a democratic society is one which limits the demands of power politics, and responds to the capacity of IT to make valuable contributions in business and administration, and in all our community lives.

Part 3
Towards an Ethical Framework

11 The Ethics Industries

SUMMARY

In this chapter we examine more closely the types of societal and cultural responses that may assert intellectual integrity with regard to information technologies, starting from the view of Fromm (1968) that intellectual integrity is supported by what he calls a "humanistic technology". A humanistic technology is one that meets human needs because we take action in technology development and applications to evaluate, alter and monitor its impact. Simultaneously communities give their support to the formation of those social institutions which will ensure the efficacy and effectiveness of the humanistic input. We make use in this chapter of Masuda's (1981) work on "ethic industries" in the context of a humanistic technology. What are the ethics industries? What set of vocations and organizations can act as ethical agents? Where are they found? Why are they important to the transition to an information society? We discuss their importance to individualism, decentralisation, democracy, and empowerment, and look at some examples of activities which have subjected IT applications to human valuation and meaningful adaptation to the needs of everyday life. At the same time we challenge the pessimism of Ellul's (1964, 1990) warning that technological determinism will swamp human morality, because all the significant pressures in society are pushing in that direction.

WHO, WHAT AND WHERE ARE THE ETHICS INDUSTRIES?

Yoneji Masuda has played a central role in Japanese academia and government, in the analysis of developing situations and formation of policies to mould the advancing "Information Society". He is not a commentator on the past, but a futurist, seeking to project how nations will progress with new technologies, in relation to the decisions governments and society at large make to steer the process of technology change. His work (1981) on post-industrial society tracks four stages to the growth of an information society, or what he views as the industries of the future. The first covers the formation of "information-related industries", including the IT and data industries. The second stage is the build-up of "knowledge industries", incorporating computerised knowledge-based systems. The third is the expansion of "arts industries", which in his description appear to contain the equivalent of the tribal memory, the national archives, a community's cultural heritage. The fourth stage is the establishment of an ethics industry. Masuda is referring to those organizations concerned with values and behavioral standards, thought, and religion – as well as ethics. Human behaviour, the focus of the ethics industry, is portrayed as providing the scientific base for the final stage of computerization in society. Within this framework is a concern with personal behaviour, the environment and human rights.

If Masuda is the visionary of a society based on the moral use of IT, Ellul (1964) reflects the opposing, pessimistic viewpoint. He argues that morality is inoperative in everyday life, and premised that of the four curbs to the coming of the technocratic, deterministic state, morality could be dismissed, and public opinion, social structure, and government all favour technological development. Ellul's warnings seem to find a greater spark of recognition in the United States than in other countries, but here, as elsewhere, we sense the importance of challenging such a gloomily deterministic approach, and argue that morality has a reasonable chance to curb what Ellul calls "La Technique".

The likely content of the ethics industry, in the sense of what organizations and influences make up its component parts, seem set to be highly sensitive to local or national culture, social organization, traditional ways of making changes, and national policies. In Japan there is a place, says Masuda, for philosophy and religion, but also for "spiritual training industries . . . yoga . . . tea ceremony . . . flower arrangement". The set of ethical components for Britain and the United States could include comparable culture-specific aspects, though some broad themes are clear. In the United States voluntarism, voluntary organizations and churches have a primary social role. In Britain, perhaps also in other societies that have experienced the impact of socialism, ethical issues undergo an extensive political debate, in the media, in Parliament, and often in specially formed committees. Government action on ethical matters shows strong variations in both countries. In Britain, for example, some topics (religious beliefs, technology transfer) are kept at a distance, others (homosexuality, divorce, drugs) are tackled, and occasionally (as with the death penalty) Parliament takes a strong moral line in defiance of known public views. In most western nations there are core values which will impinge on any ethical debate – a reverence for life and respect for human dignity, individualism alongside collectivism, and human choice. They are combined with a belief that participation and membership are primary social goods, experienced most directly in a democratically organized society. Joseph Weizenbaum (1976) has written that reference to God, grace, and morality as a basis for ethical judgements invites solitary confinement, ridicule, and the risk of being put down as a comic fool. Yet in circumstances where making no response simply colludes with the onward push of technocratization, such references are sensible and essential.

One broad observation about western society is that a number of major economic developments, or new industries, have, in turn, provoked the growth of parallel ethics industries. One of the most structured examples is that of nuclear power in Britain, where the organization of nuclear industries for military and peaceful uses caused the reactive formation of numerous organizations to monitor or oppose nuclear developments. From a very early stage the risks and moral dilemmas of nuclear production were recognised, groups like the Campaign for Nuclear Development (CND) achieved mass followings, and the issues moved centre stage. There are other examples, like reactions to the exploitation of the raw materials of Third World countries, or, topically, the issues of pollution and conservation around the fuel and timber industries, or the formation of governmental and voluntary teams to confront the impact of tobacco.

There is a notion here of "twinning", of a profitable economic development being "twinned" or "shadowed" by an ethical counterpart. Some characteristics of the arrangement are observable. The ethical agenda for an economic development may not become immediately apparent, so there is a delay in its formulation. Many people would see the demolition of the world's rain forests as an example, where the concerns with conserving animal and plant life, and providing an acceptable alternative for those who aid the demolition as the only route to a minimal standard of living, have perhaps come too late to be effective. There is almost always a massive disparity between the wealth and power of the economic developers and the ethics shadowers, so that for the latter the task of mobilising resources, getting adequate media coverage, organising activities or setting up effective pressure groups is a continuing struggle. The initiators and leaders of ethics movements put themselves at risk, just occasionally literally at risk of their lives, but more commonly at risk of being pilloried, ridiculed and forced out of those areas of activity which they are desperately seeking to integrate more usefully and acceptably into community structures. Nevertheless, once the ethical shadow is around, visible and ever present, a different relationship may form between the twins. Just occasionally hostility continues unabated, because the two sides seemingly have nothing in common – witness Christian CND members in Britain seeking to break into cruise missile and nuclear warhead sites. More frequently negotiations open up, issues are debated on all sides, and compromises are made.

Where does this leave IT? The industry has grown so fast, and our reactions been so correspondingly slow, that the twinned IT ethics industry has scarcely started to develop, except in the areas of governmental interest in data protection. Public involvement has so far been limited. Nevertheless signs of change can be spotted. Regular IT conference goers are aware of the growing sensitivity on ethical matters. Some of the idealistic, inventive and imaginative people who led the technology revolution are now turning to reassess the impact of their work, and its value to society. Perhaps, as we have argued, we have institutionalized an unbalanced compromise between the interests of the IT industry and those of the societies in which IT operates, but there remains scope and evidence of a willingness to review and adjust the position.

In pursuing these ideas it is relevant to note that the ethics industry, at least as Masuda used the phrase, is not the same as the ethics business. In all societies there are a few well-identified groups who see their task as establishing and maintaining moral standards. They are the professionals in the business, and are dominated by religious sects. To an extent religious morality is unhelpful in coping with IT, both for practical and philosophical reasons. At a practical level priests are involved in the moral (often also physical, mental and emotional) health of their flocks, but more fundamentally their business is with saving souls. The future for them is not about the advance into the information age, but about preparing for salvation and fearing damnation. The future is about heaven and hell, the community of souls, rather than about people and computers on earth. If the forward view is other-worldly, the contemporary earthly perspective is dominated by the role of religions as the guardians of ideals of moral purity, with origins deep in history. Had the Ten Commandments come down to us on a floppy disk, we might have looked around for a data company to tell us something of the credit rating of Moses. The Disciples would have been logged on police files as potential subversives. The comments are flippant, but the argument is serious. Church people can argue about the rights and wrongs of women priests or contraception because they are perceived as impinging on traditional models of "good" societies: it seems that to date IT has not been awarded that status or relevance.

The smaller component of the ethics business is the community of moral philosophers, with, from the viewpoint of IT, an important sub-group committed to analyzing what lies ahead. These are called "futurists" because they seek to project current events in order to highlight where they are leading us, and then raise the issues which need to be resolved according to whether we want to go with or reverse the trend. This is more than forward planning: it is about pinning down the continuity of values, and raising awareness about gradual changes in value systems. Futurism has a tenuous foothold in Europe, though a more widely acknowledged role on the other side of the Atlantic and in Japan. Yet despite its apparent weakness, especially in comparison with religion, the futures movement is particularly suited to handling the moral issues of IT. Its methods are appropriate – broad projections, global overviews, careful but speculative analysis: it shows deep understanding of the complex interfaces of people and machines: and its ranks include international figures with wide-framed IT expertise (Masuda, Naisbitt, Toffler, and a high proportion of the writers cited in this book).

Groups who perhaps straddle the boundary between the ethics business and some other activity include judges, counsellors and social workers. There are others, noticeably in a range of advisory services (bank managers, insurance brokers, doctors), but the listed groups are significant because they personify two important relationships for ethics, with law and welfare. One of the simplistic equations many of us might like to be able to accept is that our nation's legal system = justice = a sound moral structure. In reality our scepticism on this point is illustrated by such sayings as that "the law has nothing to do with justice". Nevertheless, legal systems do take note of ethical matters, and frameworks are being put into place to cope with IT. As an example, Britain has now tackled three areas, albeit after lengthy debate, mainly about the possibility of absorbing IT abuse into existing laws covering, for example, fraud and copyright. In chronological order the first law (Data Protection Act, 1984) established a registration system for holders of personal data, with some rights of access and correction for data subjects (albeit with many exemptions regarding access – to police records, for example). As discussed elsewhere, once the broad criteria and procedures for registration have been followed, the law appears above all to protect the claim to ownership of the personal material made by data companies.

Copyright was tackled in the UK in 1988, extending protection to programs and screen displays, with subsequent case rulings beginning to introduce the more loosely defined concept of "look and feel". The industry has itself moved to strengthen the application of the law by setting up FAST, the Federation Against Software Theft, with a policy of reacting aggressively against software theft (pirating). Most recently, in the Computer Misuse Act, 1990, hacking ("unauthorised entry" in official jargon) has been outlawed, whether or not there is intent to facilitate a crime or make program modifications, like introducing a virus. This gives very strong support to the industry, especially since Britain has a traditional ambivalence about punishing the *intent* to commit an offence.

Overall, as part of the ethics business, the British example shows a willingness to look at the concerns of the IT industry, noticeable in the areas of copyright and hacking. The industry is further supported by a decidedly weak framework (from the consumer viewpoint) for data protection. It is hard to avoid the conclusion that the law has employed its ethical role as the IT industry's friend. Do the subjects of personal data and those on the receiving end of IT activity have a friend in the ethics business? This is a role which might be filled by counsellors and social workers, or within the wider system of welfare.

Pastoral counselling, like the work of the priesthood, has a primary focus on the lives of individuals and families. A principle behind most therapies is the adjustment of the individual to society, rather than an attempt to evaluate, adjust and change society's standards. In this sense what exists and occurs in society is taken as fixed, so the contribution to ethical development is restricted. In another context, however, counsellors and social workers relate to community groups, and many social workers go a stage further to assign themselves a role of representing the interests of under-privileged people in the functioning of society. The United States has a tradition of community action illustrated, for example, by the teaching and tactical planning of Saul Alinsky (Horwitt, 1989). In Britain the notion of advocacy by social workers, for example on behalf of people with learning difficulties, is still gaining ground. In these ways staff in welfare services, whether salaried professionals or untrained volunteers, do enter the ethical debate. Issues surrounding the efficacy of residential or community care for groups like abused children and adult schizophrenics extend across into human rights. Welfare worker organizations campaign on their own and in liaison with self-help groups for a consumer voice to be heard.

The problem with social workers, counsellors and other staff of the welfare services is that many of them are thought to have been attracted in this vocational direction as a way towards the personal and human, and to keep the impersonal and technological at a distance. So although their ethical standpoint may be clearly identified, their involvement in debate about IT is inhibited by their supposed (maybe real) ignorance of the subject. The mixture of apathy and resistance which they show to technology is documented (e.g. Glastonbury, 1985). At the same time, technology issues are now aired in professional journals on both sides of the Atlantic, with a consistent quality of eschewing technical themes in favour of discussing practical applications and principles.

The ethics industry, in Masuda's broadly based concept, extends into areas of society characterised as much by what they practice as by what they preach, though some, like the environmental movement, have a strong profile in both activities. Small groups, networks, sometimes sub-cultures, are a feature of modern society, facilitated to a degree by the availability of modern communications and market choice. Within the context of broad philosophies, about themes such as pollution, pacifism and animal welfare, they establish lifestyles which are a moral statement. In many instances staff in ethics industries are trained to deal with people as people, that is, as individuals with personality. Workers value, assess, appraise, and treat each human situation, using prayer, meditation, therapy, ritual, confession, mutual support, and ethical analysis amongst their methods.

Two frameworks to analyze the personal situation and enter into a helping relationship are used in the United States by a number of workers. They coincide with frameworks which are anticipated to be at the centre of information society values. One is based on thinking about the balance between and among all life forms on earth. It emphasizes an exploration of all known influences and effects during the analysis and design of alternatives for successful adaptation. It can be called an ecological perspective. The second perspective grew out of a recognition of the complexity of life forms and their organization. It emphasizes an exploration of the network of relationships of life events as a process which structures future events. It has been called the general systems perspective.

Despite the debates about the virtues and deficits of such perspectives, they have been used fruitfully to develop a view of what must be considered when dealing ethically with the human situation. For example, variations of ecological and general systems perspectives are presently used to understand the frame of reference which a helper might consider when assisting an unemployed person, drawing on the person's financial, physical, mental, familial, educational, experiential, and religious circumstances in a holistic approach to unemployment.

IT's CONTRIBUTION TO THE ETHICS INDUSTRY

The judgements we make in and around the people's lives, and the problems and opportunities humans experience, are very complex: information technologies are not up to dealing with the complexity of everyday human life. They are presently too primitive. The IT applications that are available have largely been those classes of applications which have already been developed in business, industry, and the military, and what will be valuable, for example, in automating an office or guiding a missile, may have little use with people, even if we bypass the principle involved in seeking to automate and guide humans.

Many of these IT applications have been used, as in their organization of origin, to eliminate discretion, to standardize and structure decisions, to enforce rules and impersonality, and to contain cost. There is a real sense in which the limits of the IT applications define what is being done by humans. In this situation, the organization, worker, and service are forced to adapt to the available technology. We would argue that this is not what needs to take place. When it occurs, it is a clear example of what Winner (1978) has called reverse adaptation. There is a clear framework to the ethics of adaptation: humans should adapt to the environment, or risk destroying it: machines should be adapted to humanity, or we will be forced to behave like robots for most of our waking hours. Back to Penzias' view that if we don't want to be treated as machines, don't behave like them!

Yet no one has faced up to planning the development of information technologies more capable of supporting the ethical provision of service. Why? Perhaps because the required investment, though essential, is substantial, and would require valuing humans more than profit. It is useful to return to the question of investment. When an investment is considered, the value of the investment is determined in a number of ways, some rational, some emotional. For example, to pay tax to government on a social insurance scheme is an accepted way of investing against needs in old age or disability. To pay tax to incarcerate a murderer is an investment, though not generally satisfying, against having such a person in your neighbourhood. To pay tax to support the poor? This is not generally understood in industrial society as an investment, but as an expense, a cost. Consequently, it is believed that the investment required to limit this cost has to do with protection from fraud, limiting eligibility for benefits, and assurances of possible future productivity. Information technologies are then directed toward these investment goals, as illustrated in Britain throughout the 1980s, where the Government appeared more determined to catch the few who tried to cheat the welfare benefits system, than to encourage applications from the many who did not take up benefits available to them. In this example it was left to private initiative to use IT to help poor people.

What are the consequences? What is missing? Within this framework some countries have been blind to investments in human capital to address need, entitlement, justice, dignity, community and equality. These are investments in the personal. The consequences of a lack of investment are more visible now than in any other period since the Second World War. In the United States examples of negative outcomes are abundant. As one brief example, the country has not invested in universal prenatal, delivery, parenting, and child health services. A relatively high percentage of ethnic minority persons are poor. Their babies are more likely to be born in deprived circumstances. One baby in five lives below the poverty line. New York City, arguably the centre of American culture, resembles a Third World country. It is a city of great wealth flirting with financial and moral bankruptcy. A child born in Bangladesh has a better chance of reaching five years of age than a child born in Harlem. Nutrition among school age poor is a serious problem. Yet American taxpayers pay $9 for a Congress member's lunch, $3 for a prison convict's lunch, and 59 cents for a child's school lunch. Later, as youth, a high percentage of ethnic minority children drop out of school at early ages. As young adults, negative statistics for these people accumulate – they are more likely to be in prison, to be unemployed, or to be poor.

While the investment in health and other services throughout a person's life cycle is expensive, the consequence of not investing is doubly expensive. The American, and to an extent the British alternative is to invest in the costs of supporting impoverishment, disease, ignorance, and crime; that is, a welfare system that does not nurture, empower, shelter or feed, a pervasive investigatory system, a health system that does not treat, an educational system that does not teach, and a growing set of police forces, prisons, keepers and prisoners. In its own right, all of this costs enormous amounts of money. IT applications in these circumstances tend to support the systems as they are, not as they need to be. For example, there have been rapid advances in surveillance, computer database matching, and high technology monitoring to catch out wrong doers, but much less attempt to use these same IT capabilities to identify and help people who need life enhancement.

In the last resort it comes down to a question of values, investment, and outcomes. The outcome of universal prenatal, delivery, parenting and child health care is healthier, more intelligent babies, the probability of improved parenting and child care, empowerment of the family, and a child better able to participate in production, community, and democracy. The more distant outcome of not doing so is a country which has a growing, guilt-provoking volume of people who are outsiders, massively deprived, unable, maybe unwilling to contribute to society, disenchanted by what "their" society has to offer them, and justifiably resentful of their treatment. Such a society will have spent much of its human capital. The near outcome is a country which is progressively less able to support community, democracy, and empowerment – growing terror in the streets, a work force in prison, ignorance the common currency. Information technologies in these circumstances are more likely to be useful to large bureaucracies and the military, with social control a major issue.

Social control may be a priority even in the face of great deprivation and poverty. For example, in the United States social welfare system, fears that persons receiving food benefits may be cheating has led to the use of information technologies. Each state has a large computer system which connects local data about recipients for enforcement of the rules. The state system data can be matched with other databases in order to check earning records, tax , and motor vehicle data. In this way, IT can be used as a part of an alienating system, just as is the British preoccupation, mentioned a few paragraphs back, with the possibility that some poor people may get a little more than their entitlement.

The purpose of this particular argument is not to imply that people do not cheat: they do. Nor is it to argue against enforcement. Effective enforcement systems are essential. But what constitutes effective enforcement of hunger? The point is that if one is interested in moral decisions in regard to reducing welfare cheating in the long run, then other applications of information technologies are called for in this situation. If one is interested in feeding the hungry, then efforts to use IT to connect hungry people with available sources of food warrant at least as much attention. In conditions of abundance, only when everyone is fed is it time to check whether some are getting double helpings.

VOLUNTARISM AND NON-PROFIT

Societies organize ways to meet unmet human needs through governmental intervention in the form of any number of government programs – unemployment centres and social welfare offices are examples – in the areas of welfare, health, and education. But as we have tried to argue, governments have additional preoccupations which lead them to develop policies linked to enforcing social controls, combatting corruption and standardizing us into serried ranks of collaborative citizens. Private companies often give most generously to charitable causes, but their core motivation and concern is making money. Both governments and companies contribute to the formation of economic infrastructures which determine our basic living standards. In short, they are most commonly benevolent, but when the chips are down their priorities, as Ellul indicated, may not be the local neighbourhood's priorities. Governments and companies are willing to pay a human price for technology solutions, and are prepared to compromise on matters of ethical principle.

In contrast volunteers and non-profit groups are likely to have different objectives. Non-profit organizations are particularly badly named, because in real human terms they are the *profit* groups, those who measure their outcomes in terms of profit to humanity rather than cash in the bank. In the United States in particular, the political philosophy which has inhibited government human service provision has placed increasing pressures upon the massive network of voluntary organizations, which are legally termed to be non-profit organizations. Members of the governing board are not paid for their work in the organization. They are volunteers. They are often a combination of community people from different backgrounds who have an interest in the problem with which the organization will deal. The organization will also rely heavily on volunteers for day-to-day functioning, for teaching, counselling, helping in the community, or whatever. Administration and professional services are likely to be staffed by people who have been trained to operate in this type of organization and are paid for the work they do. Their rate of pay is most often much lower than the prevailing wage for similar jobs in for profit organizations. In this sense, they are also volunteers. Revenues for the organizations are either raised by community activities and donations, or, in the United States, by organized community fund raising and allocation bodies called United Ways. These organizations contribute more to education and health than the United States Federal Government, but less in the area of social services. The total revenues raised by the independent sector in 1987 were $327 billion US (Hodgkinson and Weitzman, 1989). Volunteers provided an estimated 20.5 billion hours of service, worth $170 billion (Hodgkinson and Weitzman, 1990). Another context for volunteers are self-help groups, where staffing and membership is likely to be made up of people whose personal circumstances and needs (or now met needs) match the purposes of the organizations.

These two types of organization exist at the heart of human service provision in most communities in the United States, and in a noticeably more peripheral context in the British welfare system. It is estimated that there were 900,000 such organizations in the United States in 1987 (Hodgkinson and Weitzman, 1989). Self-help groups, voluntary organizations, and other forms of citizen participation will have a consequent and successive impact on the support required for people to gain or retain control of their own destiny. As such, these types of organization are critical steps toward the development of new social institutions.

The British equivalent in the welfare framework are organizations based on local authorities. British social services departments are government agencies in the sense that they are funded from central and local taxation, set up through national legislation, and accountable to elected local government councillors. Nevertheless, they are not so clearly governmentally directed as their American counterparts, and have a major and long standing role as the repositories of professional (especially social work) values. Staff in British social services and probation departments are, like their American non-profit colleagues, not well paid, and there is still a tendency to assume a vocational component to this type of work, as there is also to nursing and school teaching. There is a British dimension which sees social services workers as part of the forces of law and order, of social control, but still within the framework of a welfare value system. There is only minuscule for-profit activity. In a real sense, therefore, the British welfare scene represents professional service values and the interests of the deprived members of society – a strongly embedded and firm ethical standpoint. Only in the last few years has the right wing (Thatcher) government sought to fragment this bastion, by introducing an independent sector of profit and non-profit arrangements, though even here the strongest motivation is probably to save public money rather than take the electorally high risk path of weakening the welfare state philosophy.

Within this overall framework a growing role is being played by IT. Handsnet is an example of a voluntary organization in the United States that is a national computer based system designed to help organizations serving homeless people. In various States the network is also used to help homeless people directly by allowing service providers to share data about available homes, shelter beds, or other resources. Denmark has an example of a comparable system (Lindstrom, 1991), locally based but more diverse. It operates on the same principles of helping people to exchange information and match what they need or can offer against the circumstances of others. CompuMentor in San Francisco is a voluntary organization that matches non-profit organizational needs with IT experts. The experts donate their time and efforts to helping the organization with their IT problems.

In these examples, the human is the capital, and the programs lead to social benefit, with the benefit being much more than the sum of the parts. The use of IT occurs in a humanistic manner, and the activities of social benefit, mutual assistance, and IT are complementary.

TWO CASE EXAMPLES

In the Japanese national information policy (Matley and McDannold, 1987), those projects which were designed because they were thought most likely to "trigger" and lead the transition to the information society were not industrial or commercial – they were a medical telecommunications system, an educational system, and a government database project. The Japanese showed an early awareness of the significance of schemes which incorporated social values. Such approaches can also have important impacts on project design in the application of information technologies. At this point we want to look in detail at two examples of projects incorporating social values, not from Japan, but from the USA and Britain.

ElderInfoNet is a project started in Denver, Colorado in 1987. It was mounted in order to provide a more effective manner of serving the needs of elderly persons for information about available services and appropriate referral to those services (called I&R in the States). All major organizations in the metropolitan area were invited to participate. When they began, they endorsed the following principles:

1. There is a need for a well designed comprehensive and coordinated I&R for the elderly.

2. Such an I&R need not be a single integrated system (although it could be) but at a minimum it should be a well co-ordinated arrangement with all components linked together in a co-operative or collaborative venture.

3. There should probably be a central locus of responsibility for the gathering and updating of information to be included in the basic database. There could be some specialized sub-databases (e.g. housing for the elderly or nursing home slots) which could be maintained by a separate entity – but would be linked directly to the other databases and user agencies.

4. The system should be computer based state of the art with software having the capability of both immediate on line electronic access and publication capacity.

5. The system should be Denver metro area wide.

The participants were concerned that whatever system was implemented it needed to have people talking to people, not to machines or recordings. The components of the system took more form within a year. The participants were looking for technology that appropriately met their goals. The system characteristics were expanded to include the following:

1.   A telephone network which allows for calls to be automatically forwarded to the first available phone line of any participating organization, a call transfer capability to allow calls to be transferred to any organization in one uninterrupted call, and an ability to conduct a three way or more conversation to handle caller problems, with the caller participating in the discussion without hanging up.

2.   A public access system through the public library network.

3.   Telecommunications capability between participating organizations.

As the design process moved on, a set of philosophic principles were assembled by the project designer which represented issues contained in the discussions and design up to that time. They were stated in short hand fashion as:

> Rights of access as opposed to rights of ownership need to be stressed.
>
> Users need to control the system.
>
> The system needs to be interactive.
>
> Participants must be accountable for the use of the system. The system must be able to document use in such a way that human needs can be followed up in order to see if they were met.
>
> System participation must be voluntary and co-operative.
>
> Elderly persons must be able to participate in the system.
>
> Rights of privacy must be discussed and respected in the design and use of the system.
>
> The database must be distributed in a manner that respects the autonomy of the participants and makes them accountable for system success.

Once designed, the system moved into an implementation phase and became operational in late 1990. The system designer was able to summarize the development of system principles up to that point, and the agenda for ongoing review, as follows:

1.   Advances in the data system must be evaluated continuously by the effects that they have on the lives of the staff and the clients.

2.   Equipment must be purchased which does not present a health hazard to the person who uses it.

3.   The value of traditions, ways of doing things, and customs must be examined prior to the implementation of new IT applications.

4. Data systems must be used to support, respect, and uphold democratic principles.

5. Any data system or part of a data system which is challenged as being disruptive must be subjected to study and changed or approved.

6. Data systems or parts of data systems which diminish freedom and control will not be accepted or implemented regardless of their benefits.

7. Data systems whose technical or economic viability is ambiguous should not be implemented.

8. Any added centralization use must be accompanied by an added decentralized use.

9. The data system must be created and directed by the people who use the application and the people who will be affected by the application.

10. The data system must be understandable to the people who use the system and the people who will be affected by the system.

11. All aspects of the data system must encourage participation, responsibility, contribution, and empowerment.

A few points to be made in passing are that this form of design is unlikely to have come out of the typical design process taught to technologists today. Second, there was a long, human, participative process. Third, the IT was used to support the project goals, not to drive the project goals. The use of the telephone in much more effective ways to problem solve among humans and meet human needs is an example. Finally, the centrality of evolving, continuous human participation, judgement, and evaluation of human outcome cannot be minimized or overlooked. It is clearly more important to the project than the information technologies they will use.

A different example is Maximiser, a computer program built over many years by Ferret Information Systems in Britain. In some ways it is the archetypal knowledge based system, emerging from the interactions of system design and programming with profound subject expertise, in this instance in the welfare benefits schemes operated by the British Government and local authorities. Whereas ElderInfoNet sought to emphasise humanity in the way its designers handled the design process, and the principles embedded in the system, Maximiser flags up its ethical commitment in the objectives and output of the program. Its aim is to help people whose current or longer term poverty might make them eligible to receive benefits to check this out, either directly and privately with a computer, or with the help of an intermediary like a welfare worker. Maximiser asks questions, some of them intimate and personal, and then advises whether the respondent is eligible for benefits, if so which ones, and how much cash should be received. It offers a printout of the calculations as a personal record or for taking to the benefits office to support a claim, but no computer record is retained, so the system does not link in any way to personal databases.

Prior to the existence of Maximiser (or one of the other programs now in operation, like Lisson Grove or ICL's Welfare Benefits Assessor) a claimant for benefits had the status of ill-informed supplicant. Armed with a computer calculation the claimant now has the information and security to interact with the benefits office staff, and appeal if all does not come out as expected. Tools like Maximiser, therefore, both improve the effectiveness of the human services operation, in bringing benefits to a higher proportion of those who need them, and give empowerment to underprivileged groups.

Unlike ElderInfoNet, Maximiser is not a network, and is not, therefore, facilitated by the telephone system. Such an approach would, in any event, have been inappropriate in Britain, given the fact that poor households do not have telephones, and all calls, local or distance, are charged. Instead it is set to operate on basic minimal cost technology of the sort which even the smallest community groups can afford. The most complex version of the program, which is likely to require the presence of someone with knowledge of the benefits system to get best value from it, runs on a PC or clone. Simpler versions run on small hand-held battery driven computer/calculators, with the advantages of mobility.

There are differences between Maximiser and the other similar programs, Lisson Grove and Welfare Benefits Assessor, but they have certain features in common. They all directly address the customer, the potential claimant of benefits, rather than agency staff. They all have easily called up help screens, offering simple and precise background information, on the relevant law, for example. They all give the security and privacy which comes from wiping out the record when the calculations are made, so there is no question of a relationship with another database, or personal material getting onto other files (Why, it may be relevant to ask, don't other IT users, like banks, who ask personal questions to establish eligibility for a service take the same subsequent action?). They all look as professional as anything on the market, so do not give the user the impression of a low class program designed for poor people – they give users a sense of self-respect. In short, while they do not share the explicit commitment to a planned value system which is such an important aspect of the ElderInfoNet project, they achieve the same outcome in a different way, by modelling the values to which they are committed.

SELF-FULFILMENT, DEMOCRACY AND DECENTRALIZATION

What ElderInfoNet and Maximiser have in common is that they are programs for the people, contributing to individual self-fulfilment, democratic processes, and the decentralization of bureaucratic systems. Masuda might see these projects as fulfilment of the prediction that a trend in computer and communication uses will proceed to address the needs of the individual. In this view, individual human beings, their lifestyles, their thinking and their behaviour, are the ultimate subject of information technologies – not war, science, business, or government. Ten years ago Manfred Kochen (1981) pointed out what "tasks and potentials" might be the focus for IT if it were directed toward individualism and self-fulfilment. We may expect these technologies to be used, claimed Kochen, to amplify an individual's intellectual abilities, to regulate and control an individual's feelings, and to provide new forms of communication in society.

The knowledge base for these developments is building in the behavioral, biological, and interdisciplinary sciences, using tools from what have become known as the sciences of the complex. Researchers in artificial intelligence and robotics are contributing a great deal to the gathering change. As Heinz Pagals (1989) points out, the interdisciplinary sciences, the primary tool of which is IT, are increasingly used to solve social problems. For example, in medical care, clinical systems for rural areas are being put into place utilizing information technologies for diagnosis, treatment, consultation, training, and messaging. In fact, this was the first type of system developed in Japan under their information society plan. Elsewhere regional health systems have been developed which rely upon computer interaction. Client assistance systems help facilitate the education, training, transportation, and child care needs of single mothers receiving public welfare assistance. The development of individual abilities through planned educational, research, and library systems is already functioning in a few countries.

It is interesting to note that what Kochen called the tasks or potentials of information technologies are not just directed toward the human problems we experience in everyday life, but include problems arising from the individual and institutional stresses sustained by the application of technologies. For example, computer conferencing has been used to facilitate debate about a particular community issue by having people linked together through TV sets in their own homes. But a person running the computer conference can influence the debate simply by providing pauses, diversions, or selected views of the participants themselves. This can exacerbate as easily as resolve conflicts.

As long as the human problems engendered by IT applications have not been balanced by any corresponding caring, growth, or change in social institutions, people will feel increasingly deeper emotional strain. What are the human needs that are to be met? The list of human needs seems simple: as Maslow (1954, 1962) has presented them, they are survival, security, a sense of belonging, materialism and prestige, and self-actualization. Social institutions, such as the family, school, work place, neighbourhood or community, and government exist to meet these needs. The family, regardless of its form, is where human needs and their providential interaction with other social institutions is processed and enacted. The work place may primarily provide security in terms of money or goods, but, in its optimal sense, the workplace can meet human needs at every level.

Getting people working together is a fundamental part of the ethics agenda for IT and industry, as is a form of governance that includes citizen participation, much like the voluntary and self-help group organization. Citizen participation is the opportunity for all persons to take part – directly and indirectly, both in large and small measure – in the decisions that affect themselves, others, and the larger communities of which they are a part (Gross, 1980; Ellul, 1964). Participation is a democratic process. It is a process that begins and is sustained at a personal level. In turn, the anticipation of future participation will increase co-operation and collaboration. Participation is a prerequisite to balancing the strong tendency of information technologies to support centralized, authoritarian approaches to government. It is the infusion of the micro-system of individual human interactions to modify and fragment the macro-system represented by global IT, and its characteristics of standardisation, categorisation and impersonality.

Jeremy Rifkin (1980), in writing about the development of the technological society, argues that its size, complexity, and sheer use of energy will lead to a deterioration of society. He predicts that people will give up on it and choose to return to a simpler, decentralized life. He assumes decreased technology. The French, in their telematics plan, try to develop a notion of centralized decentralization, where telematics is regulated and communication is in State control, but with access assured for all citizens. We would argue that in order to meet personal, individual needs, and to assure participation, decentralization must be the predominant organizational format. Whether the French model is meaningful is debatable.

Schumacher (1973), and many since him, have seen decentralisation as more than guaranteed access to central systems, stressing the virtue of smallness, familiarity and manageability at the individual human level. In this sense decentralisation is also important because it can anchor family and neighbourhood life. These make up the support system for our lives, a setting in which human values can be supported. People can learn from each other. Democracy can be nurtured through learning by doing in a local setting to human scale. To build an everyday understanding of the information society in the common person, there is perhaps truth in the view that concepts cannot be presented, they have to be part of you, a part of your action frame, so that they can be realized through doing. In this manner, the information society can also be shaped by the common person.

Therefore, the important questions are ones that are central to society and to the ethics industry today. What can be done to empower others, so that participation is increased? How can self-help movements and citizen action groups of all types be extended and strengthened? How can they avoid the dangers of being overtaken by other organizations or becoming bureaucracies? How do we become more democratic? It is essential to understand and appreciate how the ethics industries of today can develop the personal, individual, professional, and organizational experience to provide leadership in this area and to raise ethical sights. As Peter Drucker (1988) has argued, it is the managers of America's non-profit organizations who have the leadership abilities, the management skills, and the social values often found lacking in the leadership of major for-profit corporations. It is they, and their equivalents in other communities, like Britain's social services departments, who have experience with the development and administration of the ethical organization. In addition, voluntary, self-help, and citizen action organizations share a singular trait in regard to ethics. The organizational goals always include ethical goals.

The primary social problem for the contemporary ethics industry worker will be to participate in resolving problems specifically related to information technologies and their work. As the transition proceeds, information technologists may believe maturity will be reached when IT is used as a knowledge navigator. This is not so. One sign we can take for maturity will be when IT applications, subjected to ethical analysis, can be used as a means to solve day-to-day problems and as a tool which contributes to individuality and empowerment.

Derek Bok (1990) has probably summarized the American view better than anyone when he talks of the failure of America to come to grips with issues like poverty. In his book on the future of America, he calls for a strengthening of individual virtues, ethical virtues, and civic virtues on the part of individuals. Many European countries have a code of humanistic ethics contained within their national welfare philosophies. Perhaps it is in the context of a resurgence of the welfare ethic that we will find a value system for IT.

NATIONAL PLANNING FOR IT

An alternative route is to establish a national plan and policy around what is known or projected about the forward path of IT. We have already noted that two countries, Japan and France, have made direct efforts to develop plans for an information society which are based upon considered visions of the role of IT rather than a narrower product-based approach. Brazil can make some claim to be added to this list. The Japan Information Society Plan was published and adopted in 1972. It has three objectives closely linked to the transition from industrial to information society:

1.   To promote knowledge industries over smokestack industries;
2.   To develop solutions to the problems of industrial age industry; and
3.   To focus upon software rather than hardware solutions.

In order to achieve these objectives a number of activities were set in motion in the period from 1972, including measures to control pollution, increase the supply of intellectual personnel, decrease information gaps in society, form a National Council for Information Society Development, promote national understanding about computers, and prepare to mitigate the bad effects that the increasing use of information technologies would have upon people. The equivalent of about $65 billion (£40 billion) was allocated for the effort.

The plan considered carefully the role of government participation. One model, later adopted, put government in the role of offering guidance, co-ordination, and funding. This model was thought to offer the best chance of achieving the growth rate of information investments needed to maintain the project. It also had the best potential for influencing industry to work in concert with the plan, and for co-ordinating and facilitating a uniform development. A second model was based on government and private industry co-operating, but without direct government financial investment. This was not seen as satisfactory to meet the needs of accommodating to the fast moving fields of information technologies. Development would be uneven and slow. The model seemed likely to ignore important areas such as health, education, and welfare.

The laissez-faire model allowed market forces to prevail over development, so was also judged inappropriate because it most probably would not address the long-term projects which were important to society. Little would be done for the individual, with most benefit going to business and industry. The model was held to promote a potentially unstable economy, with a focus on automation and commercial information services as the major areas for computerization.

After adoption of the government guidance model, non-profit firms, fully funded by the government, were created to take on projects which were of a societal nature but not of interest to private industry. Other projects were to be contracted with private for-profit firms. A major commitment was made to avoid the possible outcome of a centralized and controlled society, particularly since the study identified this as a strong tendency in computerization. A National Congress for Information Society Development was convened with members from all sectors of the society, including business, labour, and consumer groups. A technical expert review system was set up to examine government policies in the area of computerization. A Citizen's Policy Participation System was begun to allow citizens to participate in the process.

The Japanese Government decided to focus initially on telecommunications networks in health and education. In what, for the early 1970s, was a rather remarkable insight, they realized the need to improve the standards of intellectual activity for everyone, so that as many people as possible could appreciate, understand, and benefit from and use the products of the information society. Proposed projects were subjected to a rating system of merits and demerits. Merits included congruence with the goals of the plan. Demerits included loss of privacy, information monopoly by government, computer crime, worker displacement through automation, and no national oversight system. Three projects were seen as central for the plan, most critically in the manner of their implementation. These were a remote medical care system, school computerization, and a national database network.

The French plan is similar to the Japanese one, particularly in the sense that it addressed the issue of moving toward an information society. The plan asserted that computerization should be controlled in the public interest, and indicated that the absence of adequate preparation would provoke struggles within core areas of tradition, culture, and knowledge. The study anticipated that industrial jobs would contract and intellectual jobs expand: small decentralized facilities would multiply and those large organizations that survived would contract. People would be living in smaller, decentralized communities. Home based work would increase. Under these circumstances, there would be more isolation. There might be a class effect in society as knowledge workers laid claim to higher wages. Computer networks would contribute to a change in language as well as knowledge, and would vary according to an individual's participation and access to the network.

These were seen as important cultural markers, similar in effect to the cultural changes which occurred as a consequence of writing and printing. The ability of everyone to access and use data was vital to the French idea of equality. The only way that traditional values could be assured for the future would be by individual users becoming part of the process that generates, processes, and distributes data. The study called this a democratization of information, and they felt it could only come about by design. Like the Japanese plan, the French realized the central role that education must play. Education needed to provide the context for the information society, so that people would be able to understand and be responsible for computerization, yet maintain their human characteristics.

The French anticipated 30 per cent job losses in some employment areas, like banks, insurance and clerical sectors of public services. New employment would be created in high technology areas. The study predicted that the workplace would move from a hierarchical, isolated, centralized model to less concentration, decentralization, and worker autonomy. Power relationships in organizations would change, as would the responsibilities of the individual worker.

The French government was expected to become the holder of most personal data, as well as owner of the major communications network. This was viewed as a possible threat to individual freedom, and arguments were advanced that this type of government involvement would have to be subjected to care and democratic procedures, to avoid repression and centralization of power. Like the Japanese plan, the study further pointed out the necessity to counter the strong pressure in the direction of structured, centralized networks.

The French wanted to set standards for their system and establish national suppliers. They also decided to establish national data banks free of foreign control. They planned to use a mixture of government and private firms in their projects. The government decided to computerize its own operations, so becoming a guaranteed large customer for the new national industry. Through ownership of the telecommunications system, the government would be in a strong position to support industry and encourage innovation.

In Brazil in 1976 the Commission for the Co-ordination of Electronic Activities began to prepare an overall policy which was designed to protect the domestic computer industry. In 1984, the passage of the National Informatics Law continued the series of protective steps to preserve its market. The law delineated the role of government as one that would guide, co-ordinate, and develop IT. The Law established citizen access to data as a right, whether the data system was private or public. Citizens also have a right to correct data that is being kept about them in a databank. Data systems with personal data are to be protected and confidentiality assured.

The Brazilian plan, of which the National Informatics Law is part, is essentially a combined economic and cultural design, like that of the Japanese and the French. It is one that maps out and implements notions of what the culture must be, in order to control and implement the nation's movement into an information society world.

The Japanese Plan is working. There are available critiques and studies of its progress (Japanese Government Economic Planning Agency, 1983). We would argue that much of the plan needs study, particularly since major elements of it may be relevant to the situation that we face in our own societies. In contrast the trends which we have studied in England and the States indicate that Ellul and other technology determinists have made salient points. Barber (1988), in a brief exposition concerning the future of technology and democracy, outlines three possible scenarios. In all scenarios the assumption is that the future of democracy is uncertain, and that society's dominant theme is the encounter with technology.

The first scenario is based upon the situation much as it is in the United States and Britain. The best hope for society is to rely on market forces to take technology in socially useful directions, in the absence of planning of any kind. In fact, our experience is that market forces have tended to undermine social values. The second scenario is based on the government exacerbating and spreading the worst free market trends, resulting in a surveillance society, capable of both the benign and hostile enslavement of its peoples. The third scenario is based upon the use of the democratic process. In this scenario, Jefferson's belief that the inadequacies of democracy are best cured by more democracy is put into practice. The process depends upon education and sharing, using the notion that the more you anticipate having to share in the future, the more you will tend to co-operate now. Barber points out that this scenario is least likely, because it requires that "citizen groups and governments take action in adapting the new technology to their needs" (p. 187).

Ultimately the survival of democracy and individual self-fulfilment depends upon humans not machines. Barber talks of establishing independent public corporations as a remedy. In the French, Japanese, and Brazilian plans, special note is made of controls on the pace of change. Change can be brought to heel with democratic processes which provide direction and guide implementation. As Barber suggests, it is the will not the way that is missing. If we are serious that we want to shape society differently, we will need to create a forum which, in part, enables us to identify our aspirations. Perhaps John McHale (1975) was right when he pointed out that the social thinking to apply our capacities in humanly desirable manners is undeveloped. It may be equally and simultaneously true that IT "is transforming the way in which individuals in Western society think and act . . . . that some of the traditional assumptions about the democratic process are being undermined or revised, for good or ill" (Street, 1988, p. 13).

One thing is clear, the ethics industry needs to grow and flex its muscles. Masuda (1981) has a vision that the society we are moving toward is global, in which different communities of citizens, participating voluntarily in shared goals and ideas, exist simultaneously throughout the world. This will not occur by itself. Nor need it be dismissed as utopian. Many interests, corporate, commercial, and governmental, have invested much in a vision of society that is quite different. Perhaps these visions can exist together, perhaps not. Our concern is that in the absence of a global humanistic vision efforts to separate humans from intelligence, to put it in machines, will move ahead unfettered.

12 A Bill of Rights

SUMMARY

On the basis of the analysis in earlier chapters of the strengths and weaknesses of existing value and legal systems in coping with IT, this chapter summarizes, draws together and argues priorities for the factors which must be taken into account in the construction of a code which is both enabling and protective for IT designers, developers, producers, employers, consumers, data subjects, or those who simply have to live with whatever is set up. From there it moves on to identify a draft Bill of Rights for our information age.

SETTING PRIORITIES

In the following paragraphs we list, with brief comments, what we see as the major priorities or routes towards ethical IT; but simply stating them begs the question of strategy. How can we move to get them implemented? We have already identified some possible choices. Certain aspects of IT development and usage can be subject to legal codification, as Britain has tried with data protection, controls on access and copyright. More comprehensively there is clearly a role for national IT policies, or long term development plans. America has never tried this. Britain perhaps had an opportunity with the Alvey project, but saw it hive off into a focus on technology. Japan and France are clearly now showing the beneficial results of their foresight, in their range of applications and IT industry, as well as in their recognition of a social responsibility. If the notion of planning and policy-making is unattractive, then promoting or reinforcing futurism is a way forward, at least to an understanding of what is going to happen to us, and what issues should come into focus. The United States owes much to the work of people in groups like the World Future Society.

At other points in this book the focus has been on the past, not the future. Here we present arguments that culture has its own rate of change, which has a lot to do with our ability to incorporate values into culture through tradition, ritual, morality, the humanities, education, religion, story telling, and myth. The study, interpretation, understanding, and passing on of values is a process which takes time, much more time than the rush of technological invention has allowed us. We must continue to find both enough time and the widest forum for their discussion and meditation in the steps towards cultural adaptation. Slow though it may be, it is the human manner of assuring that the human intelligence includes new values as part and parcel of its integrity. We want to assert by proposing a Bill of Rights that these values are as important as IT itself. We hope that the ethics industries will provide leadership for the discussion and implementation of these priorities and the Bill of Rights.

However, while individual societies need leadership for coping with the impact of IT, there remains a vital global dimension. In the wealthier industrial countries it is easy to confine analysis to internal issues, about the effect of IT on the structure, functioning and future of the national society, and on the multitude of individuals, families and groups who make up that population. We can forget that just as poor countries are removing the shackles of a colonialism which thrived on the exploitation of their agriculture and raw materials, so they are threatened by a new colonialism, based on control of technology deployment and global communications. So often poor countries were diagnosed as poor because they did not have an industrial base: now they will stay poor if they fail to obtain an adequate IT infrastructure.

Is there a strategy for ethical IT in a global context? An obvious path here leads towards international organizations, especially the United Nations, as the existing forums in which matters of importance to all our futures can be debated, perhaps resolved. The United Nations, perhaps picking up on the example of the United States and many other democratic countries, has seen merit in Declarations of Rights. As a non-governing body, United Nations Declarations stand as a testament, a set of principles, rather than part of a legal code, or legally enforceable guidelines. Always hopeful that human rights can be enforced, we have called our statement a Bill of Rights. But first the priorities on which it is based.

The first priority is that IT be subjected to an analysis, from the developmental stage onward, which takes into account social, historical, cultural, and ethical factors, and which assesses their potential contribution to an agreed set of social goals.

The usual situation is that IT applications are not being developed with enough thought and consideration given to human benefits and costs. They tend to reflect purely market considerations, the creative ideas of designers, or pressures to make use of the capacities of leading edge hardware. As Norbert Wiener (1967) commented, IT must serve humans first, technology second.

The second priority is to assess IT developments for their potential impact on democratic principles and individual freedom.

Our analysis indicates, on balance, that IT has augmented the powers of dominant groups in society, whether in organizations or government, and that its use has increased what Gross (1980) calls "friendly fascism". More importantly IT has the capacity both to encourage democratic processes, and to strengthen overt dictatorships. Therefore this priority is preventive and looking to future threats.

The third priority is to set an agenda to identify and guide the emerging characteristics of societies that use information technologies.

There has been considerable debate concerning the issue of whether or not the form of society which is developing is a different form of industrial society, an information society, a technocratic society, or a post-modern society. The difficulty with emerging paradigms is that they often cannot be assessed from the prevailing point of view of, for example, industrial forces and problems. Nevertheless, whatever is emerging is presently far enough along to suggest to us a number of problems, all of which need investigation. The most important of these seem to be the potentially destructive impact on humans, and issues about the control of IT and the role of government. We must change our view in order to work on this priority, from one that treats IT as a series of products and services, to one that views it within the context of social development.

The fourth priority is to recognize and evaluate the human choices which are being made in the application of information technologies in terms of moral values.

The application of IT is not moving along of its own accord. We are not subject to a form of technological determinism that threatens our individualism and form of government: we are making choices that do so. These choices are being made by the forces that were in charge before information technologies came into widespread use. What feels out of control to the common person are the vagaries of being driven by market forces, commercialism, and material interests.

The fifth priority is to subject those same choices to an economic and social audit as to their sustainability, to identify and feed into decision making clear statements about who will profit or lose, in what ways, and to what extent

The results of purposeful choices have both costs and benefits. Benefits have been realized by commercial and corporate interests. Airplane reservation systems, banking and trading systems, military devices, and surveillance systems have all benefited. The costs include problems of alienation, worker exploitation, unemployment, militarism, displacement, homelessness, poverty, starvation, and ignorance. Whether we want to accept it or not, the choices being made in the use of information technologies reflect not only the social values of those who are choosing, but the values of those who acquiesce to their consequences. If subliminal messages to consume a product or view an advertisement on TV are being displayed, we need to be able to make informed choices about subjecting ourselves to these suggestions. Much like a drug, we need to know the direct and side effects of IT use.

The sixth priority is to subject all IT developments and applications to scrutiny regarding their impact on forms of discrimination.

When there is a rapidly growing sensitivity to issues of discrimination, in areas of race, gender and disability. Despite the contribution of IT to improving the lives of some people who endure disabilities, the overall position is that IT appears insensitive to notions of equal opportunities, and riddled with examples of serious discrimination.

The seventh priority is to create a set of evolving guidelines which lead to accurate, detailed product descriptions for IT applications, in a wide range of user languages, and composed in terms which are widely understood and free of mystique or technical jargon.

Earlier, in Chapter 3, we argued that IT has the quality of influencing our perceptions. We need to be clear about the assumptions of any IT model of reality or intelligence with which we interact. While this may seem to be difficult to achieve, we argue that it is possible to specify what is going on in a common sense, easy to understand manner.

The eight priority is to establish national IT plans or policies.

Our argument has been that countries which have given attention to the development of IT plans tend to have gained more benefits and experienced fewer disadvantages. Further, the planning process allows for the introduction of concerns (e.g. "people" issues) which usually get excluded from the narrower and fragmented framework of free market decision making.

The ninth priority is to seek an international system, or a structure for regional or bilateral agreements, which sets IT firmly within a sympathetic framework of open technology transfer as a form of international aid, not market exploitation.

We have argued that there is a role for bodies like the United Nations, but more fundamentally that IT has become enmeshed in a system of technology transfer which is restrictive as a result of political decision and over-pricing, and too closely allied to the international arms market. IT has strengthened the divisions between rich and poor through massive discrimination against Third World countries, and ignores the need for technologies and their transfer to be sensitive to the social characteristics of recipient communities.

The tenth priority is to recognise that as well as a global arena and agenda, there is a localised, personal, family and community arena, which sets IT firmly on the path of integration with the valued parts of existing daily life patterns

Throughout this book we have sought to establish that there is not a single set of values for IT, with a single frame of reference. On the one hand there are global principles and priorities, but on the other, there are cultures and ways of living which vary widely across the world, and are equally cherished by those who enjoy them. These should play their part in determining the future of IT. At the same time there is deprivation, again both in a global and theoretical sense, as well as in the details of daily lives in many communities. We have no interest in preserving deprivation, but see a major challenge for IT in combatting it.

RIGHTS FOR PEOPLE

In his book *Protecting Privacy in Surveillance Societies* David H. Flaherty (1989) draws up (p. 8) a succinct list of rights derived from the privacy interests it is reasonable for all of us to expect in relation to data about ourselves. He lists rights:

> to individual autonomy
> to be left alone
> to a private life
> to control information about ourselves
> to limit accessibility
> to exclusive control of access to private realms
> to minimize intrusiveness
> to expect confidentiality
> to enjoy solitude
> to enjoy intimacy
> to enjoy anonymity

to enjoy reserve
to secrecy

For all of us as citizens these are vital issues, because they are so closely personal to our daily lives. They are humanity's cry of exasperation and desperation about IT's invasion of work, home, relationships, personality, and deepest feelings. They are a challenge to the IT industry to put its house in order, and to the ethics industries to draw up a coherent set of standards. In our proposed Bill of Rights we have tried to incorporate some sense of the threat to the individual, alongside principles which would have the effect of enabling and regulating the IT industry. The Bill does not aim or claim to be all-embracing. Specifically it excludes subjects which are more appropriately part of other arrangements, usually because they are not unique to IT. Examples are payment for the use of personal data, and matters affecting employment within the IT industry, which ought to be covered by, respectively, commercial and employment codes. Nevertheless, we have tried to range as widely as possible within the IT framework, and acknowledge that the consumer viewpoint, however important, is not the only one. We have also sought to keep clear of emotion and conviction, to suggest instead a Bill stated in cool language, with as much objectivity as we can muster.

A Bill of Rights for the Information Age

1. Human rights, as declared in the Universal Declaration of Human Rights, should be reasonably and prudently considered in all processes of IT development, use, and application. The consideration should take place in the widest public forum feasible, and involve representatives of all of those who will be affected, as well as appropriate expert, legally mandated, and ethical authorities.

2. Decisions which directly affect a human being may not be made by an IT device alone. IT systems can be used as an aid to decision making, but only in circumstances where a designated person is accountable for the decision.

3. Humans affected by IT device-aided decisions should be fully informed at all times, and have an incontrovertible right to appeal all such decisions through the courts of law or through formal appeal processes.

4. Personal data is the property of the person who is the subject of

the data, or that person's legal parent or legal guardian where that person is a juvenile or unable to act on his or her own behalf. Such property rights are irrevocable. Permission must be obtained from the owner for use of personal data for all uses, including personal reports, aggregated formats, linkage to other data or transfer to other computer systems.

5. Unintended or unrecognized consequences of any type resulting from the application of information technologies are the responsibility of those who have implemented the application, and subject to remedy and compensation for actual or perceived damages. A court should be able to award damages to an individual or group.

6. If IT devices or applications displace human workers, they should be compensated and provided retraining within their local communities. If the IT usage is unsatisfactory and a worker is to be employed again, the displaced worker should be given the first right to the job.

7. All IT devices and applications should be accompanied by a full, complete, and understandable written statement of operating instructions, the functions and performance of the device or application, and any known or suspected hazards connected with use. The written statement should be provided in all languages in use within the community where marketing occurs. Statements about the performance of devices or applications which prove to be unwarranted should be open to redress through court action.

8. All IT applications should conform to best equal opportunities standards, as should the IT industry.

9. An independent Commission should be established to register and review the content and use of all networks and databases containing personal material, and to register all new applications. The Commission should have power to seek modification, ban or proceed to court action in relation to any failure to meet appropriate standards or the terms of this Bill of Rights. Given a reasonable warning, devices or applications currently in use must conform or be dismantled.

10. All IT applications and devices for which a purpose or use is surveillance should be regulated in the public interest. No private or commercial sale of such devices to the public should be allowed. All use of such instruments by any government for any reasons should be approved by a court of law prior to use.

11. Specific legislation should be passed to ensure the protection of personal data, prevent unauthorised access to computer systems, and protect the copyright or patent rights of IT designers, except that no such copyright or patent shall be issued which infringes upon the human tradition of knowledge sharing or limits the common good.

12. Customers in any country should have the right to purchase equipment or programs from manufacturers at the lowest price the manufacturer offers in any location, with due allowance for differences relating to costs of transport, installation and local taxation.

13. Information technologies should be confined to developments for peaceful uses and should be freely transferrable to all countries. An international aid fund should be established to assist in technology transfer to poor communities, with an expert sub-committee charged with responsibility for establishing sensitive processes for cross-cultural transfers.

14. An independent body, linked to the Commission identified in 9 above, should be established to keep this Bill of Rights under review, and to co-ordinate and in other ways enhance the ethical soundness of IT progress.

15. The rights of individuals stated in this Bill should be the entitlement of all people of whatever country.

Bills of Rights are fine notions, an outward sign of democracy at work, though they often make dull businesslike reading. They are, however, a necessary and regular reassertion of humanity's control over its own scientific inventions. John Stuart Mill expressed the true emotions with grace and insight – "I am not charmed with an ideal of life held out by those who think that the normal state of human beings is that of struggling to get on; that the trampling, crushing, elbowing, and treading on each other's heels, which form the existing type of social life, are the most desirable lot of human kind, or anything but the disagreeable symptoms of one of the phases of industrial progress." Let us overcome those disagreeable symptoms, bring out the greatness of these new technologies, and have them flow with us, gently, sensitively, creatively, a help and companion to all peoples, a technology to support and sustain humanity.

Bibliography

Allman, W. (1986). Computerworks. *Science 86*, May, 23–31.

Association for Computing Machinery Special Interest Group on Computers and Society (1991). *Computers and Society*. Vol. 21, Nos. 2, 3 and 4.

Bagdikian, B. (1989). Global media corporations control what we watch and read. *The Nation*. June 12, 1989.

Barber, B. (1988). Pangloss, Pandora or Jefferson? Three scenarios for the future of technology and democracy. in *Information Technology: the Public Issues*. ed. Plant, R. *et al*. Manchester University Press.

Bell, D. (1973). *The Coming of Post-Industrial Society*. Basic Books, New York.

Beniger, J. (1986). *The Control Revolution*. Harvard University Press, Cambridge, Mass.

Bok, D. (1990) *Universities and the Future of America*. Duke University Press, Durham.

Bowen, M. (1986). EQUAL – A Special Interest Group on Computers and the Disabled. *Computers Users in Social Services Network Newsletter*. Vol. 6, No. 1, 9.

Brand, S. (1987). *The Media Lab*. Viking, New York.

Carlson, W. (1989). How media literacy is taught. *Education Forum*. Winter, 1989.

Childers, T. and Post, J. (1975). *The Information-Poor in America*. Scarecrow Press, Metuchen.

Cooley, M. (1987). *Architect or Bee? The Human/Technology Relationship*. Chatto and Windus, London.

Computers: A Global Report (1989). *Financial Report*. November 28, 1989.

Computers: Japan Comes on Strong (1989). *Business Week*. October 23, 1989.

Computers and Privacy (1990). *The Christian Science Monitor*. March 21, 1990.

Dawkins, R. (1976). *The Selfish Gene*. Oxford University Press, New York.

Dery, D. (1981). *Computers in Welfare: the MIS-match*. Sage, Beverly Hills and London.

Drexler, E. (1986). *Engines of Creation*. Doubleday, New York.

Drucker, P. (1988). *Managing the Non Profit Organization*. Harper Collins, New York.

Edelman, G. (1987). *Neural Darwinism*. Basic, New York.

Ellul, J. (1990) *The Technological Bluff* (tr. G. Bromiley). Eerdmans, Grand Rapids.

Ellul, J. (1964) *The Technological Society* (tr. J. Wilkinson). Knopf, New York.

Epstein, J. (1984). Project for the Research Institute for Consumer Affairs. Summarised in Information Systems and the Consumer in Glastonbury, B., LaMendola, W. and Toole, S. (Eds). (1987). *Information Technology and the Human Services*. Wiley, London.

Fjermedal, G. (1986). *The Tomorrow Makers*. Macmillan, New York.

Flaherty, D. (1989). *Protecting Privacy in Suveillance Societies*. The University of North Carolina Press, Chapel Hill.

Frenkel, K. (1990). The politics of standards and the EC. *Communications of the ACM*. July 1990.

Fromm, E. (1968). *The Revolution of Hope: Toward a Humanized Technology*. Bantam Books, New York.

Furlong, M. (1989). Crafting an Electronic Community: The SeniorNet Story. *Internationaal Journal of Technology and Aging*, Vol. 2, No. 2, 125–133.

Glastonbury, B. (1985). *Computers in Social Work*. Macmillan, Basingstoke.

Glendinning, G. (1990). *When Technology Wounds*. William Morrow, New York.

Gross, B. (1980). *Friendly Facism*. South End Press, Boston.

Habermas, J. (1971). *Toward a Rational Society* (trans. by J. Shapiro). Heinemann, London.

Hasenfeld, Y. and English R. (1974) Organizational Technology. In *Human Service Organizations* (ed. Y. Hasenfeld and R. English). University of Michigan Press, Ann Arbor.

Hawkings, S. (1988) *A Brief History of Time*. Bantam Press, London.

Healey, M. (1976). *Minicomputers and Microprocessors*. Hodder and Stoughton, London.

Hedlund, J., Vieweg, B., and Cho, D. (1985). Mental Health Computing in the 1980s: II. Clinical Applications. *Computers in Human Services*, Vol. 1, No. 2, 1–22.

Hodgkinson, V. and Weitzman, M. (1989). *Giving and Volunteering in the United States*. Independent Sector, Washington D.C.

Hodgkinson, V. and Weitzman, M. (1990). *Dimensions of the Independent Sector: A Statistical Profile*. Independent Sector, Washington D.C.

Horwitt, S. (1989). *Let Them Call Me Rebel: Saul Alinsky, His Life and Legacy*. Knopf, New York.

Illich, I. (1973). *Tools for Conviviality*. Harper & Row, New York.

Japan Computer Usage Development Institute. (1972) *The Plan for Information Society: A National Goal Toward Year 2000*. JCUDI, Tokyo.

Japanese Government Economic Planning Agency, Social Policy Bureau (1983). *The Information Society and Human Life*. Printing Bureau, Tokyo.

Kidder, T. (1981). *The Soul of a New Machine*. Little & Brown, Boston.

Kochen, M. (1981). Technology and communication in the future. *Journal of the American Society for Information Science*, March 1981, 148–157.

Kropotkin, P. (1914). *Mutual Aid*. New York University Press.

Levy, S. (1984). *Hackers*. Doubleday, New York.

Lindstrom, M. (1991). EDP in Social Work in Denmark. *New Technology in the Human Services*. Vol. 5, No. 3.

Littler, C. (1982). *The Development of the Labour Process in Capitalist Societies.* Heinemann, London.

Lovins, A. (1980). Soft energy paths. In *The Schumacher Lectures* (ed. S. Kumar). Blond and Briggs, London.

Lynn, J. and Jay, A. (1984). *The Complete Yes Minister.* Book Club Associates by arrangement with the British Broadcasting Corporation.

Lyotard, Jean-Francois (1979). *The Postmodern Condition: A Report on Knowledge.* tr. by G. Bennington and B. Massumi. University of Minnesota Press, Minneapolis, Minnesota.

Marcuse, H. (1964). *One Dimensional Man.* Beacon, Boston.

Marlett, N. (1988). Empowerment through computer telecommunications. In *Information Technology and the Human Services* (ed. B. Glastonbury, W. LaMendola, and S. Toole). Wiley, London.

Maslow, A. (1962). *Toward a Psychlogy of Being.* Van Norstrand, Princeton.

Maslow, A. (1954). *Motivation and Personality.* Harper and Row, New York.

Masuda, Y. (1981). *The Information Society as Post-Industrial Society.* World Future Society, Washington, D.C.

Matley and McDannold (1987). *National Computer Policies.* Computer Society Press of the IEEE, Washington, D.C.

McHale, J. (1968). *The Changing Information Environment.* Westview Press, Boulder.

McLoughlin, I. and Clark, J. (1988). *Technological Change at Work.* Open University Press, Milton Keynes.

Miles, I. *et al.* (1988). *Information Horizons* Edward Elgar, Aldershot.

Miller, C. and Cordingly, E. (1988) Structuring Initial Conversations on Expert Systems between Social Work Staff and Software Engineers. In *Information Technology and the Human Services* (ed. B. Glastonbury, W. LaMendola, and S. Toole). Wiley, London.

Moravec, H. (1988) *Mind Children.* Harvard University Press, Cambridge, Mass.

Mumford, L. (1966). *The Myth of the Machine: Technics and Human Development.* Harcourt, Brace & World, New York.

Mumford, L. (1970). *The Myth of the Machine: The Pentagon of Power.* Harcourt Brace Jovanovich, New York.

Naisbitt, J. (1982). *Megatrends.* Warner Books, New York.

Orwell, G. (1969). *1984.* Signet, London and New York.

Otos, S. and Levy, E. (1983). Word Processing "This is not the final draft". in Zimmerman, J. *The Technological Woman.* Praeger, New York.

Pacey, A. (1983). *The Culture of Technology.* Basil Blackwell, Oxford.

Pagals, H. (1989). *The Dreams of Reason.* Bantam Books, London.

Penrose, R. (1989). *The Emperor's New Mind.* Oxford University Press, London.

Penzias, A. (1990). *Ideas and Information.* Simon and Schuster, New York.

Qvortrup, L. (1988). Electronic village halls – IT and IT-assisted Services for Rural Village Communities. In *Information Technology and the Human*

Services (ed. B. Glastonbury, W. LaMendola, and S. Toole). Wiley, London.

Randell, B. (Ed.). (1973). *The Origins of Digital Computers: Selected Papers.* Springer-Verlag, Berlin.

Rifkin, J. (1980). *Entropy.* Viking, New York.

Sackman, H. (1971). *Mass Information Utilities and Social Excellence.* Auerbach, Princeton.

Sackman, H. (1967). *Computers, Systems Science, and Evolving Society.* Wiley, New York.

Sande, T. (1984). Micro computers and the Third World. *DERAP Working Papers.* Chr. Michelsen Institute, Norway.

Sanders, J. (1987). Do your female students say "no thanks" to the computer? *Women's Action Alliance,* New York.

Schumacher, E. F. (1973). *Small is Beautiful.* Blond and Briggs, London.

Shurkin, J. (1984). *Engines of the Mind.* Norton, New York.

Silverstone, S. (1990). Values: A conversation with Alan Kay. *Aldus.* September October 1990.

Skinner, B. F. (1971). *Beyond Freedom and Dignity.* Knopf, 1971.

Street, J. (1988). Taking control? Some aspects of the relationship between information technology, government policy and democracy. in *Information Technology: the Public Issues* (ed. R. Plant *et al.*). Manchester University Press.

Suzuki, D. and Knudtson, P. (1989). *Genethics: The Clash Between The New Genetics and Human Values.* Harvard University Press, Cambridge, Mass.

Toffler, A. (1970). *Future Shock.* Random House, New York.

Turkle, S. (1984). *The Second Self.* Simon & Schuster, New York.

UNESCO (1980). *One World, Many Voices.* Unipublications, New York.

Wacks, R. (1989). *Personal Information.* Clarendon Press, Oxford.

Wiener, N. (1965). *Cybernetics.* MIT Press, Cambridge, Mass.

Wiener, N. (1967). *The Human Use of Human Beings.* Avon, New York.

Weizenbaum, J. (1976). *Computer Power and Human Reason.* Freeman, San Francisco.

Williams, J. (1984). Technology and the Handicapped. *American Education,* Vol. 20, No. 5, 27–30.

Willoughby, K. (1990). *Technology Choice.* Westview, Boulder.

Wilson, E. O. (1978). *On Human Nature.* Harvard University Press, Cambridge, Mass.

Wilson, E. O. (1975). *Sociobiology.* Harvard University Press, Cambridge, Mass.

Winner, L. (1978). *Autonomous Technology.* MIT Press, Cambridge, Mass.

Wright, R. (1988). *Three Scientists And Their Gods.* Times Books, New York.

Author Index

Subject Index